Law, Governance and Technology Series

Volume 41

The *Law-Governance and Technology Series* is intended to attract manuscripts arising from an interdisciplinary approach in law, artificial intelligence and information technologies. The idea is to bridge the gap between research in IT law and IT-applications for lawyers developing a unifying techno-legal perspective. The series will welcome proposals that have a fairly specific focus on problems or projects that will lead to innovative research charting the course for new interdisciplinary developments in law, legal theory, and law and society research as well as in computer technologies, artificial intelligence and cognitive sciences. In broad strokes, manuscripts for this series may be mainly located in the fields of the Internet law (data protection, intellectual property, Internet rights, etc.), Computational models of the legal contents and legal reasoning, Legal Information Retrieval, Electronic Data Discovery, Collaborative Tools (e.g. Online Dispute Resolution platforms), Metadata and XML Technologies (for Semantic Web Services), Technologies in Courtrooms and Judicial Offices (E-Court), Technologies for Governments and Administrations (E-Government), Legal Multimedia, and Legal Electronic Institutions (Multi-Agent Systems and Artificial Societies).

More information about this series at http://www.springer.com/series/8808

Ian Berle

Face Recognition Technology

Compulsory Visibility and Its Impact on Privacy and the Confidentiality of Personal Identifiable Images

Springer

Ian Berle
Sutton, Surrey, UK

ISSN 2352-1902 ISSN 2352-1910 (electronic)
Law, Governance and Technology Series
ISBN 978-3-030-36886-9 ISBN 978-3-030-36887-6 (eBook)
https://doi.org/10.1007/978-3-030-36887-6

This Springer imprint is published by the registered company Springer Nature Switzerland AG.
The registered company address is: Gewerbestrasse 11, 6330 Cham, Switzerland

Preface

The book examines the use of personal identifiable images, bioethics and privacy law together and applies them to biometrics generally and face recognition specifically. My interest in bioethics and privacy law developed whilst working as a clinical photographer and medical illustration department manager in a large NHS teaching hospital. The principal concern being the prevention of unregulated and unconsented clinical photographs being taken with cell phone cameras by clinical staff and medical students, when professional clinical photographers are striving to maintain high standards of privacy and confidentiality that were embodied in local codes of responsible practice. These codes of practice are *de facto* codes that have no legal status apart from their adherence to data protection law and Article 8 of the Human Rights Act.

Clinical photographs are paradigmatically associated with face recognition biometrics, because they are both personal identifiable images and when unconsented a person's privacy and confidentiality are abused. Subsequently the book discusses how the privacy and confidentiality of personal identifiable images is affected by face recognition technology, whereby when personal images are reified into data they can be reconstituted by the technology into identifiable images. This functionality removes the possibility of consent when image capture is unknowingly obtained, especially when there is no expectation of privacy in public, and the civil liberties issues that this incurs.

The book expresses my view that in an increasingly data-dependent and concomitantly risk-averse society there is evidence that privacy is being eroded in the trade-off against national security. To balance this trade-off and to ameliorate the threat to privacy, I believe that the *moral* right to privacy needs to be more widely understood and examined. Because, without adequate public accountability and transparency, face recognition technology and its automated processes will continue to diminish citizen autonomy, especially whenever public debate and approval is denied. Consequently, this will likely lead to the majority in democratic western societies losing their understanding of and their ability to control the use of their personal identifiable images in the form of digital data despite the EU General Data Protection Regulation.

The book has been written for those interested in privacy law, image rights and the ethical use of face recognition technology. This would not have been possible without the support of my wife Judy who gave me special leave of absence from domesticity to pursue this project. And, also the encouragement of my various mentors and teachers who have helped contain and shape my concern for the privacy and confidentiality of personal identifiable images. These include Professor Geoffrey Hunt, Dr. Yasemin Erden, Dr. David A. Jones, Professor Merris Amos and Professor Richard Ashcroft. Furthermore, special mention must be made of Len Doyal, formerly Professor of Medical Ethics at The London Hospital Medical School, who supported and inspired my quest to establish ethical and responsible practice of clinical photography in healthcare. This motivated my return to study, in the pursuit of achieving a theoretical and orthopraxic basis for applying privacy and its philosophical frameworks to the uses of personal identifiable images.

All the authors and publishers of copyright material which are included in this book are gratefully acknowledged, with thanks to all the rights assistants known and unknown who have helped with the permissions processes.

Sutton, UK Ian Berle

Acknowledgements

Permission to use the various sources and extracts listed is gratefully acknowledged.

Association of American Geographers
Curry MR (1997) The digital individual and the private realm. Annals of the Association of American Geographers 87.4: 681–699. Published by Taylor and Francis, reprinted by permission of the publisher (Taylor & Francis Ltd., http://www.tandfonline.com)

Association of Computing Machinery
Zhao W et al (2003) Face Recognition: A Literature Survey. ACM Computing Surveys, Vol. 35, No. 4, December 2003, pp. 399–458. ©2003 Association for Computing Machinery, Inc. Reprinted by permission.

Cambridge University Press
Dworkin G (1988) (reprinted 1997) The Theory and Practice of Autonomy. ©Cambridge University Press 1988. Used by permission.

Waldron J (2005) Moral Autonomy and Personal Autonomy. In: Christman J, Anderson J (ed.) Autonomy and the Challenges to Liberalism, New Essays. ©John Christman and Joel Anderson (2005), published by Cambridge University Press. Used with permission Cambridge Books Online. https://doi.org/10.1017/CBO9780511610325.015

Mann M (1984) The autonomous power of the state: Its origins, mechanisms and results. European Journal of Sociology, 25(2), 185–213 © Archives européennes de sociologie 1984, published by Cambridge University Press. Used by permission.

Center for Democracy and Technology
Seeing is ID'ing: Facial Recognition & Privacy. © Center for Democracy and Technology. Used with permission

https://cdt.org/files/pdfs/Facial_Recognition_and_Privacy-Center_for_Democracy_and_Technology-January_2012.pdf

David Brin
©Brin D (1998) The Transparent Society. Reading, Massachusetts: Addison-Wesley. Used with author's permission

European Court of Human Rights
Davourlis v. Greece 27 BHRC 420, [2009] EMLR 16, [2009] ECHR 200 ©Council of Europe/European Court of Human Rights – Conseil de l'Europe/Cour européenne des droits de l'homme. http://hudoc.echr.coe.int/sites/eng/pages/search.aspx?i=001-90617

Lupker and others v. The Netherlands, no. 18395/91, para.5 ECHR, Decision of 07.12.1992

©Council of Europe/European Court of Human Rights – Conseil de l'Europe/Cour européenne des droits de l'homme. http://hudoc.echr.coe.int/eng?i=001-1433

Gene Watch UK
The UK Police National DNA Database. Used with permission http://www.genewatch.org/sub-539478

Hart Publishing
Amos M (2006) Human Rights Law ©Merris Amos 2006, Human Rights Law, Hart Publishing, an imprint of Bloomsbury Publishing Plc. Used by permission

Wicks E (2007) ©Elizabeth Wicks 2007, Human Rights in Healthcare, Hart Publishing, an imprint of Bloomsbury Publishing Plc, p. 122. Used by permission

Irma van der Ploeg
Ploeg, Irma van der (2005) Biometric Identification Technologies: Ethical Implications of the Informatization of the Body Biometric Technology & Ethics, BITE Policy Paper no.1 (unpaginated draft paper used with author's permission) http://www.academia.edu/6039558/Biometric_Identification_Technologies_Ethical_Implications_of_the_Informatization_of_the_Body

John Tagg
Tagg J (1988) The Burden of Representation: Essays on Photographies and Histories. Basingstoke: Palgrave-Macmillan. ©John Tagg and used with author's permission.

LIBERTY
LIBERTY, 'Liberty, Privacy International, Open Rights Group, Big Brother Watch, Article 19 and English PEN briefing on the fast-track Data Retention and Investigatory Powers Bill', Liberty 80 para 13. https://www.liberty-human-rights.org.uk/sites/default/files/Briefing%20on%20the%20Data%20Retention%20and%20Investi gatory%20Powers%20Bill.pdf. Used with permission.

MIT
Turk M, Pentland A (1991) Eigenfaces for Recognition. Journal of Cognitive Neuroscience, 3:1 (Winter, 1991), pp. 71–86. © 1991 by the Massachusetts Institute of Technology, published by the MIT Press.

Nelson LS (2011) American Identified: Biometric Technology and Society. © 2010 Massachusetts Institute of Technology, published by the MIT Press.

Martinus Nijhoff
Marshall J (2009) Personal Freedom through Human Rights Law? Autonomy, Identity and Integrity under the European Convention on Human Rights. Leiden: Martinus Nijhoff. Republished with the permission of Martinus Nijhoff Publishers. Permission conveyed through Copyright Clearance Center, Inc.

Velu (1970) quoted by Loukaidēs, L. Cited by Vermeulen M (2014)

See: Loukaidēs L (1995) Essays on the Developing Law of Human Rights (International Studies in Human Rights). Martinus Nijhoff Publishers. Republished with permission of Martinus Nijhoff Publishers; Copyright permission conveyed through Copyright Clearance Center, Inc.

Mitchell Gray
Gray M (2003) Urban Surveillance and Panopticism: will we recognize the facial recognition society? Surveillance & Society 1(3): 314–330 Used by permission.

https://ojs.library.queensu.ca/index.php/surveillance-and-society/article/view/3343

New Scientist Magazine
Rutkin A (2015) The rise of on-body cameras and how they will change how we live. https://www.newscientist.com/article/mg22730314-500-the-rise-of-on-body-cameras-and-how-they-will-change-how-we-live/. New Scientist, vol 227 issue 3031.

New York University
Gates KA (2011) Our Biometric Future: Facial Recognition Technology and the Culture of Surveillance. New York and London: New York University Press; ©New York University. Used by permission.

Oxford University Press
Chesterman S (2011) One Nation under Surveillance: A New Social Contract to Defend Freedom Without Sacrificing Liberty. Oxford. By permission of Oxford University Press

Wacks R (1989) (revised 1993) Personal Information: Privacy and the Law Oxford. By permission of Oxford University Press. Clarendon Press Oxford

Rule JB (2007) Privacy in peril. Oxford. By permission Oxford University Press USA.

Palgrave Macmillan
Hunt G (2013) Civil Servants and Whistle-Blowing: Loyal Neutrality and/or Democratic Ideal?' In: Neuhold C, Vanhoonacker, S, Verhey L (ed) Civil Servants and Politics: A Delicate Balance. Palgrave Macmillan. Reproduced with permission of SCSC

Republished with permission of Palgrave MacMillan from Doyal L, Gough I (1991) A Theory of Human Need. MacMillan Press Limited, Basingstoke and London. Copyright permission conveyed through Copyright Clearance Center, Inc.

Peter Lang
Eike-Henner W. Kluge (2001) The Ethics of Electronic Patient Records. ©Peter Lang Publishing Inc., New York. Used with permission

Penguin Random House
Approximately five (5) words from THE TRIAL by Franz Kafka, translated by Idris Parry (Penguin Books 1994, Penguin Classics 2000) Translation copyright © Idris Parry, 1994. Used by permission. Excerpt(s) from THE TRIAL: A NEW TRANSLATION BASED ON THE RESTORED TEXT by Franz Kafka, translated by Breon Mitchell, copyright ©1998 by Penguin Random House LLC. Used by permission of Schocken Books, an imprint of Knopf Doubleday Publishing Group LLC, a division of Random House LLC. All rights reserved.

Michel Foucault (1977), p. 213. Approximately three hundred and forty-five (345) words from DISCIPLINE AND PUNISH: The Birth of the Prison by Michel Foucault, translated by Alan Sheridan (First published as 'Surveiller et punir: Naissance de la prison' by © Éditions Gallimard, Paris, 1975; Penguin Books 1991). Translation copyright © Alan Sheridan, 1977. Used by permission; also used by permission of Pantheon Books, an imprint of the Knopf Doubleday Publishing Group, a division of Penguin Random House LLC. All rights reserved

Princeton University Press
Republished with permission of Princeton University Press from Van de Veer D (1986) Paternalistic intervention: The moral bounds of benevolence. Princeton, New Jersey: Princeton University Press. Permission conveyed through Copyright Clearance Center, Inc.

Routledge
Republished with the permission of Routledge extracts from Merris Amos (2014) The impact of human rights law on measures of mass surveillance in the United Kingdom. In: Davis F, McGarrity N, Williams G (ed) Surveillance, Counter-Terrorism and Comparative Constitutionalism. London and New York: Routledge (2014). With permission conveyed through Copyright Clearance Center, Inc.

Republished with permission of Routledge, from Mill JS 'On Liberty in Focus'. Edited by Gray J and Smith GW. Routledge, London & New York 1991. Copyright permission conveyed through Copyright Clearance Center, Inc.

Gray J (1991) Mill's Conception of Happiness. In: On Liberty in Focus. Republished with permission of Routledge, from Mill JS 'On Liberty in Focus' edited by Gray J and Smith GW. Routledge, London & New York 1991, p. 197. Copyright permission conveyed through Copyright Clearance Center, Inc.

Royal Academy of Engineering
Royal Academy of Engineering. (2007) Dilemmas of Privacy and Surveillance Challenges of Technological Change. Used by permission.

http://www.raeng.org.uk/news/publications/list/reports/dilemmas_of_privacy_and_surveillance_report.pdf, p. 33

SCRAN
Bentham, J. (1791) Letter II 'Panopticon or Inspection-House'. Used by permission

http://www.scran.ac.uk/ada/documents/castle_style/bridewell/bridewell_jeremy_bentham_panoption_vol1.htm

Science Direct
Accardo J, Chaudhry Ahmed M (2014) Radiation exposure and privacy concerns surrounding full-body scanners in airports. This article was published in Journal of Radiation Research and Applied Sciences, Vol 7, pp. 198–200, ©The Egyptian Society of Radiation Sciences and Applications 2014. http://www.sciencedirect.com/science/article/pii/S1687850714000168. Used by permission

Select Books
©Whitehead JW (2013) A Government of Wolves: The Emerging American Police State. New York: Select Books Inc. Excerpted with permission from the publisher

Springer
Driessen B, Dürmuth M (2013) Achieving Anonymity against Major Face Recognition Algorithms. In: De Decker B, Dittmann J, Kraetzer C, Vielhauer C (eds) Communications and Multimedia Security. © CMS 2013. Lecture Notes in Computer Science, vol 8099. Springer, Berlin, Heidelberg. With permission of Springer.

Gordon N (2002) On Visibility and Power: An Arendtian Corrective of Foucault. In: Human Studies, vol. 25, no. 2, 2002, pp. 125–145. Reprinted by permission from Springer

Stanford Law Review
Republished with permission of Stanford Law Review from Samuelson P (1999) Property as intellectual property. Stanford Law Review pp. 1126–1173. 52 Stan. L. Rev. 1125.

Permission conveyed through Copyright Clearance Center, Inc.

Taylor and Francis Limited
Pink T (2011) Thomas Hobbes and the Ethics of Freedom. In: Inquiry: An Interdisciplinary Journal of Philosophy, Volume 54, 2011 - Issue 5: The (Vexed and Contentious) History of Autonomy. Reprinted by permission of Taylor & Francis Ltd. http://www.tandfonline.com pp. 541–563 https://doi.org/10.1080/0020174X.2011.608886

The Journal of Privacy and Confidentiality
Acquisti A, Gross R, Stutzman F (2014). Face Recognition and Privacy in the Age of Augmented Reality. ©Journal of Privacy and Confidentiality, 6(2). https://doi.org/10.29012/jpc.v6i2.638. Used with authors' permission

The Times and Sunday Times Newspaper
© Sarah Harris 'Computer to sales staff: VIP approaching' News Licensing, The Sunday Times 14 July 2013. http://www.thesundaytimes.co.uk/sto/news/uk_news/Tech/article1287590.ece

© Richard Ford 'Photos of innocent kept by police despite court ruling' News Licensing, The Times 19 December 2014. https://www.thetimes.co.uk/article/photos-of-innocent-kept-by-police-despite-court-ruling-3rh25pxwj59

United Kingdom

Campbell (Appellant) v. MGN Limited (Respondents)

[2004] UKHL 22 on appeal from: [2002] EWCA Civ 1373

http://www.publications.parliament.uk/pa/ld200304/ldjudgmt/jd040506/campbe-1.htm

Contains Parliamentary information licensed under the Open Parliament Licence v3.0.

Intelligence and Security Committee of Parliament (ISCP)

Privacy & Security: A modern & transparent legal framework. Report 2015 para 277

Contains public sector information licensed under the Open Government Licence v3.0.

University of Chicago

Republished with permission of University of Chicago Press from Petit P (1996)

Freedom as Antipower. In: Ethics, Vol. 106, No. 3 (Apr. 1996), pp. 578–604. Copyright permission conveyed through Copyright Clearance Center, Inc.

Verso

Bentham J (1789) The Panopticon Writings. Bozovic M (ed)

London: Verso, 1995, 29–95. Used by permission.

Wiley-Blackwell

Brennan P, Berle I, (2011) The ethical and medical aspects of photo-documenting genital injury. In: Gall J, Payne-James J (eds) (2011) Current Practice in Forensic Medicine. Chichester: ©Wiley-Blackwell. Used by permission

Yale University Press

Solove DJ (2011) Nothing to Hide: The False Trade Off between Privacy and Security. ©Daniel J. Solove, published by Yale University Press, New Haven & London. Reproduced with permission of the Licensor through PLSclear.

Yale Law Journal

Gavison RE (1980) Privacy and the Limits of Law. The Yale Law Journal, Vol. 89, No. 3 (Jan. 1980), pp. 421–471. Used with permission

Figure 2.1 by Maria Averburg/www.shutterstock.com.

Contents

Abbreviations

ACLU	American Civil Liberties Union
ADDPRIV	Automatic Data Relevancy Discrimination for a Privacy-sensitive video surveillance
ANN	Artificial Neural Network
ANPR	Automated Number Plate Recognition
CCTV	Closed Circuit Television
CDT	Center for Democracy and Technology
CIGI	The Centre for International Governance Innovation
CPDA	Copyright, Designs and Patents Act
DHS	Department of Homeland Security
DMV	Department of Motor Vehicles
DNA	Deoxyribonucleic acid
DPA	Data Protection Act
DRIPA	Data and Investigatory Powers Act
DVLA	Drivers and Vehicles Licensing Agency
ECHR	European Convention on Human Rights
ECtHR	European Court of Human Rights
EEOC	United States Equal Employment Opportunity Commission
EPIC	Electronic Privacy Information Center
EU	European Union
FISA	The Foreign Intelligence Surveillance Act
FRT	Face Recognition Technology
FTC	Federal Trade Commission
GAO	United States Government Audit Office
GDPR	General Data Protection Regulation
GMC	General Medical Council
GPS	Global Positioning System
HIPAA	The Health Insurance Portability and Accountability Act
HRA	Human Rights Act 1998
IAFIS	Integrated Automated Fingerprint Identification System

ICAO	International Civil Aviation Organisation
ICO	Information Commissioner's Office
ISA	Intelligence Services Act
ISCP	Intelligence and Security Committee of Parliament
LDA	Linear Discriminant Analysis
MRS	Market Research Society
MRTD	Machine Readable Travel Documents
NGI	Next Generation Identification
NSA	National Security Agency
OECD	Organisation for Economic Co-Operation and Development
PACE	Police and Criminal Evidence Act
PCA	Principal-Component Analysis
RFID	Radio Frequency Identification
RIPA	Regulation of Investigatory Powers Act
UNSC	United Nations Security Council Sanctions Committee
US PATRIOT ACT	Uniting and Strengthening America by Providing Appropriate Tools Required to Intercept and Obstruct Terrorism Act

List of Figures

Table of Cases

Table of Statutes

Chapter 1
Introduction

Abstract The emergence of digital photography in the 1980s and the invention of Adobe PhotoShop© in 1987 revolutionised photography and subsequently enabled the informatisation of the body. Without digital photography, imaging dependent biometrics would not be possible because the sensors that have replaced film quantify physical components of bodies in the process of informatisation, that film and its analogue processes cannot accomplish. Ultimately quantification converts what can be seen into data and completes the cycle of informatisation. When bodies are informatised, face recognition, irises and fingerprint biometrics are obtainable and regularly used for border control, surveillance and personal access applications. This chapter therefore, briefly describes how Face Recognition Technology (FRT) is founded on digital photography, and reviews how FRT has impacted privacy and confidentiality. The ethical and legal implications of FRT, and how personal autonomy in terms of consent and choice are also considered.

This chapter briefly describes how Face Recognition Technology (FRT) is founded on digital photography, and reviews how FRT has impacted privacy and confidentiality. The ethical and legal implications of FRT, and personal autonomy in terms of consent and choice are also considered.

1.1 The Digitised Image and Face Recognition Technology

The emergence of digital photography in the 1980s and the invention of Adobe PhotoShop© in 1987 revolutionised photography. Until then photography was an analogue process that used silver halide or chromatic dye products to record images onto film and paper, which then needed (and still needs) chemical processing to reveal the recorded images. The invention of digital photography has replaced the largescale use of film, and made the taking of photographs, or rather the capturing of images an instantaneous event when viewed on the camera's screen. Consequently, the rapid improvements in digital photography have exceeded that of earlier photographic processes, to the extent that digital cameras and other image capture devices

I. Berle, *Face Recognition Technology*, Law, Governance and Technology Series 41,
https://doi.org/10.1007/978-3-030-36887-6_1

are everywhere, and film-based photography is only practised by enthusiasts or by professional photographers.

The digitised image is no longer simply a captured moment of time but has become a means of informatising the body that goes beyond the mere recording of a resemblance. Thus, without digital photography imaging dependent biometrics would not be possible, because the sensors that have replaced film quantify physical components of bodies in the process of informatisation, that film and its analogue processes cannot accomplish. Ultimately quantification converts what can be seen into data and completes the cycle of informatisation. When bodies are informatised, face recognition, irises and fingerprint biometrics are obtainable and regularly used for border control, surveillance and personal access applications when entering restricted areas.

1.2 Face Recognition Technology

This book considers some of the impacts and potential impacts of face recognition technology (FRT) on privacy and confidentiality, and how the drive to securitise identity using this technology interferes with personal autonomy. The emphasis on FRT and not other biometric artefacts, is because faces unlike other physical features are easily seen and recordable, therefore, when faces are informatised they are analogous to barcodes when scanned and processed.

FRT is a biometric software application designed to identify a specific person in a digital image. This involves the capture of facial biometrics, to create a searchable biometric database of facial images to verify the identity of an individual. It may also be used to either authorise a person's access to their secure personal information, or allow entry to a secure location, or to identify a person on a security or crime watch-list. However, not all aspects of FRT are benign because it potentially diminishes autonomy to the extent that liberty, privacy and choice are interfered with and threatened. This may happen as individuals lose control of their own facial image whenever their image data is acquired by coercion, persuasion or acquiescence, or when data minimisation is impossible. From the perspective of civil liberties, any involuntary or surreptitious image capture affects privacy rights and exacerbates the tension between civil liberty campaigners and governments. This is especially when any secondary purposes of the image capture are unknown, or when images are published or distributed without the subject's consent or knowledge—for example, the publication of Naomi Campbell's photograph[1]; Campbell illustrates the potential and actual disconnection between privacy and the right to one's own image; and is further described ethically and legally in the cases cited below. Moreover, this is further evident when the secondary uses are permitted in the terms and conditions of

[1]See Sect. 7.6.

use; or are tolerated by the inadequacies of privacy protection which defaults to coercion or acquiescence.

Therefore, the following chapters examine the *potential* for a new form of invasion of privacy. Providing hard evidence of *actual* cases in the specific case of FRT is not easy. One may say that the absence of evidence shows that there is nothing to be concerned about. However, that would be problematic for two reasons:

(1) We are here largely in the area of State surveillance, and the associated secrecy that history has provided ample evidence for in other spheres. For example, the American whistle-blower Edward Snowden's revelations, and the landmark challenge in the UK brought by MPs David Davis and Tom Watson to the Government's surveillance law, whereby the High Court ruled in 2015 that DRIPA was unlawful.[2]
(2) Parallel cases of such undermining of privacy are in fact to be found with other modern technologies. For example, using mobile phones to maliciously circulate sexually intimate photographs of ex-partners; and the unregulated photography of patients in healthcare settings.

1.3 Face Recognition Technology and Privacy

This book draws new parallels on the general deployment of FRT from the basis of what we already know about the dangers of State handling of personal information and the parallel scenarios of unconsented or inadequately consented photography that invade privacy and breach confidentiality.

It may also be questioned as to whether there has ever been a general recognition of the value of privacy of personal images. If no-one values the privacy of personal images, then there is no reason to be concerned about FRT in this respect. But, the answer is that there is clear evidence of such a concern in a parallel scenario. Indeed, I point out that an interesting parallel from more familiar territory, which helps to ground my argument for privacy in relation to personal images, is the necessity of informed consent to clinical photography in healthcare. There is a standard of responsible professional practice which is noted in the UK's General Medical Council's (GMC) guidelines referred to below. The necessity of consent to clinical photography evolved to prevent unauthorised photography, storage and disclosure of clinical images. Subsequently, since 1986 clinicians are required to explain the purpose of photography to the patient. Clinical photographers are duty bound to confirm consent before taking the photographs.[3] Undergirding this practice is the duty of confidence, the adherence to data protection law and the right to privacy.[4] Moreover, since safeguarding vulnerable and exposed people is essential, the same

[2]DRIPA (Data and Investigatory Powers Act).

[3]Cull and Gilson (1984), pp. 4–9.

[4]Berle (2002), pp. 106–109.

protection is evident in schools, colleges and leisure centres (in the UK) to prevent unconsented and unauthorised photography.

From a UK perspective however, whilst patients and others are protected from the unauthorised uses of photography, the situation is quite different outside the healthcare, education and leisure domains. Beyond the boundaries of those domains, the 'ordinary' image of the citizen remains unprotected and vulnerable to unconsented use. While this discrepancy might be partly explained by the very personal nature of imagery used in healthcare, this alone cannot account for vulnerability that comes from a lack of protection. This vulnerability has been challenged in the courts by celebrities, such as Naomi Campbell and Princess Caroline of Monaco, who have established their right to privacy, but this has not created a precedent for ordinary citizens, and the dichotomy remains between the latter and celebrities. From this vantage point a disparity in how autonomy is exercised can be seen. That is, that citizens as patients are required to make informed choices, but outside patient-hood citizens cannot exercise that choice of image protection. An exception is that citizens who happen to be wealthy celebrities can take measures to protect their physical and informational privacy from intrusion and (or) unauthorised disclosure. However, privacy is conceptually difficult and nuanced, and has been variously described in the literature,[5] and is discussed below in Chaps. 4, 5, 6 and 7.

Given such disparities, the following challenges the pervasive image capture for face recognition purposes and scrutinises the impact which such technology has on privacy and autonomy. It further considers redressing the balance in favour of establishing the right to one's own image (especially in the UK), whilst recognising the conditionality of such a right. Again, informed consent in healthcare offers a pertinent comparison here. For example, the GMC's '*Making and using visual and audio recordings of patients*' guidelines recommends what is essentially a dialogue between the provider and the client.[6] Something similar could be adopted in the FRT discourse. From this perspective, the aim is to provide a framework that addresses the disparities noted above, by highlighting the loss of autonomy and choice, as described by Dworkin[7] that has evolved from my previous work on responsible practice in clinical photography, and which seeks to examine how the notion that the right to one's own image is morally and legally justified. Moreover, this would appear to be consistent with that practice in EU countries,[8] and which the UK may need to adopt.[9] Doing so acknowledges human dignity and personhood, and those values which are evident in healthcare, such that they are espoused by all the healthcare professions, such as medicine and nursing.

Moreover, although it is generally assumed that facial images do not need the same protection that other data is afforded, this concomitantly affects personal

[5]Nissenbaum (2010), Wacks (1989, revised 1993) and Westin (1967).

[6]General Medical Council.

[7]See Chaps. 4 and 5.

[8]See Sects. 8.4 and 11.7.

[9]Chapter 7.

choice because personal data is dichotomised at the initial stages of data capture. This would be alleviated if personal image rights are available. By valuing the status of the image as personal data, protection is possible and would be subject to the European Union's General Data Protection Regulation (GDPR). However, the GDPR has made the status of the image conditional on the image context and not all images may have the same protection.

1.4 Face Recognition Technology and Surveillance

Surveillance of people and populations is not new, but it has been enhanced by technologies that are designed to increase its efficiency. With the potential for combining numerous bits of data, FRT enhanced surveillance can interfere with privacy. Especially when surveillance includes those data gathering activities by the State or organisations that observe or seek to predict behaviour, much of which has been critiqued and commented upon. In 'Surveillance Surveyed'[10] the contours of the current discourse are discussed and reviewed.

1.5 Face Recognition Technology and Its Ethical and Legal Implications

The pervasiveness of FRT and often its unknown unconsented use by large social media networks and others has cultivated the general assumption that facial images do not need the same protection that other data is afforded, and thereby affects personal choice. However, this lack of awareness and choice has changed with the implementation of the General Data Protection Regulation (GDPR), but only for new images. Earlier volumes of personal identifiable images already available may not qualify, as the extent of retrospective permission and the enormity of the task lessens the prospect of their inclusion. Therefore, it's possible that most non-qualifying images will remain unconsented and their data subjects will remain outside the scope of the GDPR, since the image data cannot be pseudonymised. Herein is the dilemma, if new images are only protected and older pre GDPR images are not, because consent is not possible or that images are cached and distributed beyond reach, is there therefore, the possibility that either the data processing per GDPR is unlawful because of the unconsented content or will the data be GDPR compliant by other means? These other means could be simply assuming the data was consented when the provider's terms and conditions were agreed to, but this could be either coercion or acquiescence if the service user was persuaded or was nonchalant. Moreover, where State agencies are the recipients of the data, the

[10]Chapter 4.

safeguards necessary to protect the historical data have yet to be tested, especially if the data is held beyond the reach of EU jurisdiction. The question rests on whether further processing of images as defined in Article 6 of the GDPR is lawful.

1.6 Face Recognition Technology and Personal Autonomy

The concept of personal autonomy espoused by philosophers such as Immanuel Kant and Gerald Dworkin and the notions of liberty described by John Stuart Mill and Isaiah Berlin, assist the ethical framework required in a society that is becoming increasingly compulsorily visible. The antidote to such visibility is a radical reassessment of the value of personal identifiable images, that acknowledges the dignity of the data subject thereby protecting them from excessive intrusion and restores a greater degree of choice where appropriate. Yet, for a variety of reasons to choose or not to choose may not be optional, but where it is possible the default should favour opting *in* rather than *out*. By having a choice, individuals will have the opportunity to assess the advantages or disadvantages of their selection, especially where informed consent is valued as an autonomous act.

Moreover, Dworkin's claim that an individual's liberty, power and control are necessary conditions for autonomy to be exercised, also needs to be balanced against the Millian notion of harm that is possible when individuals lose control of their data. On those occasions liberty, power and control are lost and the individual is no longer an autonomous agent. But could the possibility of this happening be remedied by the GDPR?

1.7 Face Recognition Technology and Big Data

Hilbert et al.[11] calculated that in 2007 Big Data comprised a total storage capacity of 295 exabytes (295 billion gigabytes or about 404 billion CDs) and the demand for information-processing capacity is growing exponentially, that by 2025 it is estimated to be 163 zettabytes[12] (1ZB equals 1 trillion gigabytes). Each new development requires more storage capacity or processing power which further diminishes control by both the consumer (data subject) and the retailer (data controller). The loss of control is associated by the potential need to contract out the data management to third parties, or to install systems that are managed by contractors. Furthermore, as an individual's personal details are repeatedly required by each database the need for interoperability maybe advocated or encouraged to either rationalise databases, or to verify identities across platforms and improve performance. Therefore, the need to

[11]See Hilbert et al. (2011).

[12]Cave (2017).

regulate data processing to protect the data subject's information and to improve organisations' accountability is paramount especially when considered from the perspective of face recognition technology, and the concomitant expansion of Big Data that exceeds Dostoevsky's (1864) vision of pre-determined actions that are orchestrated by the laws of nature, thereby eliminating personal responsibility and choice, and resulting with the need to tabulate the actions and indexing them in "encyclopaedic lexicons" that would be required to administer and publish the actions, because everything would be calculated to comply or adhere to the laws of nature.[13] This compliance or adherence is predetermined by algorithms that control online behaviour and choices.

Such is the nature of Big Data, which in some applications is used to make decisions on our behalf: such as continuous credit card payments or prompt an action set by the algorithms. Moreover, large amounts of this data comprise of tracking and targeting cookies that record browsing history and is the reason why pop-up advertising or recommendations appear regularly in mailboxes. This marketing is effective because of the surveillance that is triggered when individuals are active on the web. Facebook is one such large surveillance enterprise and apart from its advertising, its global reach of 350 million photographs per day[14] allows Facebook, using face recognition software to automatically identify or tag people by matching new images to those previously uploaded.[15] And when coupled with Big Data, tagged individuals can ultimately be associated to other information that completes their demographic profile. The aggregation of data will be unlawful if it breaches Article 6 of the GDPR.

The various uses of Face Recognition Technology are discussed in the next chapter.

References

Berle I (2002) The ethical context of clinical photography. J Audiov Media Med 25(3):106–109

Cave A (2017) What will we do when the worlds data hits 163 zettabytes in 2025? https://www.forbes.com/sites/andrewcave/2017/04/13/what-will-we-do-when-the-worlds-data-hits-163-zettabytes-in-2025/#3114fd17349a. Accessed 6 Aug 2019

Cull P, Gilson C (1984) Confidentiality of illustrative clinical records. J Audiov Media Med 7(1):4–9

Dostoevsky F (1864) reprinted 2015 Notes from underground and other stories (trans: Garnett C). Wordsworth Classics, Ware

Facebook (2017a) How many photos on Facebook. https://www.brandwatch.com/blog/facebook-statistics/. Accessed 6 Aug 2019

Facebook (2017b) How does Facebook suggest tags? https://www.facebook.com/help/122175507864081. Accessed 6 Aug 2019

[13]Dostoevsky (1864 reprinted 2015), p. 471. See Sect. 6.6.

[14]Facebook (2017a).

[15]Facebook (2017b).

General Medical Council. Making and using visual and audio recordings of patients. https://www.gmc-uk.org/ethical-guidance/ethical-guidance-for-doctors/making-and-using-visual-and-audio-recordings-of-patients. Accessed 24 Sep 2019

Hilbert et al (2011) Global data storage capacity totals 295 exabytes: USC study. https://www.eweek.com/storage/global-data-storage-capacity-totals-295-exabytes-usc-study. Accessed 6 Aug 2019

Nissenbaum H (2010) Privacy in context: technology, policy and the integrity of social life. Stanford University Press, Stanford

Wacks R (1989) (revised 1993) Personal information: privacy and the law. Clarendon Press, Oxford

Westin AF (1967) Privacy and freedom. Bodley Head, London

Chapter 2
What Is Face Recognition Technology?

Abstract Face recognition technology is one of several biometric tools or modalities used for person identification and verification. Broadly, it is mainly a monitoring and security technology designed to facilitate or control access used by governments, law enforcement agencies, and commerce. It has many other uses already in play, and many others are on the horizon. The chapter begins with a discussion of the technology and is followed with an overview of a few large-scale utilisers of FRT.

2.1 Introduction: What Is Face Recognition Technology?

Face recognition technology (FRT) is a biometric image capture tool that is used for either identity verification or to identify a person in order to connect them definitively to their indexed data. The former matches a person's face against an image database of known faces and verifies (confirms) their identity, and the latter is a query methodology that compares a face image against that of an identity being claimed.[1]

It is, for example, commonly used at airport security gates. Whilst this application is beneficial in terms of increased efficiency it is dependent on the processing power and application of the system. Yet, the development of the technology is especially problematic ethically and legally when secondary uses of the digital images are not consented or authorised, since it is possible to aggregate and distribute data without the individual's knowledge; this would potentially breach data protection and rights law when a conventional passport photograph would not.

For verification purposes FRT relies on a voluntary enrolment process or other initial capture system in order to build the image database. Whatever the mechanism of enrolment it is essential to submit to photography or supply an authenticated photograph, and either of these resultant images will be uploaded to the image database. Ultimately, the purpose is to provide a secure identification system that

[1]See Patil et al. (2010), pp. 74–78.

I. Berle, *Face Recognition Technology*, Law, Governance and Technology Series 41,
https://doi.org/10.1007/978-3-030-36887-6_2

solves "the problem of 'disembodied identities', or the existence of visual and textual representations of individuals that circulate independent(ly) of their physical bodies".[2] Hence, if faces are display devices[3] that computers should be able to read, the only limitations to achieving that objective are the variables of computer processing, which is also discussed below. There is also an apparent circularity in verifying an image against the 'same' image, which is indicative of the technology's potential for failure and error. If the template image is a fake, then the whole point of the process is undermined.

Principally, the technology is used for identification and identity authentication purposes by law enforcement agencies, border control, access control and secure logging-in processes. Large scale applications, such as the Indian unique identification number project[4] involve recording every citizen's personal and biometric details to strengthen economic and social inclusion, and thereby building a national database which is used to empower access to healthcare and banking. Another application of FRT is analytics and video screening which are the features of smart surveillance (discussed in Chap. 10). Whatever the application the technology operates by analysing facial features.

Allied to face recognition is face detection. Face detection is the means by which faces are detected in an image which is not necessarily a portrait or ID photograph. The computational algorithms needed to either detect and or analyse faces are related, and face detection is the stepping-stone towards that goal. Furthermore, the application of face recognition in surveillance necessitates the need to identify one individual in a group or scene, not just to detect whether faces are present in the camera's field of view. For example, in the USA suspects who have jumped bail have been identified at sports events such as football matches by means of FRT.[5]

2.2 How Does Face Recognition Work?

In 1991 Turk and Pentland[6] developed a "near real-time computer system that can locate and track a subject's head, and then recognise the person by comparing characteristics of the face to those known individuals". Essentially their system was an information theory approach that decomposed face images into a smaller set of characteristic features which they called 'eigenfaces'.[7]

This was achieved by extracting relevant information from a face image and encoding it to an existent encoded image located in an image database, thereby

[2]Gates (2011), p. 12.

[3]*ibid* p. 200.

[4]AADHAAR Unique Identification Authority of India.

[5]Rogers (2016).

[6]Turk and Pentland (1991).

[7]*ibid* pp. 71–72.

matching the new image with the stored image. Mathematically, an algorithm was devised to analyse the four variables of an "input image and its pattern vector" to determine whether or not a face image is present.[8] The term *eigenface* is derived from the German word *eigen* meaning proper or characteristic.[9]

Turk and Pentland further discuss some elements of biology and neural networks which later researchers have developed. Further detailed discussion of these developments is beyond the scope of this book. Yet, because face recognition relies on computational analysis, some discussion of the diversity of algorithms is required and follows below.

But before considering how the algorithms function, face recognition technology is generally perceived as benign and beneficial, because photographs are socially and culturally acceptable, that they are non-disclosive and are already collected and verified routinely as part of the Machine Readable Travel Documents (MRTD) application form process in order to produce a passport to International Civil Aviation Organisation (ICAO) Document 9303 standards.[10,11] However, these benefits raise ethical questions, depending on the particular application and its use, especially when there is no conscious interaction required from passengers, or people generally in other scenarios. Therefore, at first glance these claimed benefits seem reasonable, yet the assumption that a photograph is socially and culturally acceptable should not be simply applied to FRT without considering the ethical consequences. These include the validity of consent, human dignity and how the technology affects second-order choices and the coercive nature of enrolment.

2.3 Face Recognition Algorithms

Face recognition algorithms can be defined as a process or set of rules to be followed in order to calculate or analyse facial characteristics, especially by a computer. As with any rules, there is always the question of interpretation and exceptions.

Shang-Hung Lin[12] explains that in most cases, face recognition algorithms are divided into at least two functioning modules: a face image detector which locates human faces and a face recogniser which identifies the person. This is accomplished when image pixels are converted into a representational vector and the pattern recogniser searches the database to find the best image match.

Therefore, face recognition is a form of pattern recognition,[13] by which the process analyses the measurements of a person's facial characteristics that are

---

[8] *ibid* p. 76.

[9] Syed Navaz et al. (2013).

[10] Slevin (2013).

[11] International Civil Aviation Organisation.

[12] Lin (2000).

[13] Dangi (n.d.).

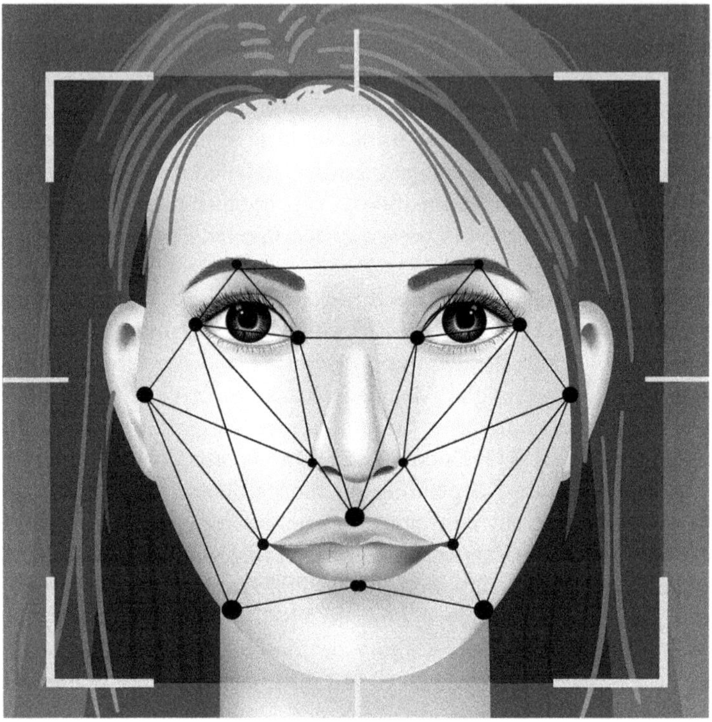

Fig. 2.1 Proprietary algorithm

captured by a camera. The pattern recognition process then synthesises the overall facial structure, using distances between the pupillary centre of the eyes, nose, mouth, and jaw edges including the chin. These measurements calculated by proprietary algorithms, illustrated in Fig. 2.1, are stored in a database and used as a comparison the next time a person stands before a camera.

Driessen and Durmuth's[14] description of the process assists in conceptualising the process:

> First, one needs to find the approximate position of the face in the image; this is called face-detection and a separate line of research. Most work on face recognition considers this job to be completed before; commonly used face image databases such as the FERET database[15]

[14]Driessen and Dürmuth (2013).

[15]The FERET program started in 1993 and ran until 1997. Sponsored by the Department of Defense (sic) Counterdrug Technology Development Program through the Defense Advanced Research Products Agency. Its primary mission was to develop automatic face recognition algorithms that could be employed to assist security, intelligence and law enforcement personnel. The FERET dataset was assembled to support government monitored testing and evaluation of face recognition algorithms using standardised tests and procedures. The final set of images has 3300 images from 1200 persons, with varying mimical expressions, from different dates, under semi-controlled conditions. The dataset is available for research related to face recognition. Cited by Driessen and Dürmuth (2013).

> annotate the images with the eye coordinates. Second, images are normalized, which usually includes an affine transformation [that is, the vectors between points of the space] to align the eyes, histogram equalization, and sometimes masking of the background. Third, in feature extraction algorithm-dependent features the probe image [is] extracted. Representing an image by a set of features can be seen as a step-in data reduction that aims at extracting a compact but discriminating description of the image. Ideally, the output of this step is at the same time robust against changes in posture, lighting, face expression, etc. Finally, the pre-processed probe image is matched against gallery images....the output of a face recognition algorithm is a list of identifiers, where the algorithm estimates that the first identifier (e.g. name) is the most likely one, matching the subject on the probe image.[16]

This can be generically summarised as: acquisition and pre-processing, feature extraction, classification, and verification/identification.

Possible algorithms are very many and a brief survey of papers since 2000 is instructive. For Shang-Hung Lin the principal benefit of biometric identification is its resistance to forgery.[17] He describes two biometric ID methods, the physiological and the behavioural. The former includes fingerprints, face and DNA; the latter includes keystroke and voice print. In their exhaustive survey, Zhao et al.[18] categorise techniques by applying guidelines used in psychological studies of how humans recognise faces whereby "holistic matching methods use the whole face region as raw input to recognition system" such facial representations are otherwise known as 'eigenfaces'. Alternatively using "feature-based (structural) matching methods [by which] local features such as the eyes, nose and mouth are first extracted and their locations and local statistics (geometric and/or appearance) are fed into a structural classifier".[19] Additionally, a combination of these two methods hybridise the systems[20]; and that within these classifications further sub-classification is possible. Noting that using principal-component analysis (PCA), "many face recognition techniques have been developed"[21] and only one of these is eigenfaces which uses a nearest neighbour classifier[22] that is based on the Euclidean distance.[23,24,25]

Driessen and Durmuth[26] responding to the need to achieve anonymity against face recognition algorithms, especially in the context of improving privacy in social networks and other on-line albums, note that the eigenface algorithm "still provides very competitive performance for images taken in a moderately controlled

---

16 Driessen and Dürmuth (2013), p. 3 *op cit.*

17 Lin (2000), p. 1 *op cit.*

18 Zhao et al. (2003), pp. 399–458.

19 *ibid* p. 409.

20 *ibid* p. 409.

21 *ibid* p. 409.

22 Turk M, Pentland A *op cit.*

23 Euclidean space is the space in which distances and angles matter.

24 PCA Principal component analysis is a technique to reduce the complexity of a data set, namely reducing its dimensionality (in some sense, less variables).

25 Shah Zainudin et al. (2012), p. 51.

26 Driessen B, Durmuth M *op cit.*

environment. Also, it forms the basis for a wide range of algorithms, including Linear Discriminant Analysis (LDA) which can be applied after PCA and the Bayesian classifier…".[27] Bayesian face recognition differs from most algorithms, because "in order to recognise a face the algorithm iterates over all stored persons (not faces), and for each decides if this is the correct person or not",[28] and is therefore based on an inferred "probabilistic" similarity.[29]

2.4 Other Approaches

Since the year 2000 various others have continued to publish their analyses and therefore the superiority of one or another approach remains debatable, given the regular benchmarking and competition amongst developers and researchers. The debate centres on whether PCA or LDA is more useful for face recognition, that is, whether feature classification (PCA) or data classification (LDA) is the most suitable approach.[30]

However, Syed Navaz et al.[31] report that there are some benefits of using PCA with an Artificial Neural Network (ANN). Their particular algorithm it is claimed, more accurately identifies input face images of an individual already stored in the database and is therefore capable of recognising new face images[32] and also tolerates some variation in the new appearance. Similarly, the application of this combination using proprietary patented algorithms has been demonstrated and is available[33] whereby the impact of smiling or the wearing of a hat or glasses is reduced during the matching process. This advance is now being exploited commercially by retail, leisure and hospitality companies.

Yet, such variations of system adoption are potentially problematic legally, if they fail expectations or claimed efficiencies. Also, if system errors cause unnecessary or unsubstantiated interference with freedom of movement or access they are ethically problematic. Subsequently, the following discusses the weaknesses of face recognition technology and the developments to minimise them.

[27] *ibid* p. 3.

[28] *ibid* p. 5.

[29] Moghaddam et al. (2000).

[30] Shah Zainudin et al. (2012) *op cit.*

[31] Syed Navaz et al. (2013).

[32] *ibid* p. 254.

[33] NEC.

2.5 Weaknesses and Failures of FRT

Biometric face recognition relies on the ability of the algorithm to identify a known individual. Yet, all forms of biometrics have error rates that affect the accuracy of the method and the overall performance between the computed dataset and the working system used in the real world. These error rates consist of either incorrectly accepting or rejecting an individual when presented for verification. An incorrectly accepted result or false positive is known as the False Acceptance Rate (FAR) and an incorrectly rejected result is known as the False Rejection Rate (FRR).[34] These measures are inversely proportional; that is the threshold of one affects the other, for example by tuning the system to reject impostors and thereby minimising FAR, it may also affect the FRR and reject some authorised users.[35] These rates are determined by the designer or operator, and are functions of the system's 'decision-threshold'.[36] For example, this could mean a 1:25 chance of not unlocking your mobile phone when switching it on (the false negative) or a 1:1000 chance of someone else doing so if your phone was lost or stolen (the false positive). Moreover, the 2010 NIST Interagency Report 7709[37] noted the improvement in accuracy of face recognition algorithms, whilst maintaining a False Acceptance Rate (FAR) of 0.001, False Rejection Rates (FRR) are falling—2002: FRR of 0.2; 2006: FRR of 0.01; 2010: FRR of 0.003. On that 2010 basis an individual has a 1:3000 chance of rejection at an airport e-gate. Or as Carl Gohringer reported in 2016, most European e-gates operate with an FRR of approximately 6% (0.006) set against a corresponding FAR of 0.1%.[38] Although the weaknesses and failures have yet to be *entirely* eliminated, which may be impossible in practice, we can see there have been significant improvements. Whilst this is good news for travellers, there is one difficulty that remains, in that, the false rejection rate can be influenced by poor quality images (photographs or video capture stills) and the false acceptance rate can be influenced by spoofing using a photograph of a registered user, which exposes the legitimate data subject to harm such as the risk of injustice, identity theft or fraud.

2.6 Face Recognition Vulnerability

An ethical and legal risk exists when biometric face recognition is compromised when an impostor circumvents the system by spoofing the identity of a registered user. The ethical and legal risks are predicated by poor safeguarding and security of the system used, and the potentially fraudulent activity the access allows. Face

[34] Gregory and Simon (2008), p. 22.

[35] Lin (2000), p. 12 *op cit.*

[36] Acharya and Kasprzyk (2010).

[37] Grother et al. (2010).

[38] See Gohringer (2012).

spoofing by photograph is the most common abuse of the system.[39] The 'photo-attacks' occur when a photograph is presented to an unmonitored system. Biggio et al. note that this can be either a hard-copy or an image displayed on a smartphone or portable computer. Given that the face is an unconcealed biometric feature that is readily and easily obtainable, either directly by photographing the registered user or by copying their image from social network websites, the system is clearly exposed to spoofing attacks. I see no reason why such an ethical/legal risk should not increase as the public becomes more aware of the vulnerabilities of the system. Additionally, the advent of three-dimensional (3D) printers and the determination of the impostor increases the vulnerability of face recognition systems to the faking of facial-images by wearing a mask manufactured using a 3D printer. Indeed, whilst the risks of a successful attack maybe limited or countered by either increasing the decision-threshold or by human vigilance, counter-measures are required to protect systems from attack. The counter-measures can be either more robust uni-modal algorithms or supplementary biometrics to support face recognition identification: the so-called multi-modal techniques which include liveness detection.

Moreover, the rates of false positives and false negatives in the application of FRT is clearly an ethical issue. A false positive in certain circumstances (such as criminal investigation) could lead to wrongful police and judicial action against an innocent individual. A false negative, in similar context, could allow a criminal to go undetected and commit crimes. Since no system is perfect there will be some rate of 'false identifications' and the question then arises what false/positive rate is acceptable, not only for FRT but also for all biometric modalities.

A utilitarian calculation might be done as in all matters of policy dealing with populations rather than individuals. To that end, personal autonomy would be curtailed for the benefit of the greater good, such as might be determined to improve security and manage risks. But, how would such a rate be set? Ideally, the 'false identification' rate should cause less harm than alternative approaches to identification or, minimally compared with no identification technical screening system at all. Such a calculation would not appear to be feasible, since too many variables would be involved not to speak of the tangle of social values involved. Nevertheless, policy-makers, and those applying FRT, should at least give some thought and discussion. From the perspective of state paternalism, a more detailed consideration of what this might involve continues below in Chap. 9.

2.7 Face Spoofing Counter-Measures

In so-called 'spoofing' someone attempts to gain access to information or a location by pretending to be the authorised user. Spoofing counter-measures can be broadly categorised as: *Motion analysis:* the detection of movement that is discernible in real

[39]Biggio et al. (2012), p. 5.

faces; *Texture analysis:* the comparison between natural (skin) and unnatural texture patterns (paper); *Liveness detection:* the capture of signs of life such as eye-blinks.[40]

Other multimodal methods include fingerprints. This approach is based on the assumption that an impostor would need to circumvent two or more biometric systems. Rodrigues et al. however, have shown false acceptance rates increase when either mode is spoofed.[41] Given the need to eliminate spoofing attacks, Zhang et al.[42] and Kant and Sharma[43] propose liveness detection solutions based on biological and physiological attributes only evident when a valid user is present.

Zhang et al. propose using multi-spectral lighting because skin reflectance at 850 nm and 1450 nm (nanometres) differs from that of a photograph, however when used to test genuine faces against mask faces, the 'distribution distances' evident in a photograph are not as significant, due possibly to the variety of materials available for mask faces and also the three-dimensionality of masks. Kant and Sharma propose using a fusion of thermal imaging and skin elasticity to detect spoofed faces. Skin elasticity is measured by capturing several face images at pre-determined intervals and comparing the images to detect liveness. In addition, presumably to avoid the use of several fake images mimicking elasticity, thermal imaging is used to detect the heat property of the image or subject.

Clearly the 'arms race' is already under way. These anti-spoofing proposals are examples of an expansive literature, and they appear to offer promising solutions because they use recognisable biological and physiological attributes. They also confirm the fact that face recognition is not merely identity photography but a biological index capable of quantifying identity for subsequent verification and presents new ethical and legal vulnerabilities.

2.8 Current Uses of Face Recognition Technology

2.8.1 Passports and Other Government Uses

Electronic passports (e-passports) containing a digital image of the passport holder's photograph have become essential. The passport is used to cross automated gates (e-gates) that use face recognition technology. Moreover, the International Civil Aviation Authority (ICAO), a United Nations agency, has endorsed the need for the e-gates to be globally interoperable; and the American US-VISIT programme requires passports to have an integrated data chip that contains the information from the data page.[44] In addition to e-passports, Germany has introduced mandatory

[40] Anjos and Marcel (2011).
[41] Rodrigues et al. (2010).
[42] Zhang et al. (2011).
[43] Kant and Sharma (2013).
[44] Acharya and Kasprzyk (2010).

electronic ID cards or *Personalausweisgesetz*. The cards contain a radio-frequency enabled chip that stores personal information including a digital photograph, fingerprints and an electronic signature. The card is also valid for travel within the European Union. Similarly, Portugal has a 'Citizen Card' which contains a digital photograph and electronic signature.[45]

The Indian government[46] has initiated its Unique Identification Project (UID) and has commissioned the Unique Identification Authority (UIDAI) to assign a unique identification number to each resident. The enrolment stage known as 'Aadhaar' captures each resident's identity information and is matched against every other previously enrolled resident to avoid duplication. This process is called 'de-duplication'. Because of the population size (1.2 billion), de-duplication using ordinary demographic fields such as name, address, age and gender, were deemed to be surrogates of identity and therefore too vulnerable to loss or corruption. Consequently, to prevent duplication, biometric technology was adopted to support the issuance of a unique identity number and also to pre-empt any fraudulent use of demographic information. The UID uses multimodal biometrics and comprises of face, ten fingerprints and both irises. Irises are included because those working in manual occupations can have degraded fingerprints, and irises offer more stability where multimodal verification is required. They can also be collected from children as young as 5 years old.[47] Similarly, with a population of 172 million, the Indonesian government has initiated its 'National Electronic ID (e-KTP) Programme'[48] which is currently being implemented using multimodal biometrics comprising of face, signature, ten fingerprints and irises. The card will be multifunctional and will initially facilitate e-government activities such as e-voting; by 2016 the card will function as a driving licence, a bank card for ATM banking use and also facilitate access to social services.

By statute in the UK,[49] the principal use of multimodal biometrics is for visa holders who stay longer than 6 months. These 'Biometric Residence Permits' are mandatory for visitors applying to stay a minimum of 6 months or are applying for 'indefinite leave to remain' to settle in the UK.[50] Likewise prior to travel Canada, Australia, Japan and most European countries have similar schemes for visa applicants.[51] Additionally, Israel has a biometric passport and ID card with an optional fingerprint scan on each document.[52]

Given the need to enhance or expand existing systems, the United States has adopted an overt interoperable approach that functions as a law enforcement

---

[45] *ibid.*

[46] UIDAI (2012).

[47] *ibid.*

[48] Priyanto (2012).

[49] UK Borders Act 2007 c.30 §.5 8.

[50] Biometric Residents Permit.

[51] Government of Canada 'International use of biometrics'.

[52] Kamisher (2017).

capability. Similarly, the UK Borders Act 2007 authorises law enforcement agencies to control immigration and cross-check the status of visitors. The accrual of data that identity card programmes initiate is cause for concern when considered from the perspective of rights and justice and is paradigmatic of the DNA database discussed in Chap. 10.

2.8.2 Law Enforcement

Law enforcement agencies are the operational divisions of government policy, regulation and legislation. These agencies use biometrics for crime prevention and detection, border control and immigration. For instance, the US Federal Bureau of Investigation (FBI)[53] operate numerous systems and databases denoted by their acronym, such as 'IDENT',[54] IAFIS,[55] NGI,[56] and 'US-VISIT'.[57] In 2012 these databases held more than 100 million records each, which is more than one third of the US population.[58] Whether there is the likelihood of duplicated records amongst each database is unknown. Many of the records are fingerprints that have accrued since the FBI developed and implemented the automated fingerprint identification system (IAFIS) in 1999. Currently the system also includes both biometric identifiers, such as footprints, palm-prints, fingerprints and photographic images that have been taken for authorised purposes, or are the latent identifiers collected from locations or items associated "with criminal activity or a lawful investigative or national security interest".[59] The overall objective is the interoperability of systems and databases that will assist the prompt and seamless sharing of biographic information and biometric data.[60] Generally, communication between the systems will simplify sharing of data such as fingerprints and biographic details on identifiable groups or individuals, and specifically when full biometric operability is achieved, every authorised IAFIS/NGI operative in the Department of Justice (DOJ) will have access to the system.[61]

This level of interoperability necessitates the need to capture images in live situations and scenarios; and this has driven the pursuit of innovative technologies to supply law enforcers with the tools to achieve their objectives in crime detection

[53]FBI Privacy Impact Assessment.

[54]Automated Biometric Identification System.

[55]Integrated Automated Fingerprint System.

[56]Next Generation Identification.

[57]United States Visitor and Immigrant Status Indicator Technology.

[58]Lynch (2012).

[59]FBI *op cit.*

[60]FBI *ibid.*

[61]FBI *ibid.*

and prevention. One such American company, BI^2 Technologies[62] has developed its Mobile Offender Recognition and Information System (MORIS™) which is a handheld device that can recognise and identify individuals' irises, faces or fingerprints. The device is attached to an Apple iPhone for uploading to an existing database, which can potentially be used to create a new record that can subsequently be shared via the FBI/NGI system. These devices and the potential cascading of data have provoked civil liberties concerns which will be discussed below in Chaps. 3 and 5.

By comparison, UK face recognition biometrics is (currently) confined to border control and immigration. The former allows British e-passport holders to re-enter the UK via e-gates. The latter requires visitors or non-British residents to have a biometric residence permit in addition to their visa if they are to remain legally in the UK for longer than 6 months. The biometric data is stored on a central database and is checked against government records in compliance with UK data protection law.[63]

2.8.3 *Commerce*

Numerous companies use face recognition as part of their services to improve customer experience and/or to maximise efficiency and profits. Social networks such as 'Facebook' and 'Google+' tag names to photographs by prompting users to identify their friends whom they communicate with the most.[64] And by 2018, more than 250 billion photos have been uploaded to Facebook, equating to 350 million photos per day.[65] These photos are further tagged at a rate of 100 million labels per day.[66]

This rate of expansion is probably driven by Facebook's use of the photographs as training images to generate the labelling, although it is not explicitly stated. Instead they admit to using face recognition software "similar to that found in many photo editing tools to match your new photos to other photos you are tagged in. We group similar photos together and, whenever possible, suggest the name of the friend in the photos".[67] Because of this default setting, there is an ethical issue here. The purpose of suggesting that others confirm friends' names avoids having to get consent from the individuals being tagged and allows Facebook to extract biometric data from the uploaded image. Though even if only friends are permitted to confirm identification there is the potential for abuse by automatic face

---

[62]BI^2 Technologies.

[63]Data Protection Act 2018.

[64]Center for Democracy & Technology (2012).

[65]Smith (2019).

[66]Welinder (2012), p. 173.

[67]Facebook (2011).

recognition,[68] and therefore this practice by Facebook appears unethical because it denies individuals the right to control the dissemination and identification of their images, even though it is possible to change personal preferences after being tagged.[69]

Facebook and Google+ generate income from advertising targeted at specific members who have been sorted by their profiles. For instance, photographers may see adverts from photographic dealers, or offers from post-production companies. Whilst this maybe innocuous, what drives it is not necessarily so. For example, it is now possible for stores and hotels to identify visitors and clients using face recognition systems. One such system requires the customer to enrol on the basis of improving the customer experience from a tailored service. The system created by NEC IT Solutions works by analysing facial images captured when a customer enters the store. The image is then checked against a database of clients previously enrolled images, and once identified their details are available to the store's staff. The details might include names and shopping preferences. Chris de Silva, a vice-president at NEC IT Solutions, said: "We're trialling the system in general retail, which would include hotels and anything where the public are walking in..." [yet privacy concerns aside customers would be] "quite happy to have their information available because they want a quicker service, a better service or a more personally tailored service"; tests had also proven that the system cannot be defeated, inasmuch that facial hair or other changes do not affect the system's accuracy.[70]

The assumptions expressed by De Silva lack any sensitivity to the consequences of unconsented intrusion and are indicative of the coercive nature of the project's objectives, and which relate to the burgeoning privacy issues that face recognition software causes. The fact De Silva is satisfied that the software can potentially overcome efforts to avoid being identified is on one hand arguably acceptable when applied to counter terrorism, but on the other hand ethically problematic when the software is used for commercial gain. Ethical aspects of this dichotomy follow in the ensuing chapters, yet I am not advocating a form of moral relativism but rather noting that the ethical considerations are context dependent which necessitates careful examination of the moral dilemmas, especially when considered in terms of compulsory visibility (Chap. 6). But could be remedied by affirming the status of personal identifiable images as having property rights that are protected or at least auditable provenance.

More pressing, however, is the fact that NEC[71] have developed a neural network algorithm that effectively reduces error rates (see Gohringer above) and making this commercially viable is significant, (and is also of moral significance given the ethical dichotomies of the various applications). Subsequently Universal Studios in Japan are using NEC's Access Control System for processing customers who are visiting

[68]Welinder (2012), p. 174.

[69]Facebook (n.d.).

[70]Harris (2013).

[71]NEC.

their theme park. Their theme park attracts eight million visitors per year, of whom 500,000 apply for an annual pass. Prior to the introduction of automated access control each annual pass was processed manually and involved an ID photograph being taken, and this took 2–3 h to complete. Currently, applicants collect their annual passes and proceed to an entry gate where the control system captures their image on first entry; once enrolled, subsequent entry by scanning the annual pass and capturing the visitor's image takes mere seconds. Universal Studios report that by using this system costs have been reduced by thirty percent (30%).[72] Similarly, Disney's theme parks have progressed from hand or finger shape scanning[73] to face recognition[74] for access and enrolment to process its 59 million visitors per year.[75] These burgeoning numbers drive the need for fast and accurate access to these large theme parks and therefore justify using biometrics. This is not without its critics and the potential for encroaching civil liberties is sufficient grounds for concern. For example, it would arguably be an infringement of civil liberties if or when data was used subsequently for purposes not directly associated with the original purpose for collection, an activity that the Disney Corporation is supposedly complicit with and which is discussed below in Chap. 3.

2.8.4 Gambling and Banking

At the interface of commerce and crime prevention is the use of face recognition technology in the gambling industry. Generally used to reduce financial risks, assist social responsibility and enhance customer service, casinos covertly photograph visitors as they pass through their registration desks. The images are then scanned by the face recognition software to identify gamblers who have either voluntarily enrolled on an exclusion list or is used to identify gamblers who are known cheats. For example, one developer's suite of face recognition software includes a module which is claimed to have "the ability to run operational real-time facial recognition scans of any individual on their property against a law enforcement-verified database of criminals numbering in the millions… Our data is based on data feeds from about 2,000 different jurisdictions of verified law enforcement data at the city, county, state level, and federal or international correctional or wanted data" "gives access to a database of active professional card counters, slot machine and table game cheats….exclusion lists, gaming scams and cheating devices" also this product "collects information from multiple sources and …provides daily database updates via the Internet" and another module "enables the sharing (sending and receiving) of

[72]NEC.

[73]Harmel (2006).

[74]Occupy Corporatism (2012).

[75]Niles (2012).

real-time information to help alert and identify suspicious patrons and devices".[76] At casinos regulated by The Ontario Lottery and Gaming Corporation, when a match is found a silent alarm is triggered and the matching photographs displayed on a security guard monitored computer screen, after which the visitor's identity is confirmed and if necessary the visitor is escorted out of the casino.[77]

In addition to casinos, the banking industry's next generation automated teller machines (ATMs) will use face recognition access to prevent fraud and identity theft. These machines will connect to the customer's mobile phones or tablet computer, and their real-time image will be matched to a database of pre-enrolled images to confirm the customer's identity. The software uses anti-spoofing algorithms to confirm the presence of a registered user to further prevent the fraudulent use of the machines.[78]

At face value the financial and gambling sectors' use of face recognition technology might be morally justified (assuming that gambling itself is not immoral), given that it protects the sector's interests and allegedly prevents excessive gambling by those who have self-excluded themselves. Although any broadening use of the sector specific software risks increasing the fears and misconceptions of the technology.

References

Acharya L, Kasprzyk T (2010) Biometrics and Government. https://lop.parl.ca/Content/LOP/ResearchPublications/06-30-e.pdf. Accessed 6 June 2018 (unavailable 6 Aug 2019)

Anjos A, Marcel S (2011) Counter-measures to photo attacks in face recognition: a public database and a baseline. http://ieeexplore.ieee.org/document/6117503/. Accessed 7 Aug 2019

BI2 Technologies Biometric Intelligence & Identification Technologies. http://www.bi2technologies.com/. Accessed 7 Aug 2019

Biggio et al (2012) Security evaluation of biometric authentication under realistic spoofing attacks. p 5. https://pralab.diee.unica.it/it/node/667. Accessed 7 Aug 2019

Biometric Residents Permit. https://www.gov.uk/biometric-residence-permits. Accessed 18 Sept 2019

Biometrica (n.d.). https://biometrica.com/casinos/. Accessed 7 Aug 2019

Center for Democracy & Technology (2012) 'Seeing is ID'ing: facial recognition & privacy' https://cdt.org/files/pdfs/Facial_Recognition_and_Privacy-Center_for_Democracy_and_Technology-January_2012.pdf

Dangi R (n.d.) Face recognition. https://www.engineersgarage.com/articles/face-recognition. Accessed 6 Aug 2019

Driessen B, Dürmuth M (2013) Achieving anonymity against major face recognition algorithms. In: De Decker B, Dittmann J, Kraetzer C, Vielhauer C (eds) Communications and multimedia security. CMS 2013. Lecture Notes in Computer Science, vol 8099. Springer, Berlin. Photo credit, figure 2.1: ©Ian Berle

---

[76]Biometrica (n.d.).

[77]Elash and Luk (2018).

[78]Finextra (2013).

Elash A, Luk V (2018) Canadian casinos, banks, police use facial-recognition technology. http://www.theglobeandmail.com/news/national/time-to-lead/canadian-casinos-banks-police-use-facial-recognition-technology/article590998/. Accessed 7 Aug 2019

Facebook (2011) Making photo tagging easier. https://www.facebook.com/notes/facebook/making-photo-tagging-easier/467145887130. Accessed 7 Aug 2019

Facebook (n.d.) How do I remove a tag from a photo or post I'm tagged in? https://en-gb.facebook.com/help/140906109319589. Accessed 7 Aug 2019

FBI Privacy Impact Assessment Integrated Automated Fingerprint Identification System (IAFIS)/Next Generation Identification (NGI) Biometric Interoperability. https://www.fbi.gov/services/records-management/foia/privacy-impact-assessments/iafis-ngi-biometric-interoperability. Accessed 7 Aug 2019

Finextra (2013) Facebanx unveils facial recognition tech for banks. http://www.finextra.com/news/Announcement.aspx?pressreleaseid=49488&topic=mobile. Accessed 7 Aug 2019

Gates KA (2011) Our biometric future: facial recognition technology and the culture of surveillance. New York University Press, New York, p 12

Gohringer C (2012) Advances in face recognition technology and its application in airports. http://www.planetbiometrics.com/article-details/i/1214/desc/advances-in-face-recognition-technology-and-its-application-in-airports/. Accessed 7 Aug 2019

Government of Canada International use of biometrics. http://www.cic.gc.ca/english/department/biometrics-international.asp. Accessed 7 Aug 2019

Great Britain, Data Protection Act 2018 c.12. https://www.legislation.gov.uk/ukpga/2018/12/contents. Accessed 7 Aug 2019

Gregory P, Simon MA (2008) Biometrics for dummies. Wiley Publishing Inc, Indiapolis, p 22

Grother PJ et al (2010) Report on the evaluation of 2D still-image face recognition algorithms. NIST Interagency Report 7709. http://www.nist.gov/customcf/get_pdf.cfm?pub_id=905968. Accessed 6 Aug 2019

Harmel K (2006) Walt Disney World: The Government's Tomorrowland. http://news21.com/story/2006/09/01/walt_disney_world_the_governments. Accessed 7 Aug 2019

Harris S (2013) Computer to sales staff: VIP approaching. The Sunday Times 14 July 2013. http://www.thesundaytimes.co.uk/sto/news/uk_news/Tech/article1287590.ece. Accessed 7 Aug 2019

International Civil Aviation Organisation Machine Readable Travel Documents ICAO Document 9303 part 9 section 4.1 'Primary Biometric: Facial Image' p 7-8. www.icao.int/publications/Documents/9303_p9_cons_en.pdf. Accessed 6 Aug 2019

Kamisher E (2017) Israel transitions to Biometric passports and IDs. Jerusalem Post 1st June 2017. http://www.jpost.com/Israel-News/Israel-transitions-to-Biometric-passports-and-IDs-494535. Accessed 18 Sept 2019

Kant C, Sharma N (2013) Fake face recognition using fusion of thermal imaging and skin elasticity. IJCSCIJ 4(1):65–72. http://www.csjournals.com/IJCSC/PDF4-1/Article_15.pdf. Accessed 7 Aug 2019

Lin SH (2000) An introduction to face recognition technology. Informing Sci 3(1):1, Informing Science Special Issue on Multimedia Informing Technologies

Lynch J (2012) Written testimony of Jennifer Lynch Staff Attorney with the Electronic Frontier Foundation (EFF) Senate Committee on the Judiciary Subcommittee on privacy, technology, and the law what facial recognition technology means for privacy and civil liberties. July 18, 2012, p 3. http://www.judiciary.senate.gov/imo/media/doc/12-7-18LynchTestimony.pdf. Accessed 7 Aug 2019

Moghaddam B, Jebara T, Pentland A (2000) Bayesian face recognition. www.cnbc.cmu.edu/~tai/readings/face/pentland.pdf. Accessed 6 Aug 2019

NEC. The acronym of NEC corporation previously known as Nippon Electric Company. http://uk.nec.com/en_GB/global/about/history.html. Accessed 7 Aug 2019

NEC. Face recognition. https://www.nec.com/en/global/solutions/safety/face_recognition/index.html. Accessed 6 Aug 2019

NEC. New biometric identification tools used in theme parks. http://www.nec.com/en/global/about/mitatv/03/2.html. Accessed 7 Aug 2019

Niles R (2012) Disney claims top 8 spots in 2011 global theme park industry attendance report. http://www.themeparkinsider.com/flume/201205/3073/. Accessed 7 Aug 2019

Occupy Corporatism (2012) Disney biometrics and the Department of Defense. http://www.occupycorporatism.com/disney-biometrics-and-the-department-of-defense/. Accessed 7 Aug 2019. See also Chapter 3.2

Patil AM, Kolhe SR, Patil PM (2010) 2D Face recognition techniques: a survey. Int J Machine Intelligence 2(1):74–78

Priyanto U (2012) National Electronic ID Card (e-ktp) Programme in Indonesia. https://www.scribd.com/document/240007853/1-Priyanto-Unggul. Accessed 7 Aug 2019

Rodrigues RN, Kamat N, Govindaraju V (2010) Evaluation of biometric spoofing in a multimodal system, Biometrics: Theory Applications and Systems (BTAS). In: Fourth IEEE International Conference on Biometrics: Theory Applications and Systems (BTAS), pp 1–5. 27–29 Sept. 2010

Rogers K (2016) That time the super bowl secretly used facial recognition software on fans. https://www.vice.com/en_us/article/kb78de/that-time-the-super-bowl-secretly-used-facial-recognition-software-on-fans. Accessed 6 Aug 2019

Shah Zainudin MN et al (2012) Face recognition using Principle Component Analysis (PCA) and Linear Discriminant Analysis (LDA). Int J Electr Comp Sci 12:51. http://www.ijens.org/Vol_12_I_05/1214404-05-3737-IJECS-IJENS.pdf. Accessed 6 Aug 2019

Slevin J (2013) How to measure passenger flow? Part 3 – Facial Recognition. http://blog.hrsid.com/mflow/2013/12/03/can-measure-passenger-flow-part-3-facial-recognition. Accessed 6 Aug 2019

Smith K (2019) 53 Incredible facebook statistics. Brandwatch marketing. https://www.brandwatch.com/blog/47-facebook-statistics/. Accessed 7 Aug 2019

Syed Navaz A, Dhevi Sri T, Mazumder P (2013) Face recognition using principal component analysis and neural networks. Int J Comp Netw Wireless Mobile Commun 3:245–256

Turk M, Pentland A (1991) Eigenfaces for recognition. J Cogn Neurosc 3(1):71–86. Massachusetts Institute of Technology, published by the MIT Press

UIDAI (2012) The role of biometric technology in Aadhaar Enrolment. stateofaadhaar.in/wp-content/uploads/UIDAI_Role_2012.pdf. Accessed 7 Aug 2019

UK Borders Act 2007 c.30 §.5. https://www.legislation.gov.uk/ukpga/2007/30/contents. Accessed 7 Aug 2019

Welinder Y (2012) A face tells more than a thousand posts: developing face recognition privacy in social networks. Harv J Law Technol 26(1):166–237. http://jolt.law.harvard.edu/articles/pdf/v26/26HarvJLTech165.pdf

Zhang Z et al (2011) Face liveness detection by learning multispectral reflectance distributions. http://www.cbsr.ia.ac.cn/users/zlei/papers/Zhang-FaceLiveness-FG-11.pdf. Accessed 18 Sept 2019

Zhao W et al (2003) Face recognition: a literature survey. ACM Comp Surv 35(4):399–458. http://doi.acm.org/10.1145/954339.954342. Accessed 6 Aug 2019

Chapter 3
Some Ethical and Legal Issues of FRT

Abstract This chapter considers some of the ethical and legal issues of FRT. Ethically FRT is problematic and legally challenging, ethically because of its intrusiveness and legally because the technology exceeds and tests the jurisprudential boundaries. Some examples of where and how FRT is used to illustrate the issues, and how privacy campaigners have responded to its burgeoning uses by commercial enterprises and government agencies.

3.1 Fears and Misconceptions of FRT

Here we introduce some pertinent legal and ethical concerns, looking at them from the point of view of users of FRT as well as consumers. The adoption and use of FRT by governments and commercial organisations necessitates acceptance by citizens and clients. But, it is possible that acceptance does not necessarily imply approval, because whilst fraud prevention is essential to prevent a user's account being accessed illegally, it is the secondary uses[1] of the technology by the service providers, such as Disney or government agencies, that remain beyond the control of the data subjects. The secondary uses have motivated whistleblowers and others to demand transparency and accountability, and these matters are discussed in more detail in Chap. 10.

Yet from the perspective of the theme parks and casinos owners, the degree of fraud prevention that is possible from using face recognition access and surveillance is arguably good for the company. The same system can be used for monitoring traffic flow, behaviour, and surveillance generally. Governments may mandate, or national security agencies may demand, access to the data for either to test their own systems, or to supplement existing data or create a new image data file. Ultimately, even with freedom of information requests, the actual use of the data or how it is managed is likely to be redacted from any information released.[2] Therefore, the

[1]Such as data acquisition for third party use not associated with the primary purpose of disclosure.
[2]Electronic Privacy Information Center.

I. Berle, *Face Recognition Technology*, Law, Governance and Technology Series 41,
https://doi.org/10.1007/978-3-030-36887-6_3

implications of extending the remit of use is cause for concern, but these are conceded when the popular justifications for the technology tilt towards favouring the convenience that the technology affords, for instance speeding up access or preventing fraud. The tension between the two is evident in numerous weblogs, where investigative journalists, public watchdogs or 'bloggers' reveal the covert uses of the technology.

This is evident when the distinction between identification and data collection is blurred, such as the use of photo driver licences and photo enabled ticketing; and the degree of mission creep that is possible where interoperable data access is permitted or mandated. Two American scenarios illustrate the issues and the angst felt among the on-line and print journalists, who gather respondents to their articles:

3.1.1 Disney World

Susanne Posel[3] claims that the Disney Corporation sends their customer data to the US Department of Defense (DOD) for analysis and profiling. Although unconfirmed and regarded as misinformation,[4] this potential fake news does have some credibility inasmuch that Disney uses biometrics to log customers entering its leisure centres[5] and monitors customers movements around the centres via a network of cameras. Moreover, many leisure centres photograph customers without permission whilst on the rides and attractions, these are available to purchase, yet the copyright remains the property of Disney and similar companies. However, the discretionary uses of the photographs are uncertain and blur the line between identification and data collection, because identification is proof of entitlement and data collection is proof of who the customer is during the process of creating a record of their visit. By combining these aspects of enrolment future identity verification is simplified. Subsequently, data collection when associated with an identity photograph creates a more detailed profile that may contain other information volunteered at entry, especially if the data is aggregated with unrelated personal information.

3.1.2 Driver Licences

In the United Kingdom and the United States driver licences include an identity photograph; and in the UK the Driver and Vehicle Licensing Agency (DVLA) is responsible for issuing licences and maintaining the image database. In the US this is state operated, rather than a federal function, although federal government agencies

[3]*Occupy Corporatism a.k.a* Susanne Posel (2012).

[4]Jacobs (2014).

[5]Suderman (2016).

are responsible for the collection of photographs for passports, immigration cards and military and government employee purposes.[6] Also, state agencies are empowered by their legislatures to use face recognition matching to prevent fraudulent licence applications. For instance, in Washington State,[7] this is publicised in conspicuous locations at all licensing offices and includes details of a person's right to appeal.[8] And at paragraph (4)(c) the "results from the facial recognition matching system: [m]ay only be disclosed to a federal government agency if specifically required under federal law". This clause allows the FBI via its NGI project described above, to access the data and which provides the legislative framework for biometric interoperability between state and federal agencies.

In New York State (NYS), face recognition technology was introduced in 2010. Since then, in 2013, Governor Cuomo announced that the Department of Motor Vehicles (DMV) had investigated "13,000 possible cases of identity fraud" resulting in more than 2500 arrests and over 5000 individuals who faced other enquiries.[9] The system is used to ensure "one driver, one license" functionality by reviewing new photographs against pre-existent photographs held in the DMV database. The effectiveness of the system was evaluated with the assistance of University of Albany's Institute of Traffic Safety Management and Research, and it is evident that the DMV can thwart those intending to defraud,[10] since up to 50% of applicants had multiple licences or had attempted to apply for another licence.

In 2005, the DVLA announced that it would be testing a face recognition system similar to those used by American licensing agencies,[11] but the scheme was axed in 2008.[12] Although, in the future, it maybe that the DVLA will use the 'Passport Office's Face Recognition Engine'.[13] However, whether the scheme is resurrected by whatever means, given the success rate experienced in the US, it remains to be seen. Nevertheless, the Americans have observed the effectiveness of the UK's CCTV surveillance and licence plate recognition systems, and New York's Lower Manhattan Security Initiative modelled on London's system, monitors security cameras and licence plate readers.[14]

---

[6]Smith (2013).

[7]For example: Washington State Legislature.

[8]*ibid.*

[9]Cuomo (2013).

[10]*ibid.*

[11]Homeland Security News Wire.

[12]Bowcott (2008).

[13]DVLA Strategic Plan for 2014 to 2017.

[14]Kelly (2013).

3.1.3 New York Domain Awareness System

Although not directly associated with face recognition, the Domain Awareness System (DAWS) is included because of the potential for systems convergence and interoperability. There is for instance a danger of the blending and 'cascading' of data from different sources which is a significant ethical concern. The legal authority for DAWS is the New York City Charter Chapter 18, §435(a) which gives the New York Police Department (NYPD) wide ranging plenary power to maintain law and order, by preserving the peace, preventing crime, guarding public health, and regulating the movement of pedestrian and vehicular traffic etcetera.[15] The overall remit is surveillance which includes licence plate recognition, but does not utilise face recognition technology as this would potentially constitute a search and subsequently breach the Fourth Amendment; principally because the driver is inside the car and not arguably in a public space. This nuanced approach has been considered by the Center for Democracy and Technology (CDT) in their report '*Seeing is ID'ing: Facial Recognition & Privacy*'[16]:

> Traditional Constitutional law is often read that Americans have no "expectation of privacy" in information they voluntarily reveal in public spaces. Courts justified this theory by pointing out that anybody can observe an individual in public, and therefore, the theory goes, using electronic devices such as camera to augment normal human senses and take pictures in public places is not subject to the Fourth Amendment. On a practical level, this theory is rapidly becoming outdated. CDT and others have urged the Supreme Court, in the pending *U.S. v Jones* case, to rule that government use of GPS to track a person - even in public places – is a search under the Fourth Amendment, due largely to the stark differences between GPS and human observation. In the context of facial recognition, it would require extraordinary effort to deploy a human being - even a team of human beings – 24 hours a day to capture facial details of all passersby, identify or link associated online content to the individuals, target messages to the individuals, and then retain the data for later use. It is simply no longer reasonable to equate the human eye and sophisticated vision connected to vast networks.[17]

The outcome in the case of *United States v Jones*,[18] was that the court found that the use of remote surveillance by a GPS tracking device violated the Fourth Amendment because it breached Jones's reasonable expectation of privacy due to the device being installed after the warrant permitting its use had expired. Crucially, the court appears to have considered the expiration of the warrant to be the misdemeanour that triggered the violation of the Fourth Amendment rather than the actual tracking itself and is arguably compliant with *United States v Knotts* (see below). Therefore, from this perspective any change of the legal framework that may emerge from future American case-law could result in the convergence of the DAWS and DMV systems; yet the impact of the FBI NGI data requests on the state held

[15]New York Police Department (2009).

[16]Center for Democracy and Technology (2012).

[17]*ibid* pp. 7–8.

[18]United States v. Jones.

databases may supersede the DAWS guidelines when combined with images from the DMV. Ultimately, the issues and provocations of Fourth Amendment caselaw challenge constitutional and academic lawyers alike, and the cases below[19] illustrate some of the issues.

Each of the above examples illustrates how data cascades and thereby aggregates individuals' profiles without their knowledge which arguably breaches civil liberties and the principles of data protection. Cascading[20] is a generic technical term used to describe complex data analysis and processing, whilst data aggregation[21] is the process of summarising information such as age, profession, income or location for reporting purposes. This issue is discussed further in Chap. 10.

3.2 Some Deeper Issues: FRT, Data Protection and Civil Liberties

The real ethical and legal problem is centred on privacy. In the past an addressed envelope revealed the recipient's name whilst (assuming a sealed envelope) the contents remained private; and unless the recipient was known, they were otherwise largely anonymous (to all but those determined to check residence databases and such). The relationship between the envelope and its contents are discussed in more detail in Chap. 5 (see *Privacy and Autonomy*), yet the concept is introduced here because the information age (i.e. the internet and its allied information networks such as Facebook) has spawned other forms of communication which now include face recognition modalities. The term 'modality' is used to describe its application; of itself face recognition is not a means of communication, but where it is used it can assist communication and information flows by identifying the data subject or person.

Therefore, face recognition is potentially the key that unlocks, collates or aggregates the trail of data and information that is generated by individuals. From the point of view of surveillance, the more complete 'portrait' of a person that is thereby provided is an acute privacy issue. Solove[22] points out that a piece of data here or there is not exceptionally telling. Yet, when combined, odds and ends of information start to form a personal profile that becomes greater than the parts. Therefore, the consolidated information synergises to create a more detailed profile which the disparate parts do not when isolated from each other. Aggregating data is unquestionably not a new activity, but it is more efficient and increasingly more extensive, and easier to analyse.

---

[19]Section 7.4.

[20]Orekhov (2014).

[21]Rouse (n.d.).

[22]Solove (2008, pbk 2009), p. 118.

Eventually the aggregated data grows into data repositories of personal information which Solove describes as "digital dossiers".[23] These dossiers are arguably similar to electronic patient records and accord with Kluge's[24] contention that "electronic patient records are an example of a new kind of entity: namely, that they are ontologically reified entities that function as person-analogues in information and decision-space".[25] Moreover, the governance of patient information is subject to various data protection principles; yet unlike electronic patient information, data dossiers contain a wider spectrum of data that potentially exposes the data subject to breaches of privacy and the concomitant issues of civil liberty.

Data protection regulates data sharing between individuals and organisations; whilst each nation develops their data protection regulations within their legal and cultural norms. The consequences of these differences are discussed in Chap. 7 and are previewed by this brief introduction of the British and American data protection regulations: In the UK data processing and sharing is regulated by the Six Data Protection Principles (contained in the Data Protection Act 2018) which states for instance, that processing should be lawful and fair (Principle 1), and that it should be kept securely (Principle 6).[26] In respect of data sharing, the UK ICO's Data Sharing Code of Practice (2011)[27] requires that there be "some form of active communication where the individual knowingly indicates consent" and that "if you are going to rely on consent as your condition you must be sure that individuals know precisely what data sharing they are consenting to and understand the implications for them. They must also have genuine control over whether or not the data sharing takes place".

Data sharing required by statute would be for example, a disclosure request authorised by a Chief Constable in the course of a police investigation; and for the provision of an essential service such health care or social services.

By comparison, the US scenario appears to be irregular from the UK perspective inasmuch as their legal framework, unless it is challenged, permits access to personal data by third parties without consent or at least without the knowledge of the data subject. Whilst any data requested must be authorised by federal law, the fact that personal data can be cascaded across agencies and the effect that *US v Jones* has had, is sufficient grounds to challenge the *status quo* and possibly motivate whistle-blowers to expose activities that they regard as unethical or unlawful. Yet, whistle-blowers aside, similar activities (for data sharing) are permissible in the UK providing they comply with the regulations (and do not breach Article 8 of the Human Rights Act 1998). Ultimately, face recognition technology is open to use as a surveillance tool and whatever the country, the potential for abuse remains whether

[23] *ibid* p. 119.

[24] Kluge (2001).

[25] *ibid* p. 3.

[26] Data Protection Act 2018.

[27] Information Commissioner's Office (ICO).

by employees or state initiated covert activities that are exposed by concerned individuals or by insiders in the interests of public disclosure.

3.3 Face Recognition: Civil Liberty and Public Disclosure

The potential power of new information and communication technologies, of which face recognition is one, raises critical questions of disclosure and civil liberties. There is a need to distinguish between (a) the disclosure of internal matters which may adversely affect national security and are thus unjustifiable, and (b) the disclosure of matters that affect the population at large which do not affect national security; but may reveal facts that potentially embarrass governments and organisations in a society that values democratic ideals. Face recognition technology has a new, powerful and large-scale capacity and refined capability to identify citizens, and thereby over-ride some typical expectations of anonymity. This ability to visually identify a person exceeds the capability of mobile tracking devices (i.e. smart phones) and RFID (that is used on public transport systems in London), but when used together, all are enhanced because an individual can be identified at a specific time and location. The disclosure of personal images and the 'information' that goes with them is somewhat new ethical and legal terrain. The temptation to exploit the technology for spurious reasons by those who have the resources to control and develop it raises public and professional concerns, some of which may, understandably, provoke disclosure in the public interest by whistleblowing.

In a democracy it is assumed that the legitimacy of power can be scrutinised and legitimately constrained if it exceeds the rule of law. At the same time, constraint must be achieved by reasoned debate and achieved by developing juridical responses to case law or by applying constitutional rights appropriately (i.e. Davis and Watson, Chap. 10 and above). In Chap. 7 (Data Protection and Privacy) two American scenarios (*Dionisio and Katz*) are discussed, one illustrating the power (that is the capacity and capability) of face recognition technology and the second how American case law responds to curtail or limit that power; these US and UK scenarios illustrate how overzealous use of photography or videography violates human rights legislation. Paradoxically, although governments and organisations (corporations) disdain or criminalise public disclosure, whistleblowing fosters change whereby accountability and transparency of power is enhanced. The urgency to change is evident in President Obama's response to the burgeoning use of surveillance by US intelligence services and by corporations seeking greater market penetration. President Obama noted that although corporations of all sizes and types track our online buying habits, and store and analyse our data for commercial purposes, a higher standard was expected for government surveillance, to the extent that such activity must not merely be based on trust and good intentions, not to abuse the data collected, but rather "on the law to constrain those in power".[28]

Nevertheless, rhetoric aside, arguably without occasional and controversial public disclosure heads of government or corporations would probably ignore the issues to maintain the status quo. By public disclosure, governments and corporations are held to account for their actions and are called to justify the legitimacy of their actions, doing so may garner support and citizens' consent.

3.3.1 *Public Disclosure*

To reveal state secrets is treason, but to speak out as a whistleblower against injustice is arguably a public duty, especially if in a privileged position. Hunt[29] defines whistleblowing thus:

> Whistleblowing is the public disclosure, by a person working within an organisation, of acts, omissions, practices, or policies that are perceived as morally wrong by that person, and is a disclosure regarded as wrongful by that organisation's authorities.

There is also the distinction to be drawn between the role of a 'watchdog' and a 'whistleblower'. The watchdog keeps within the law by not disclosing classified information and limits their comments to descriptive or reflective pronouncements which may be nonetheless persuasive and discursive; on the other hand, the whistleblower discloses information in ways that are deemed wrongful by the authorities, yet their disclosure is nevertheless valid where the context is identical. The difference between the two is the content[30] and the means of delivery of what is disclosed or announced. The moral justification for disclosure can only be assessed when the results or effects of the disclosure are understood.

For example, US Senator Ron Wyden, an erstwhile defender of privacy and civil liberties has warned his compatriots that the government has broadly limitless authority to collect law-abiding American citizens information.[31] Wyden's warning followed in the wake of the disclosures made by the fugitive American whistleblower (the former National Security Agency contractor) Edward Snowden,[32] who revealed that a group of government appointed judges who are responsible for decisions permitting surveillance in national-security cases had redefined the word 'relevant', to legitimise the collection of data of potentially millions of people by the NSA.[33] But, what is *'relevant'* is important. In 1991 the US Supreme

---

[28]President Obama (2014).

[29]Hunt (2013), p. 46.

[30]The depth and breadth of information disclosed.

[31]Sadowski (2013).

[32]Edgar (2017).

[33]Valentino-DeVries and Gorman (2013).

Court's interpretation of Section 215 of the Patriot Act[34] lowered the standard of what is "relevant" to mean "anything and everything",[35] which could mean everything is relevant, regardless of the volume of records and the negligible portions of data that might actually be "relevant to an authorized investigation".[36]

If, however, the low standard of relevance initiates the gathering of information that is not significant, innocent people are likely to be investigated unnecessarily. Where or when such injustices occur, whistleblowing maybe the only option, and the wrongfulness of disclosure determined by its subjectivity that requires adequate judicial representation and effective lines of accountability. Therefore, it remains to be seen whether President Obama's call for higher standards materialises and whether ostracised whistleblowers are vindicated. Hunt[37] observes that:

> Where citizens have a right to certain information that is wilfully being denied to them the conscientiousness civil servant will wish to act vicariously for the citizens, on pain of otherwise undermining the very worth and meaning of their professional role. A government which in actual practice denies freedom of information, and *a fortiori* ignores or even victimises the civil servant who takes freedom of information seriously, is corrosive of the very rationale for civil service as understood in a democracy.

Arguably, if the over-riding concern is to protect citizens from harm, governments may want to withhold information and the cycle of watchdog or whistleblower will continue; albeit within the context of the law and its application and interpretation. For instance, in respect of the separation between espionage and criminal investigations Solove[38] helpfully describes the difference between the Electronic Communications Privacy Act (ECPA) and the Foreign Intelligence Surveillance Act (FISA). The former protects privacy by requiring the government "to justify the need for surveillance by demonstrating suspicion of criminal activity", the latter legitimises intelligence gathering "where the goal is to collect information broadly". Unlike ECPA, under FISA proceedings are secret and the decisions permit the security agencies to gather information from innocent individuals, those who principally would not be justifiably suspected of criminality.

Furthermore, Solove contends that "FISA's high level of secrecy is appropriate for matters of espionage but not for matters of law enforcement in general".[39] In the UK similar separation is evident between PACE, RIPA and the ISA, however in August 2013, Schedule 7 of the Terrorism Act 2000 was invoked to detain a journalist and confiscate his laptop computer which from a public disclosure perspective is indicative of governmental sensitivities that results in seemingly inappropriate pre-emptive action. Commenting on the government's response to the

[34]USA Patriot Act.

[35]Timm (2013).

[36]USA Patriot Act at §§505, 507 and 508 *op cit.*

[37]Hunt (2013), p. 47 *op cit.*

[38]Solove (2011), p. 77.

[39]*ibid* p. 77.

journalist's detention, the UK's former Lord Chancellor Charles Falconer[40] counselled that Schedule 7 does not provide the means to detain and question journalists, simply because the state doesn't like what's published. And had exceeded its powers in doing so, and that the courts should make this clear, sooner rather later.

Whilst this remains to be clarified, the distinction between the gathering of evidence in accordance with PACE and the need to adhere to the principles contained in RIPA, is paramount if the government and state agencies are to remain accountable.

3.3.2 Public Interest Disclosure and FRT

The previous section broadly discussed the principles and purpose of public disclosure related to government and state agencies use of powers to access information. Since FRT converts photographs into machine-readable digital data, thereby becoming information, the same concerns about the access to information is identical. The FRT information merely being additional data that the data subject set contains. The data subject is anyone who has created an on-line profile, for example on a social network, an on-line shop or an on-line application for vehicle road tax. Taken in isolation, these seemingly innocuous transactions are regular activities for many people. The data is held on main servers that the state may request or even demand access to. Each provider may have fragments of data that relate to specific aspects of a person's life. Yet, when each provider supplies these fragments they begin to converge to provide a fuller picture of a person's life. In their separate elements a person maybe identifiable but remain anonymous, but in a scenario which includes face recognition anonymity is often lost. This arguably supports the detection and conviction of offenders caught on camera but is not justified otherwise because of the similarities to the retention of DNA data described in Chap. 10.

It is the 'otherwise' that requires diligence and in surveillance surveyed, that follows, the contours of the discourse beyond the immediate political and ethical issues are considered. After which, we shall return in greater depth to ethical and legal issues, especially in relation to privacy and the power of state surveillance.

References

Bowcott O (2008) Credit crunch hits plans for DVLA's facial recognition database. http://www.theguardian.com/politics/2008/nov/13/transport-economy. Accessed 7 Aug 2019

[40]Falconer (2013).

Center for Democracy and Technology (2012) Seeing is ID'ing: facial recognition & privacy. https://cdt.org/files/pdfs/Facial_Recognition_and_Privacy-Center_for_Democracy_and_Technology-January_2012.pdf. Accessed 7 Aug 2019

Cuomo AM (2013) Governor Cuomo announces 13,000 identity fraud cases investigated by DMV using facial recognition technology. https://www.governor.ny.gov/news/governor-cuomo-announces-13000-identity-fraud-cases-investigated-dmv-using-facial-recognition. Accessed 7 Aug 2019

Data Protection Act 2018, chapter 2 §35-40 http://www.legislation.gov.uk/ukpga/2018/12/contents/enacted. Accessed 7 Aug 2019

DVLA Strategic Plan for 2014 to 2017, §1.17 https://www.gov.uk/government/publications/dvla-3-year-strategic-plan/dvla-strategic-plan-2014-to-2017. Accessed 7 Aug 2019

Edgar TH (2017) Beyond snowden: privacy, mass surveillance, and the struggle to reform the NSA. Brookings Institution Press, Washington DC

Electronic Privacy Information Center: EPIC v. FBI: The Next Generation Identification. https://epic.org/foia/fbi/ngi/. Accessed 7 Aug 2019

Falconer C (2013) The detention of David Miranda was an unlawful use of the Terrorism Act. The Guardian, 21st August 2013. http://www.theguardian.com/commentisfree/2013/aug/21/terrorism-act-david-miranda-detention. Accessed 7 Aug 2019

Homeland Security News Wire 12 December 2005. Visage selected for UK facial-recognition driver license scheme. http://www.homelandsecuritynewswire.com/viisage-selected-uk-facial-recognition-driver-license-scheme. Accessed 7 Aug 2019

Hunt G (2013) Civil servants and whistle-blowing: loyal neutrality and/or democratic ideal? In: Neuhold C, Vanhoonacker S, Verhey L (eds) Civil servants and politics: a delicate balance. Palgrave Macmillan, London, p 46

Information Commissioner's Office (ICO) Data Sharing 2011, p 15 https://ico.org.uk/for-organisations/guidance-index/data-protection-act-1998/. Accessed 7 Aug 2019

Jacobs K (2014) Exposed again Suzanne Posel a.k.a. Sanne Cohen (Occupy Corporatism. Truth News International. https://truthnewsinternational.wordpress.com/2014/02/22/exposed-again-suzanne-posel-a-k-a-sanne-cohen-occupy-corporatism/. Accessed 7 Aug 2019

Kelly H (2013) After Boston: the pros and cons of surveillance cameras. https://edition.cnn.com/2013/04/26/tech/innovation/security-cameras-boston-bombings/index.html. Accessed 7 Aug 2019

Kluge EHW (2001) The ethics of electronic patient records. Peter Lang Publishing Inc., New York

New York Police Department (NYPD) Public Security Privacy Guidelines 2009, p 1 http://www.nyc.gov/html/nypd/downloads/pdf/crime_prevention/public_security_privacy_guidelines.pdf. Accessed 7 Aug 2019

Obama B (2014) Remarks by the President on review of signals intelligence. http://www.whitehouse.gov/the-press-office/2014/01/17/remarks-president-review-signals-intelligence. Accessed 7 Aug 2019

Orekhov O (2014) Complex data processing gets simpler with cascading. http://www.epam.com/ideas/blog/complex-data-processing-gets-simpler-with-cascading. Accessed 7 Aug 2019

Posel S (2012) Disney biometrics and the department of defense. http://www.occupycorporatism.com/disney-biometrics-and-the-department-of-defense/. Accessed 7 Aug 2019

Rouse M (n.d.) Data aggregation. https://searchsqlserver.techtarget.com/definition/data-aggregation. Accessed 7 Aug 2019

Sadowski J (2013) Ron Wyden's warning: America may be on track to become surveillance state. http://www.slate.com/blogs/future_tense/2013/07/23/ron_wyden_dangers_of_nsa_surveillance_and_the_patriot_act.html. Accessed 7 Aug 2019

Smith D (2013) Facial recognition and driver licenses: identification or data collection? http://jonathanturley.org/2013/07/06/facial-recognition-and-driver-licenses-identification-or-data-collection/#more-66734. Accessed 7 Aug 2019

Solove DJ (2008, pbk 2009) Understanding privacy. Harvard University Press, Cambridge

Solove DJ (2011) Nothing to hide: the false trade off between privacy and security. Yale University Press, New Haven, p 77

Suderman J (2016) A Disney dilemma – fingerprinting at the happiest place on earth. http://jeffsuderman.com/tag/epcot-center. Accessed 7 Aug 2019

Timm T (2013) Reform the FISA Court: privacy law should never be radically reinterpreted in secret. https://www.eff.org/deeplinks/2013/07/fisa-court-has-been-radically-reinterpreting-privacy-law-secret. Accessed 7 Aug 2019

United States v. Jones, 565 U.S. 400 (2012) Jones was convicted and given a life sentence. http://supreme.justia.com/cases/federal/us/565/10-1259/. Accessed 7 Aug 2019

USA Patriot Act. https://it.ojp.gov/PrivacyLiberty/authorities/statutes/1281. Accessed 7 Aug 2019

Valentino-DeVries J, Gorman S (2013) Secret Court's redefinition of 'relevant' empowered vast NSA data-gathering. http://online.wsj.com/article/SB1000142412788732387390457857189375 8853344.html. Accessed 7 Aug 2019

Washington State Legislature: Facial Recognition Matching System RCW 46.20.037 (1). http://apps.leg.wa.gov/rcw/default.aspx?cite=46.20.037. Accessed 7 Aug 2019

Chapter 4
Privacy and Surveillance Surveyed

Abstract This chapter considers how surveillance modalities affect privacy. The modalities include government sanctioned CCTV or social networks, each of which create tensions and concerns between the data subject-citizen and the data processor.

The chapter focuses on the wide uses of surveillance and considers the sociological and philosophical responses to the burgeoning levels of surveillance and its effect on personal liberty, especially, when the prevailing political view that increased surveillance and subsequent incursions of personal liberty is a societal good. The chapter also concentrates on autonomy and related privacy issues that are associated with the acquisition of images or audio recordings by selected agencies and how those images or recordings are used or disseminated.

4.1 Introduction: Privacy and Surveillance

People watching is not a historically recent development. From the creation account in Genesis where Adam and Eve were observed by God, to the spies and informants in eighteenth century France and to the modern methods deployed in the twenty-first century, the differences are a matter of degree and the depth of information. This chapter focuses on the wide uses of surveillance and considers the sociological and philosophical responses to the burgeoning levels of surveillance and its effect on personal liberty, especially, when the prevailing political view that increased surveillance and subsequent incursions of personal liberty is a societal good. The chapter also concentrates on autonomy and related privacy issues that are associated with the acquisition of images or audio recordings by selected agencies and how those images or recordings are used or disseminated.

Unlike earlier labour-intensive surveillance methods where the few were observed by the many. Automated FRT and other biometrics (such as iris scans) where the many are observed by the few, are dependent on the delivery of digital images and the technologies required for image capture, and subsequent data searching or mining. Within this context 'identity verification' is largely concerned with standardisation and conformity (that is, the ability to match a live image to an

I. Berle, *Face Recognition Technology*, Law, Governance and Technology Series 41,
https://doi.org/10.1007/978-3-030-36887-6_4

image in a dataset). However, Simson Garfinkel[1] suggests that identity is about bodies not people. This poses the question 'are identity and identification conceptually different?' For the purposes of this book it may be useful to think in terms of bodies as *identified* and persons as having an *identity*, the former is extrinsically *a posteriori* knowledge (within a limited understanding of that term, and in terms of material bodily existence), but the latter can be variable and multi-faceted. And therefore, for the purposes of surveillance, CCTV surveys bodies and face recognition software reveal their identities. However, errors such as false positives can occur that lead to situations of mistaken identity when someone is detained erroneously because they share the same name as a person on a 'watch-list' or look like a person of interest.[2] Nevertheless, surveillance assisted security is passively consented to because individuals believe it is beneficial and when requested are prepared to handover information in exchange for security and convenience.[3]

Most biometric systems require enrolment and participation, an individual submitting to a scan or photography. This appears to have a wide degree of acceptance among the population(s) at large.[4] Yet, the burgeoning use of FRT in social networks, for example, is only possible when users agree to the networks' terms and conditions often without due regard to the implications of acceptance that include unconsented secondary and tertiary uses of personal data. Responding to this, Yana Welinder[5] seeks to improve privacy in social networks by highlighting the need to maintain the contextual integrity of consented personal data and regulating the use of face recognition technology.

Contextual integrity and regulation are maintained by prohibiting unconsented uses and giving users more control of their accounts. This has been implemented in EU General Data Protection Regulation (GDPR), which encompasses Welinder's call for improved privacy by making consent mandatory. Moreover, whilst a social network appears to personalise individuals and develop relationships, ultimately every user becomes a data subject and is depersonalised by the system inasmuch that they are surveilled as targets for unsolicited advertising or phototags. Whilst the GDPR protects privacy and confidentiality individuals will need to be proactive with their choices when enrolling or using social networks; but they may also be subjected to face recognition processes that are beyond their control.

---

[1]Garfinkel (2000), p. 65.

[2]Sullivan (2014).

[3]Chesterman (2011), p. 12.

[4]Gregory and Simon (2008) and El-Abed (2010).

[5]Welinder (2012).

4.2 The Data Subject and Surveillance

Surveillance is not a new activity. It has however become more ubiquitous and encompassing, that it reaches virtually every aspect of twenty-first century living through the technological advances in image capture and the digital footprints embedded in a multiplicity of locations. Yet, before technology there were (and continue to be) censuses and bureaucracies that record the movement of people.[6] These were labour intensive activities that required forms to be completed, logged and filed. Whilst technological advances have not completely replaced human labour, technology has increased efficiencies and is arguably more productive given the volume of data generated. However, much of this data analysis is automated and occasionally hyped-up to give the impression that it is more efficient and accurate than it really is. David Lyon[7] cautions policy-makers to beware surveillance systems that cannot deliver the efficiencies their proponents claim, which when used could affect civil liberties when systems converge, and data is integrated. This integration or aggregation of data potentially creates a culture of suspicion which was evident in the aftermath of 9/11. It was only by hindsight that the perpetrators were identified, but the legislative impacts on privacy and civil liberties are still evident and further discussed in Chap. 11.

Transparency and balanced accountability are the antidote to suspicion. For David Brin,[8] considered below, the antidote to suspicion is transparency and balanced accountability. For Lyon, the necessity to protect and secure public safety are political goals which permit or may permit the suspension of ‘normal’ conditions[9] which for Giorgio Agamben is a ‘state of exception’.[10] In this context, personal space becomes an ethical and political issue that creates a pretext for either intrusion or exclusion that is probably predicated by suspicion or prejudice, and which threatens privacy and personal flourishing.[11] Nevertheless, in 1996 Gary T. Marx[12] detected a shift towards transparency and predicted the increasing assemblage of data that would be possible in the future. The purpose of this is risk management as a means of control that affects civil liberties.[13] Viewed from this perspective, if the state informed its citizens about its intentions and uses of surveillance the tension in the relationship between the citizen and the state could potentially be relieved. This openness could nurture trust and may limit the need for whistleblowers, thereby increasing accountability on both sides. The benefits of transparency espoused by Brin have yet to be realised and Marx's detection of

---

[6]Lyon (2003, 2007).

[7]*Ibid* (2003).

[8]Brin (1998).

[9]Lyon (2003), p. 15 *op cit.*

[10]Agamben (2005).

[11]Lyon (2003), p. 34 *op cit.*

[12]Marx (1996), p. 40.

[13]Lyon (2003), p. 45 *op cit.*

transparency was short-lived although his prediction about the increasing assemblage of data was accurate.

Aside from the issue of privacy, there is a surprising link to both Bentham and Foucault, and CCTV surveillance via photography. John Tagg[14] has described the use of photography as a means of surveillance in the late nineteenth century for evidential purposes. This is now standard practice in the collection and recording of evidence at scenes of crime, or of the effects of physical assault; this in itself has an immediate singular function: the potential prosecution of offenders after the fact. Yet by extension the same practice can be paradigmatically applied to and observed in the biometric and surveillance discourses. Hence:

> . . .the body isolated; the narrow space; the subjection to an unreturnable gaze; the scrutiny of gestures, faces and features; the clarity of illumination and sharpness of focus; the names and number boards. These are the traces of power, repeated countless times, whenever the photographer prepared an exposure, in police cell, prison, consultation room, asylum, Home or school. Foucault's metaphor for the new social order which was inscribed in these smallest exchanges is that of the 'Panopticon' – Jeremy Bentham's plan for a model institution in which each space and level would be exposed to the view of another, establishing a perpetual chain of observations which culminated in the central tower, itself open to constant public scrutiny. [Bentham also advocated] a Ministry of Police, but, with the development of photography, his utopian structure was to become redundant, Bentham's 'Panopticon' was the culmination and concrete embodiment of a disciplinary technique already elaborated across a range of institutions – barracks, schools, monasteries, reformatories, prisons - in which a temporal-spatial technology, with its enclosed architectural spaces was set to work to drill, train, classify and survey bodies in one and the same movement[15]

Tagg's description is comparable to biometric data capture, the photographer has been replaced by a technician or automated device, the exposure automatically calculated, and the image uploaded. Therefore, it seems that the unwitting or unwilling individual photographed in the nineteenth century has become the so-called consenting enrolee who nevertheless is surveyed, scrutinised and disciplined to comply with governing authorities in their effort to control and collect data, and which Whitehead[16] warns is indicative of an authoritarian state. Aside from the issue of surveillance *per se,* the issue of consent is a significant aspect in the current discourse and is consistent with consent in healthcare in terms of necessity but is only superficially obtained here. For instance, Solove[17] unsurprisingly notes, that many applications require agreement or acceptance of terms and conditions; yet the terms and conditions are probably rarely read[18] in their entirety and are often accepted at the expense of privacy. Such poor privacy management is predicated by the need to access the service, regardless of any consequences. The service being

---

[14]Tagg (1988).

[15]*Ibid*, pp. 85–87.

[16]Whitehead (2013).

[17]Solove (2012).

[18]Morrison (2015).

the preference and objective; therefore, the manner of choosing according to hierarchical accounts of autonomy is not, in fact, autonomous.[19] Whilst this may be rather prosaic, inasmuch as many applications are perceived as socially beneficial given the convenience possible and therefore acceptable, they nevertheless increase on-line activity and encroach on civil liberties when the metadata is disclosed to government agencies. In respect of civil liberties (in terms of basic rights and freedoms), the US government has been criticised by privacy campaigners for the unconstitutional and unwarranted deployment of surveillance described in Chap. 3. Similarly, large groups of people are monitored by the police in the UK for the purposes of identifying known offenders or those suspected of criminality.[20]

4.3 Biometric Data and Civil Liberties

At the cusp of data, two metaphors popularly describe the broad effect of surveillance and its narrower effect on civil liberty. Firstly, George Orwell's *Nineteen Eighty-Four* is a harrowing depiction of a totalitarian society excessively watched and disciplined by a government called Big Brother. The Orwellian dystopic metaphor focuses on the harms of surveillance, such as inhibition and social control.[21] However, Daniel Solove[22] observes that it's likely that most people are not too concerned about being monitored, especially if it doesn't affect or interfere with their lives nor would they necessarily complain. Such acquiescence is evident on social networks albeit without the otherwise unknown monitoring. Because, although dissimilar to Big Brother, social networks such as Facebook are forms of inverted surveillance when users voluntarily reveal their location or their preferences for certain retail outlets to their friends on the network. Nevertheless, this data, if covertly monitored, is similar to the Orwellian panopticism of *Nineteen Eighty-Four*, but minus much of the discipline Orwell describes. Yet secondly, the data that is collected on social networks creates the potential for another literary metaphor: Franz Kafka's *The Trial.* Kafka's central character called *Josef K* is arrested but doesn't know why. He eventually discovers that a mysterious court has information about him, that is the reason for his arrest, but he is unable to learn anymore. The *Trial,* writes Solove, depicts an unknowable organisation that makes decisions about people without their knowledge, or how they have used personal information to decide their fate and denies them any recourse or participation in the decision-making process.[23] This Kafkaesque metaphor exemplifies the problems of information processing and is symbolic of inadequate accountability and transparency.

[19]See Sect. 5.3.

[20]Notting Hill Carnival; Football Supporters.

[21]See Solove (2011).

[22]*Ibid.*

[23]*Ibid*, p. 26.

Moreover, these two metaphors illustrate the pervasive nature of data driven surveillance that has diminished personal autonomy. As a result, the inability to control or influence the processing of personal data is evident when for instance, at its most benign, receiving unwanted cold telephone calls or mailshots. The least benign aspects are the effects on freedom and liberty that are caused by the current Orwellian and Kafkaesque surveillance culture that exceeds consent and potentially the rule of law.

However, limiting the impact on freedom and liberty is problematic, because according to Simon Chesterman[24] any effort "to prevent governments from collecting such information are doomed to failure because modern threats increasingly require that governments collect it, governments are increasingly able to collect it, and citizens increasingly accept that they will collect it". This he believes, will evolve into "a new social contract… in exchange for security and the convenience of living in the modern world".[25] How conjectural this observation is remains to be seen; although if laws of necessity and self-preservation, as propounded by Thomas Jefferson, the third US President,[26] are rigorously applied a state of exception could emerge. The first iterations of the US PATRIOT Act were arguably such a legal instrument[27] that disturbed Agamben[28] and Chesterman and civil liberty activists. Whitehead[29] has expressed similar views and describes the impact on American citizens by state interference, and over-zealous officials who without clear guidelines or policies interpret the law without considering its effect on an individual's freedom and civil liberty. The impact on an individual can be harmful, and if so ultimately destroys citizens' trust in governments and officials alike.

Moreover, Chesterman has compared the British experience of CCTV in public places with that of Canada and the USA, noting rather imprecisely that CCTV is outside the scope of the UK Data Protection Act 1998.[30] Nevertheless, public CCTV is normalised in the UK to the extent that it is arguably beneficial, and is not necessarily regarded as intrusive.[31] Conversely, in the US an expectation of privacy test is applied to CCTV and is somewhat subject to the Fourth Amendment; and in

---

[24]Chesterman (2011), p. 4.

[25]*Ibid*, p. 12.

[26]Cited by Chesterman (2011).

[27]USA PATRIOT Act: The Uniting and Strengthening America by Providing Appropriate Tools Required to Intercept and Obstruct Terrorism Act of 2001. See Edgar (2017).

[28]Agamben (2005) *op cit.*

[29]Whitehead (2013) *op cit.*

[30]However, more precisely, public CCTV for surveillance purposes is regulated by the Surveillance Camera Commissioner, who encourages compliance to the surveillance camera code of practice; but does not have any powers of enforcement, and any breaches of the code would likely breach human rights law and not data protection law. Moreover, CCTV in shops and company premises needs to comply with data protection law. Whether public CCTV is affected by the Human Rights Act 1998 is another matter that need not be of concern here. Ideally, the Canadian approach would address any contentious use of CCTV in public.

[31]To be discussed.

2004 Canada adopted a four-prong test: specific need, effectiveness, proportionate and permissible when no other means of obtaining evidence or information is available.[32]

Since each of these examples challenge privacy and are indicative of how transparent governments are, Chesterman considers the effects on individuals and society, noting that the wish to impede the disclosure of certain information about oneself is commonplace. But "most legal protections of a right to privacy date only to the late nineteenth century, as reaction to changes in threats, technology, and culture".[33] These two aspects of privacy—that is privacy and confidentiality—are ostensibly the self-evident basis for the concept, and the reason for the reactive nature of efforts to protect it.

By alluding to the nineteenth century, the inference would be the technological advances observed by Warren and Brandeis[34] in their response to unauthorised photography. But our present understanding and relationship to privacy is still problematic and subsequently privacy activists have been unsuccessful in "drawing lines in the sand to stop the encroachment of the surveillance state"[35] due to the difficulties in precisely defining privacy.[36] To overcome these difficulties Chesterman proposed new 'social contract' is "premised on granting access to information. . . .the benefit is not political order as such, but a measure of increased security and the convenience of living in the modern world."[37] Indeed, many individuals experience the benefits that enhanced security mechanisms enable, and the convenience that biometrics affords them. However, the revelation by Edward Snowden in 2013 presents scenarios which illustrate the tension between the need to monitor private on-line activity by the state and the alarm that intrusion provokes.[38]

---

[32]Chesterman (2011), pp. 151–153 *op cit*.

[33]*Ibid*, p. 242.

[34]Warren and Brandeis (1890).

[35]Chesterman (2011), p. 246 *op cit*.

[36]Similarly, Solove (2011), pp. 24–25 *op cit* [succinctly notes that] "privacy can be invaded by the disclosure of your deepest secrets. It might also be invaded if you're watched by a Peeping Tom, even if no secrets are ever revealed to anyone".

[37]Chesterman (2011), p. 250 *op cit*.

[38]To be discussed in Chaps. 7 and 8.

4.4 The Data Subject and Privacy

Alan Westin's[39] seminal text *Privacy and Freedom* describes privacy as the right to (or state of): 'solitude privacy, intimacy' and/or 'reserve'[40] which Ruth Gavison has further defined "as a concern for limited accessibility".[41] Similarly, Helen Nissenbaum following Gavison's *Privacy and the Limits of Law* characterises privacy as "a condition that is measured in terms of the degree of access others have to you through information, attention, and proximity".[42] Raymond Wacks[43] notes that Westin's definition of privacy has influenced the idea that privacy is associated with the ability to control personal information, and that when an individual loses control their privacy is lost. This suggests that an individual controls access. But what is it access to? From the perspective of access limitation, privacy is essentially a descriptive and neutral concept, and when applied to personal information is principally qualitative, for instance, date of birth or bank account number. Therefore, typical invasions of privacy occur when information is collected without explicit consent or aggregated or disseminated by others not connected with the original purpose of disclosure.

Nissenbaum's characterisation of privacy emphasises Wacks's analysis. That is, when an individual controls the disclosure of their personal information or prefers to be left alone, they are acting autonomously. Privacy understood in this way is self-determinative and is accordingly exercised contextually, inasmuch as an individual may disclose information in one context or setting but may choose not to in another. This presumption of privacy is based on the idea that control is possible, and that it is the ability to administer the flow of information or level of contact with others.

4.5 The Data Subject and Autonomy

The question of control, or *will*, provokes questions about *autonomy*.

Dworkin's hierarchical concept of autonomy includes the exercise of critical reflection to be truly self-determinative and therefore any loss of control from a Dworkinian perspective diminishes autonomy. According to Dworkin, the loss can occur by coercion or deception when they encroach upon an individual's actions that result in the person feeling manipulated and used.[44] Whatever the mechanism, ultimately, personal control may not be possible, especially when an individual is subjected to surveillance and not given the opportunity to exercise control other than

[39]Westin (1967).

[40]*Ibid*, p. 31.

[41]Gavison (1980), p. 423.

[42]Nissenbaum (2010), p. 70.

[43]Wacks (1989, revised 1993), p. 14.

[44]See Dworkin (1988, reprinted 1997), p. 14.

to curtail their own liberty or freedom of movement to avoid being seen. This is not very practicable given the pervasiveness of social media and the access limitations ordinarily available, and therefore personal autonomy is reduced.

For Helen Nissenbaum[45] privacy is an issue of context and from this perspective autonomy is not reduced, because what an individual discloses is a personal choice depending on the purpose or need. Subsequently, privacy is neither neutral nor normative but a matter of degree when framed within its context and is consequently variable. However, variability provokes conflict when the context is not mutually beneficial, and the data subject is unable to assert their privacy or right to choose. In this respect and to pre-empt conflicts of interest, privacy is to be defined within a moral, political or legal framework evident in the General Data Protection Regulation (GDPR). Nevertheless, Nissenbaum's observation that:

> we have a right to privacy, but it is neither a right to control information nor a right to have access to this information restricted. Instead, it is a right to live in a world in which our expectations about the flow of personal information are, for the most part, met; expectations that are shaped not only by force of habit and convention but a general confidence in the mutual support these flows accord to key organizing principles of social life, including moral and political ones. This is the right I have called contextual integrity, achieved through the harmonious balance of social rules, or norms, with both local and general values, ends and purposes.[46]

Although the GDPR addresses the insufficiencies of previous legislation and harmonises the right to privacy, Nissenbaum's description is valid given the complexities of information flows across borders and the differences of political will, especially between the EU and the USA.

The GDPR formalises the relationship between the data subject and the data processor, by acknowledging and respecting the data subject's privacy. To that end the data subject's consent is an important component of legitimate data processing, and is indicative to some degree of Dworkin's "tension between autonomy as a purely formal notion (where what one decides for oneself can have any particular content), and autonomy as a substantive notion (where only certain decisions count as retaining autonomy whereas others count as forfeiting it)".[47] Thus Dworkin's formal notion of autonomy is situated by relational ties that are based on the selectivity and inclusivity of the relationship with others, and the substantive notion is defined by the limitations imposed on individuals by others. Conflict occurs when the two notions of autonomy are conflated, for instance when a person over-reaches their right to be heard or to be considered. On this account we surmise that autonomy is an exercise of the will; privacy is the exercise of opacity or obscurity. For instance, by exercising one's will privacy becomes a choice to remain obscure or not. Thus, choice is the defining feature of autonomy and privacy (or otherwise) the effect.

---

[45]Nissenbaum (2010) *op cit.*

[46]*Ibid*, p. 231.

[47]Dworkin (1988, reprinted 1997), p. 12 *op cit.*

However, governments and organisations now have much more information about their citizens than at any other time in human history.[48] Such information can stimulate the growth of coercion by the state, whereby their powers exceed public consent (and perhaps a *de facto* state of exception evolves surreptitiously, and self-rule subsumed), or that organisations exceed the boundaries of consented data processing and use the information to further their objectives. But if the GDPR is adopted, interpreted and applied impartially, the dynamics of the relationship between citizen and state, client and organisation will be enhanced. Improving relationships by protecting data subject rights is welcome, but the issue of consent remains problematic when face recognition technology is a factor when it becomes impractical or difficult to remain unseen.

To that end Solove's[49] analysis of secrecy in terms of privacy illustrates the problem when reviewed from the USA's judicial interpretations of their Constitution's Fourth Amendment. For Solove the issue is principally that of a narrow interpretation of privacy, hence

> [T]he reason privacy has led to such a narrow scope of Fourth Amendment coverage is the secrecy paradigm. The Supreme Court conceives privacy as a form of total secrecy. Under this view, if you share your information with other people – even people you trust a lot – you can't expect privacy. If you expose your information in any way – even if the government has to go to great trouble and expense to discover it – then you can't expect privacy. . . .The secrecy paradigm has resulted in many forms of government information gathering falling outside Fourth Amendment protection. This is a big problem, because when the Fourth Amendment doesn't apply, there's often nothing to regulate the government.[50]

The secrecy paradigm is universally applicable and necessitates the need for new rules to accommodate the changing landscape, without which the expanding use of face recognition modalities potentially obliterates privacy and impacts confidentiality; and by default becomes the means towards unconsented or unintended transparency as information systems become inter-operable. In Europe the new rules are integrated in the GDPR, but future jurisprudence developed by debate, reasoned analysis and case law will determine its adequacy. But if the secrecy paradigm persists any changes to data law or surveillance law will be window dressing and progress stunted.

Underscoring this need to change however, is Whitehead's[51] reference to the case of *United States. v. Jones*:

> [B]y the time *U.S. v. Jones* reached the U.S. Supreme Court, it had generated heated debate regarding where to draw the line when it comes to the collision of privacy, technology, constitutional rights and government surveillance. The arguments on both sides were far-ranging, with law enforcement agencies on one side defending warrantless searches and civil liberties advocates on the other insisting that if police can stick a GPS on car why not on a piece of clothing, or everyone's license plate? Yet while a unanimous Supreme

[48]Chesterman (2011), p. 251 *op cit.*

[49]Solove (2011) *op cit.*

[50]*Ibid*, pp. 100–101.

[51]Whitehead (2013), p. 107 *op cit.*

Court sided with Jones, declaring that the government's *physical* attachment of a GPS device to Antoine Jones' vehicle for the purpose of tracking Jones' movements constitutes an unlawful search under the Fourth Amendment, the ruling failed to delineate the boundaries of permissible government surveillance within the context of rapidly evolving technologies.

The US Supreme Court's failure to delineate the boundaries of permissible government surveillance places a burden on future complainants to prove that an incursion is unlawful, especially as among the rapidly evolving technologies is face recognition, which when combined with surveillance cameras and a smart-phone (which is also, by default a tracking device) provides the means and the mechanism to not only track and locate an individual but also to verify their identity. Arguably this is a welcome tool when used in crime detection, but which potentially impedes civil liberty.

However, the converging technologies have accelerated the informatisation of the body that exceeds mere representation. Yet, the temptation by agencies to adopt face recognition reduces anonymity and increases *de facto* transparency. This *de facto* transparency is only part of what Brin[52] envisaged. Brin conceptualised an open society where transparency is the product of accountability and not merely the effect of investigative powers or surveillance, asserting that: "transparency is not about eliminating privacy. It is about giving us the power to hold accountable those who would *violate* it"; for this reason, the *Jones* complaint concerning the use of the GPS tracking device is justified. Though, however the complaint is framed, it is no defence against the alleged criminality.

4.6 Privacy, Informatisation and Photography

Different interpretations and expectations of privacy drive the development of legal frameworks in the UK and USA, although expectations of privacy maybe similarly applied, the discourse differs by degrees of interpretation and the different approaches to the operation of state power. Principally seen in the jurisprudence that surrounds the US Constitution's Fourth Amendment and in the UK that of Article 8 of the Human Rights Act. The difference between them is underlined by their divergent philosophies. In respect of data privacy law, the US focuses on redressing consumer harm whilst balancing efficient commercial activities,[53] and the intrusion by government agencies vis-à-vis the Fourth Amendment has been discussed in some detail above. In the EU privacy is a legislated basic right that is balanced against other competing rights and is distinct from data protection legislation which defines the governance of data held by organisations or government departments. However, any separation between privacy and data protection has with the inception of the GDPR been rectified. Moreover, in cases described below by

[52]Brin (1998), p. 334.

[53]Schwartz and Solove (2014).

Brennan and Berle,[54] the case law associated with Article 8(1) recognises the right to privacy where unauthorised or unconsented filming or photography has occurred:

> Article 8(1) provides that everyone has the right to respect for their private and family life, their home and correspondence. Herein, is the right to self-determination or autonomy and therefore any interference without consent breaches Article 8. For instance, secret filming which occurred in *R v Loveridge*[55] when the police had arranged to film appellants by video camera in a magistrate's court. The Court of Appeal held that this effectively breached Article 8(1). Similarly, in *Douglas*[56] Lord Justice Sedley perceived that unauthorised wedding photographs interfered with personal autonomy. Moreover, in *Roddy* the Family Division maintained that the protection of personal autonomy in Article 8 covered the right to determine what is or is not private [therefore]:
>
> *Article 8 thus embraces both the right to maintain one's privacy and, if this is what one prefers, not merely the right to waive that privacy but also to share what would otherwise be private with others or, indeed, with the world at large*[57]

The *Roddy* judgement emphasises the value of privacy and recognises self-determination as a quality of life expressed in terms of control which accords with Westin, Gavison and Nissenbaum. Therefore, Article 8(1) is the benchmark used to test the right to privacy in personal contexts that are not restrained by the 'secrecy paradigm' described by Solove. Paradoxically in *Roddy*, there exists a significant secrecy paradigm that could be extrapolated from the judgement, inasmuch as the judgement is very specific and may not apply in other contexts. Especially where the boundaries of the personal, intimate and private cannot be easily protected it may not be possible to maintain one's privacy, because the boundaries do not exist in the public space and hence the secrecy paradigm develops beyond the protection of Article 8(1). Article 8 is a conditional right which is divided into two parts: 8 (1) being balanced against the permissible interference of 8(2) such as the interests of national security, public safety, crime prevention and the protection of the rights of others[58] which therefore necessitates the need for proportionality when assessing claims of breach of privacy. This was recognised by the European Court of Human Rights (ECtHR) in the case of *Von Hannover v Germany* after the Court had previously reconceived the concept of autonomy to encompass a wider notion of privacy and thereby remove the secrecy paradigm that had permeated previous judgements, by stating that[59]:

> ...the guarantee afforded by Article 8 of the Convention is primarily intended to ensure the development, without outside interference, of the personality of each individual in his

[54] Brennan and Berle (2011), p. 146.

[55] R v Loveridge.

[56] Douglas & Anor v Northern and Shell Plc & Anor.

[57] Roddy (a minor); Torbay Borough Council v News Group Newspapers. This case centred on whether a 17 year old, who had a child at 13, had reached a level of maturity to decide what was private. My italics.

[58] Human Rights Act (HRA) 1998.

[59] Von Hannover v Germany. My italics.

> relations with other human beings. There is therefore a zone of interaction of a person with others, even in a public context, which may fall within the scope 'private life'

Previously in *Bruggeman and Scheuten v Federal Republic of Germany* the ECtHR had asserted that[60]:

> the claim to respect for private life is automatically reduced to the extent that the individual himself brings his private life into contact with public life or into close connection with other protected interests.

The change towards a wider appreciation of privacy and the recognition of autonomy has changed the social climate and attitude towards how, for instance, the press and the media treat celebrities (and *vice versa*). However there remains the issue of interference in other contexts and the exercise of autonomy or its loss that occurs in a variety of contexts and scenarios. Specifically, celebrities aside, any interference needs to be carefully considered especially if the level of suspicion is uncertain or the need to expose an individual to scrutiny is spurious.

Additionally, since photography can be intrusive and unwelcome, Article 8 ECHR is potentially the remedy because in von Hannover, the Court held that the right to respect for private life had been violated, which includes activities occurring in public. The case established the boundaries between the private and public divide; however, discerning the difference between publicity seeking imagery and intrusive photography is essential if the Article 8 right is not to be devalued.

UK and EU case law aside, the division between the US and the EU definitions of privacy have been addressed by Schwartz and Solove[61] in their attempt to reconcile them by redefining what 'personally identifiable information' (PII) comprises. They place information on a continuum and term their model PII 2.0, and divide data into three categories:

1. *Identified Data*. A specific individual easily identified from others. High risk of identification
2. *Identifiable Data*. Relates to an identifiable individual but with low to moderate risk of identification
3. *Non-identifiable Data*. Data not easily related to an individual and identification only remotely possible

In the UK cases cited above, the first category applies and any counter-claim that privacy was not breached would be unassailable, although when the categories are applied to Irma van der Ploeg's[62] prescient policy paper, whatever the level of risk and its remedy, it requires a broad reappraisal of privacy protections, or the monitored oversight of Ploeg's recommendations. Before considering Ploeg's paper there is in US law a distinction made between an envelope and its content.[63] The envelope

[60]Bruggeman and Scheuten v Federal Republic of Germany.

[61]Schwartz and Solove (2014) *op cit*. See Sect. 7.4.

[62]van der Ploeg (2005).

[63]Solove (2011), pp. 157–161; pp. 167–170 *op cit*.

or an email header does not have an expectation of privacy, whereas the content does. Moreover, an address reveals who the recipient is and is analogous to the secrecy paradigm; similarly, an informatised body, by virtue of face recognition technology is an envelope, the contents of which can be examined by scrutinising data, potentially without a warrant. Furthermore, an address contains a machine-readable postcode which assists sorting mail automatically by identifying the area where the recipient resides. Thus, the analogy potentially creates transparency by default when individuals are identified automatically using FRT and accords with Ploeg's depiction of social categorisation.

Irma van der Ploeg has defined biometrics as the "informatisation of the body". This she claims, "enables a clearer view of the ethical and normative aspects involved" because biometrics are "digital representations of our physical or bodily characteristics". Noting however, that because of the scale involved biometric products are suboptimal and problematic (this to some degree remains the case in 2019). Ploeg further highlights the ethical issues of social categorisation: known/unknown, legal/illegal, wanted/unwanted, low/high security risk. Moreover, an informatised body becomes a machine-readable body that can be violated when 'read' without consent. Avoiding or preventing any violation or transgression necessitates respecting the boundaries and understanding the concomitant inviolability of the body. The prevention of harm, subsequently, although not framed in the same terminology, is caveats withstanding, incorporated within the GDPR Article 9.

The prevention of harm is a laudable aspiration, yet, an informatised body becomes politicised when individuals lose their right to self-determination[64] in the miscellany of biometrics. Accordingly, Mordini and Petrini[65] in 2007, noted the increasing debate over whether biometrics offered society any substantial advantages over ordinary non-technological methods of identification, and whether biometrics threatened privacy and is potentially harmful if used by authoritarian governments.[66]

However, the effectiveness, efficiencies and convenience of biometrics can outweigh the opposing arguments and socio-political concerns.[67]

4.7 The Data Subject and Biometric Data

Biometric efficiencies and convenience have improved the mobility of travellers and access to a variety of services and utilities, such as airport e-gates and mobile phones.

---

[64]The 'politicisation of bodily integrity' is usually gender specific and relates to the women's rights discourse. I have used the term to broaden its scope and apply it to the biometric discourse in terms of consent and self-determination, which resonates within the women's rights discourse.

[65]Mordini and Petrini (2007), p. 10.

[66]See Agamben (2005).

[67]Whitehead (2013) *op cit*, p. 125.

However, e-gates require the common-place machine readable passports and phones need to record and store the owner's facial appearance or fingerprint. Whatever the modality, personal data is stored and protected. In the UK passport data is stored on a government database and is centrally administered, similarly other UK government agencies store photographic images and other personal data. Each of these databases can potentially be cross-referenced, if the overarching goal politically is the maintenance of security and protection, or crime detection. That aside, the quantity of biometric data generally has reduced the expectation of privacy even though in response to directives and laws, privacy enhancing technologies (PETs) are deployed, such as: anonymisation, pseudonyms, and pin numbers.

The vigilance required to maintain privacy is not always rewarded since the secrecy paradigm defeats that objective. This is because with the increasing compulsory visibility that everyone is subjected to, is evidence that FRT diminishes personal autonomy and choice.[68] This is analogous to unconsented or unregulated clinical photography when patients are photographed when they are at their most vulnerable or unaware.

4.8 The Socio-Political Context

The extensive use of face recognition technology as described in Chap. 2 relates to convenience and the benefits of the technology. Yet, there is a counter-benefit which commentators and critics are concerned with, namely the loss of freedom when governments and their agencies use the technology for political ends.

Therefore, the various legislative instruments described in Chaps. 7 and 8 that limit freedom and raise levels of anxiety cause Whitehead to characterise such developments as the foundation of a police state, whereby "bureaucracy, secrecy, perpetual wars, a nation of suspects, militarisation, [and] surveillance"[69] become normalised activities. From his perspective, a warning of the drift towards a state of exception can be deduced, which accords with Agamben's description of state power.

For biometric centred surveillance and other means of observation it appears that the overarching goal politically is the maintenance of security and protection that is constrained by the rule of law. For Whitehead, it is a matter of citizen engagement[70] and for Chesterman and Solove generally, accountability rests within the US Constitution, the legislature, and the courts. Although the foregoing socio-political issues

[68]See Sect. 2.2.

[69]Whitehead (2013), p. 4 *op cit.*

[70]*Ibid*, pp. 219–232.

are US focused the principles apply in UK and EU contexts and will be discussed further in Chaps. 7 and 8.

Furthermore, in this context Chesterman's *One Nation under Surveillance* conveys, with hindsight Brin and Garfinkel's envisaged concerns that have materialised. Arguably, it is the lack of accountability that Chesterman, Solove and Whitehead highlight, and the frustration that it causes which prompts whistleblowers to act. Though, remedially Nelson[71] in *America Identified* quantifies the adoption of biometric technologies and subsequent identification noting that generally, biometrics has become an acceptable aspect of identity management. Yet, also noting that "signs of a disconnect are growing between privacy advocates who warn that privacy in is peril, and a new generation of individuals who view personal information as a form of currency in social networking, communication, and a means of empowerment".[72] Within this milieu of opposing concerns is the use of face recognition technologies that challenge privacy and affect autonomy.

Concurrent to the political demands for biometric assisted or enhanced surveillance is the commercial applications for biometrics that are claimed to improve on-line security and privacy. The confluence[73] of these two somewhat opposing positions as they relate to face recognition technology and personal autonomy is the principal issue that follows and is predicated by my concern for establishing a consistent approach for protecting identifiable images from unconsented use that is compatible with protected healthcare and copyrighted images. Yet, even though Nelson and Gates apparently advocate a *'fait accompli'* because of the inescapable and inevitable use of FRT and other biometrics that are propounded to improve security. They may not dismiss privacy *per se* but may subsume it in favour of defusing the security versus privacy dichotomy. The relationship between the boundaries of the state (or corporations and organisations), personal autonomy, privacy and confidentiality discussed here, can be thus illustrated (Fig. 4.1).

Tension 1 (T1) is the boundary between totalitarian or democratic societies and Personal Autonomy (PA). Tension 2 (T2) safeguards the personal space of autonomous 'citizens' and their privacy. Since biometrics is defined as 'bodily informatisation', Tension 3 (T3) represents the notion of whether a face is information (data). The interfaces that intrude at each level represent the information flows and degree of intrusion. The next chapter considers the intersections in relation to liberty, and considers the effect on Personal Autonomy, Privacy and Confidentiality.

[71]Nelson (2011).

[72]*Ibid*, p. 3.

[73]The term 'confluence' is used to convey a mixture that cannot easily be separated.

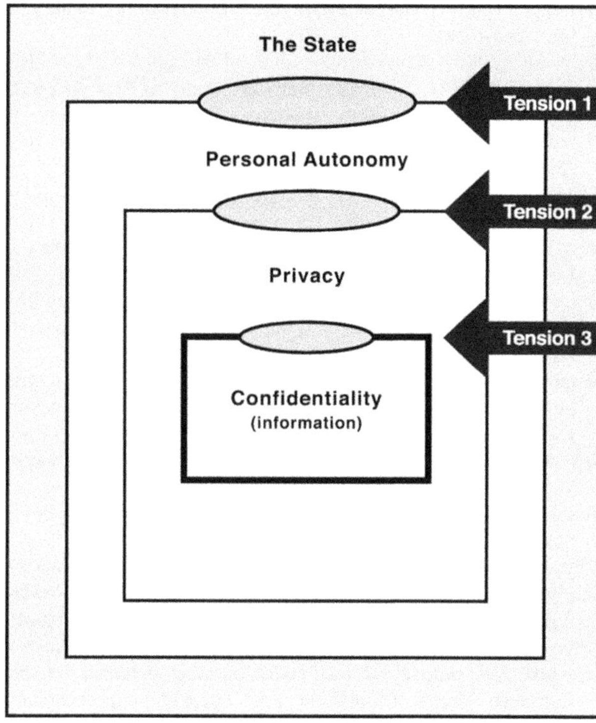

Fig. 4.1 Boundaries and tensions

References

Agamben G (2005) State of exception (trans: Attell K). The University of Chicago Press, Chicago and London

Brennan P, Berle I (2011) The ethical and medical aspects of photo-documenting genital injury. In: Gall J, Payne-James J (eds) Current practice in forensic medicine. Wiley-Blackwell, Chichester, p 146

Brin D (1998) The transparent society: will technology force us to choose between privacy and freedom. Addison-Wesley, Reading

Bruggeman and Scheuten v Federal Republic of Germany [1981] EHRR 244 at paragraph 56. My italics. http://www.bailii.org/eu/cases/ECHR/1977/1.html. Accessed 8 Aug 2019

Chesterman S (2011) One nation under surveillance: a new social contract to defend freedom without sacrificing liberty. Oxford University Press, Oxford, p 12

Douglas & Anor v Northern and Shell Plc & Anor [2001] QB 967, [2001] UKHRR 223, [2001] 1 FLR 982, [2001] EMLR 9, [2001] FSR 40, [2001] 2 All ER 289, [2001] HRLR 26, 9 BHRC 543, [2001] 2 WLR 992, [2002] 1 FCR 289, [2000] EWCA Civ 353, at 126. http://www.bailii.org/ew/cases/EWCA/Civ/2000/353.html. Accessed 8 Aug 2019

Dworkin G (1988, reprinted 1997) The theory and practice of autonomy. Cambridge University Press, Cambridge, p 14

Edgar TH (2017) Beyond Snowden: privacy, mass surveillance and the struggle to reform the NSA. Brookings Institution Press

El-Abed M et al (2010) A study of users' acceptance and satisfaction of biometric systems. IEEE International Carnahan Conference on Security Technology (ICCST), 2010, San Francisco, United States. https://hal.archives-ouvertes.fr/hal-00991086. Accessed 8 Aug 2019

Garfinkel S (2000) Database nation: the death of privacy in the 21st century. O'Reilly & Associates Inc, Sebastopol

Gavison R (1980) Privacy and the limits of the law. Yale Law J 89:421, 423. https://www.jstor.org/stable/795891?seq=1#page_scan_tab_contents. Accessed 8 Aug 2019

Gregory P, Simon MA (2008) Biometrics for dummies. Wiley Publishing Inc., Indianapolis

Human Rights Act (HRA) 1998. http://www.opsi.gov.uk/acts/acts1998/ukpga_19980042_en_1. Accessed 8 Aug 2019

Lyon D (2003) (reprinted 2004 & 2008) Surveillance after September 11. Polity Press, Cambridge

Lyon D (2007) (reprinted 2011) Surveillance studies: an overview. Polity Press, Cambridge

Marx GT (1996) Ethics for the new surveillance. In: Bennett CJ, Grant R (eds) 1996 Visions of Privacy. University of Toronto Press, Toronto, p 40

Mordini E, Petrini C (2007) Ethical and social implications of biometric identification technology. Ann Ist Super Santa 43(1):5–11. http://www.iss.it/binary/publ/cont/STAMPA%20ANN_07_02%20Mordini.1180428288.pdf. Accessed 8 Aug 2019

Morrison K (2015) Survey: many users never read social networking terms of service agreements. http://www.adweek.com/socialtimes/survey-many-users-never-read-social-networking-terms-of-service-agreements/620843. Accessed 8 Aug 2019

Nelson LS (2011) America identified: biometric technology and society. Massachusetts Institute of Technology, Massachusetts

Nissenbaum H (2010) Privacy in context: technology, policy and the integrity of social life. Stanford University Press, Stanford, p 70

R v Loveridge, EWCA Crim 1034, [2001] 2 Cr App R 29 (2002)

Roddy (a minor); Torbay Borough Council v News Group Newspapers [2004] EMLR 127, [2004] 2 FLR 949, [2004] Fam Law 793, [2003] EWHC 2927 Fam), [2004] 1 FCR 481, at 36. http://www.bailii.org/ew/cases/EWHC/Fam/2003/2927.html. Accessed 8 Aug 2019

Schwartz PM, Solove DJ (2014) Reconciling personal information in the United States and European Union. Calif Law Rev 102:877. http://scholarship.law.gwu.edu/faculty_publications/956. Accessed 8 Aug 2019

Solove DJ (2011) Nothing to hide: the false trade off between privacy and security. Yale University Press, New Haven and London

Solove DJ (2012) Privacy self-management and the consent dilemma. Harv Law Rev 126:1880 (2013); GWU Legal Studies Research Paper No. 2012-141; GWU Law School Public Law Research Paper No. 2012-141. http://ssrn.com/abstract=2171018. Accessed 8 Aug 2019

Sullivan A (2014) Mistaken identity. https://www.facebook.com/TheDishBlog/posts/837738439627490. Accessed 8 Aug 2019

Surveillance Camera Commissioner. https://www.gov.uk/government/organisations/surveillance-camera-commissioner. Accessed 8 Aug 2019

Tagg J (1988) The burden of representation: essays on photographies and histories. Palgrave-Macmillan, Basingstoke

van der Ploeg I (2005) Biometric identification technologies: ethical implications of the informatization of the body. Biometric Technology & Ethics, BITE Policy Paper no.1 (unpaginated draft paper). http://www.academia.edu/6039558/Biometric_Identification_Technologies_Ethical_Implications_of_the_Informatization_of_the_Body. Accessed 8 Aug 2019

Von Hannover v Germany Application no. 59320/00 Judgement 24 June 2004 at paragraph. 50. http://www.worldlii.org/eu/cases/ECHR/2004/294.html. Accessed 8 Aug 2019

Wacks R (1989) (revised 1993) Personal information: privacy and the law. Clarendon Press, Oxford, p 14

Warren SD, Brandeis LD (1890) The right to privacy (the implicit made explicit). Harv Law Rev:193–220. https://www.jstor.org/stable/i256795. Accessed 8 Aug 2019

Welinder Y (2012) A face tells more than a thousand posts: developing face recognition privacy in social networks. http://jolt.law.harvard.edu/articles/pdf/v26/26HarvJLTech165.pdf. Accessed 8 Aug 2019

Westin AF (1967) Privacy and freedom. Bodley Head, London

Whitehead JW (2013) A government of wolves: the emerging American police state. Select Books Inc, New York

Chapter 5
Autonomy, Liberty and Privacy

Abstract General ignorance of the range and kinds and implications of the use of FRT raises ethical and legal questions. Some general points may be widely known. For instance, how FRT is used to identify individuals by converting their facial features into digital data and comparing that real-time or recorded data with images stored in databases. The stored images have usually been harvested from individuals who supplied an identity photograph, such as for a passport, driving licence or travel pass. So far, so good. But how far does the average citizen understand that whilst this use of images in identity photographs can also facilitate the application process, it is also an integral part of the document containing other information, and the database that is created may be ethically problematic. This is especially true when used or accessed covertly by agencies without explicit consent and not directly associated with the primary purpose of the photograph. Therefore, this chapter examines how autonomy, liberty and privacy are affected by FRT and presents some elements of an ethical framework, from which FRT's impact on autonomy, liberty and privacy can be assessed.

5.1 The Concept of Autonomy

We have already scanned, in Chap. 3, some of the ethico-legal questions arising from the use of FRT. The following presents some elements of an ethical framework for a wider discussion of FRT namely the concepts of individual autonomy and liberty. I shall consider first and second-order autonomy and positive and negative liberty; opening with a discussion of the significance of the ignorance of FRT by the general public.

General ignorance of the range and kinds and implications of the use of FRT raises ethical and legal questions. Some general points may be widely known. Thus, Chap. 2 described, for example, how FRT is used to identify individuals by converting their facial features into digital data and comparing that real-time or recorded data with images stored in databases. The stored images have usually been harvested from individuals who supplied an identity photograph, such as for a passport, driving licence or travel pass. So far, so good. But how far does the average

I. Berle, *Face Recognition Technology*, Law, Governance and Technology Series 41,
https://doi.org/10.1007/978-3-030-36887-6_5

citizen understand that whilst this use of images in identity photographs, for instance, facilitates the application process it is also an integral part of the document containing other information, and the database that is created may be ethically problematic, i.e. similar to the DNA database (Chap. 10). This is especially true when used or accessed covertly by agencies without explicit consent and not directly associated with the primary purpose of the photograph.

The secondary uses of the image database have generated responses from a variety of individuals and organisations, for instance the Electronic Frontier Foundation (EFF), an American consumer rights organisation has sued the Federal Bureau of Investigation (FBI) for their failure to respond to a Freedom of Information request about secondary uses of image and other databases. The EFF's principal concern[1] is that the secondary uses, are uses which the public are ignorant of, because the "NGI[2] expands the FBI's IAFIS[3] criminal and civil fingerprint database to include multimodal biometric identifiers such as iris scans, palm prints, face-recognition-ready photos, and voice data, and makes that data available to other agencies at the state and federal levels".[4]

It is possible that the FBI is reasonably justified in keeping quiet about the uses of some of them, yet without transparency or disclosure of some kind or to some degree the harms done by secondary uses of face recognition cannot be assessed or evaluated by citizens or citizen representative bodies. One cannot assume that there are no possible harms, for at the very least some such may arise unintentionally or by the malicious intent of third parties. Public ignorance could be used by government or agencies to their own advantage and deny democratic debate.[5] Edward Snowden's disclosures (Chap. 2) have heightened public suspicion of the government use of data generally, and there is no reason why 'data' should not include images.

It is variously reported that the UK leads the world[6] in the use of surveillance cameras by all kinds of bodies; a position criticised by civil liberty activists. But these cameras have nevertheless gained widespread public approval, perhaps rather passively, that is, with a high degree of public ignorance. They have become associated with safety and security and are part of daily living in the public mind. This may be acceptance or acquiescence, by virtue of implied or even 'artificial' consent[7] rather than plebiscite. The justification that many citizens accept for such surveillance may be unfounded. It is interesting that Solove citing a Home Office report, states that the cameras had "no overall effect on all relevant crime viewed

---

[1]EFF.

[2]Federal Bureau of Investigation: Next Generation Identification (NGI).

[3]Integrated Automated Fingerprint Identification System.

[4]EFF *op cit*.

[5]Edgar (2017).

[6]Chesterman (2011), p. 145. Citing ICO and Parliamentary reports.

[7]*Ibid*, p. 150.

collectively".[8] The study further reported that the cameras fail to reduce the fear of crime. Still, the cameras do, in particular cases aid crime detection or record the perpetrators of criminal acts as in the case of the July 2007 London underground suicide bombers.[9]

Paradoxically, CCTV is not necessarily a deterrent and therefore does not prevent certain types of crime but is rather a means of recording events and incidents for later investigation. There remains, however, an ethical problem that may be couched in terms of a hierarchical distinction between first order and second-order autonomy, promulgated by the moral philosopher Gerald Dworkin,[10] when CCTV is used for purposes other than crime prevention or detection.

5.2 Freedom & Privacy

Before explaining and applying the first/second-order distinction, I have to state and explore the concept of autonomy itself since that is a central concept in this book, and that will lead us into the hierarchical distinction and its relevance to an ethical consideration of FRT.

The autonomy of the individual signifies the capacity and freedom to live one's life according to one's own sense of worth, one's own values and aims rather than having those manipulated or directed or obstructed by external forces (e.g. government bodies, powerful corporations, advertisers, the media). An abstract concept of individual autonomy is formulated in the philosophy of Immanuel Kant[11] and an influential version developed by the later philosopher John Stuart Mill,[12] who was also a utilitarian in his ethics. It is a central concept in the liberal tradition of ethics and political legal theory. The concept is admittedly very broad and consequently rather vague and open to several interpretations resulting in a plethora of controversies which are beyond the scope of this book to examine. In any case, the idea of a tension between personal control of one's life and control by forces outside one's control is easy enough to grasp; but what is and is not control, and what individual choice is or is not are not always easy to determine, as becomes apparent with regard to FRT in general, and FRT and privacy in particular.

Some of the more obvious tensions with individual autonomy are ideas, policies and actions founded on some idea of a collective good such as 'public interest' or 'national interest' or 'human welfare' or 'national security'. This is a principal tension running throughout this book. One manifestation of individual autonomy

---

[8]Solove (2011), p. 180. Citing Gill and Spriggs (2005).

[9]*Ibid.*

[10]Dworkin (1988, reprinted 1997).

[11]Kant (1781).

[12]Mill (1859).

Fig. 5.1 First-order/second-order choices

is individual privacy, and we return below to clarify that concept especially in relation to collective concepts such as 'national security'.

It is likely that 'autonomy' and 'privacy' are emphasised in some cultures more than others (in the USA, the UK and some parts of Europe, for instance), while it seems rather unlikely that privacy plays the same role or has the same meaning across the world. The role of regional cultural differences in the perception of FRT's 'autonomy and privacy problem' is not covered in this work but would be an interesting study in our globalising world. That said, I am in general using the concept of 'autonomy' in Dworkin's sense[13] of a defining feature of individual humans (people) that may be manifested in almost any aspect of their lives (such as shopping or sport), and not just the strictly moral realm (as conceived by Kant) although including that.

5.3 Dworkin's First and Second-Order Autonomy

Gerald Dworkin's work is generally situated in the tradition of liberal ethical and political theory, intimately connected with the tradition of John Stuart Mill. While not wishing here to take on board the entire Dworkian liberal thesis and its ramifications I think his distinction about autonomy operating at two levels or orders is very useful for understanding what is ethically problematic about FRT. The general idea is that one range of choices is contained within a choice which is itself one among many choices at a higher level. Thus, there is a nesting of choices, as shown in Fig. 5.1.

The choices 1, 2, 3 are constrained by the prior choice of A rather than B. This can happen because B is freely rejected on the basis of information, or because there is ignorance of the existence or availability of B and its range i, ii, and iii. Furthermore, the chooser may have its very perception of A (mass screening by FRT) distorted by an intervening factor X, or similarly with B and the intervening factor Y. In the simplest possible model, those who submit to FRT at 1 have so little information or participation that they are unaware of alternative forms of FRT application 2 and 3 (which they might otherwise prefer), and in fact the higher level determining factor A (e.g. government control, market competitiveness) is obscured by the intervening justification (e.g. preventing terrorism, enhancing customer choice). The higher-level choice of rejecting A (mass screening by FRT) in favour of selective FRT applications determined democratically does not arise at all. It cannot arise for

[13]Dworkin (1988), p. 17 *op cit.*

several reasons: lack of technical understanding, failure of attention, misunderstanding of motivation, lack education or participation, manipulation and secrecy by controllers of FRT, and so on. While it can be argued that the choosers 'have *a* choice', which is undeniable, those choices are constrained within the 'hidden' choice of A rather than B. To give a very simple example, consumers may be able to choose from 100 TV channels, but what if all those channels are either entertainment or sports? This means they are limited practically to choosing only one of those media. This is what, in other spheres, has loosely been described as 'dumbing down' or 'consumerist ideology'. This hierarchical understanding of autonomy and liberty lies in the background of much of my thesis about the ethics of FRT and is central to understanding how choice is affected and portrayed above.

The difficult question is, how are these different orders of choices to be understood? The capacity for determining one's own life as a 'free spirit', or 'self-governance', has been described and understood in various ways, some of which oppose each other, for instance is autonomy 'value/content-neutral' or is it 'substantive'. Value-neutral proponents such as Frankfurt[14] and Dworkin argue that autonomy does not require any particular set of values but is rather met through a *formal* process of critical reflection and is therefore hierarchical in nature.

Hierarchical concepts of autonomy are predicated by the need for significant levels of reflection or evaluation of the range and meaning of choices before determining a course of action by the exercising of first and second-order preferences. Thus, when determined, an act or decision becomes an effective autonomous choice. But what if evaluation is restricted or not possible? For instance, when one is required to make an immediate decision such as the request to submit to a face scan, but one is ignorant of its purpose. And what if reflection yields a negative response? Is there a real choice? Suppose what is wanted is not supported by a higher preference which is manipulated by systems and processes that are paternalistic. Therefore, in some contexts FRTs deny autonomy because choice is constrained or coerced.

Substantive views hold that values or commitments are necessary for autonomy, such as commitment to specific religious or political views, though these arguably limit autonomy because they are value driven, Dworkin recognises these as potential virtues because at worst autonomy is egoistic when defined as "substantive independence".[15]

To that extent, this may mean that individuals live according to their own choices and values based on what they regard as morally permissible. This may justify such independence and be perceived as egoistic, especially when living is in pursuit of a person's own ends and beyond any concern for others.

Conversely, when personal ends are sublimated does this imply a Kantian respect for the moral law?[16] This question changes the focus on personal autonomy to that of

[14]Frankfurt (1971).

[15]Dworkin (1988), pp. 17; 20–21 *op cit.*

[16]See Waldron (2005).

moral autonomy which at first glance appears unconnected with my contention that face recognition technologies deny personal autonomy in deference to a heteronomous utilitarianism. As I have said, I do not intend to enter the voluminous philosophical discussions about Immanuel Kant's 'moral autonomy'. Yet the two concepts are connected when applied to the issue of the 'common good' justification associated with face recognition technologies, and the Kantian critique of 'heteronomy', which includes unreflecting submission to the rule of others.[17] Although the 'common good' is a valid argument for sublimating personal autonomy, a more detailed examination of the argument is beyond the scope here. Nevertheless, it imposes a value laden context on value neutral proponents of autonomy which for them may be indicative of second- order preferences. Indeed, Jeremy Waldron[18] observes that:

> [T]alk of personal autonomy evokes the image of a person in charge of his life, not just following his desires *but choosing which of his desires to follow*. It is not an immoral idea, but it has relatively little to do with morality. Those who value it do not value it as part of the moral enterprise of reconciling one person's interest with another's; instead they see it as a particular way of understanding what each person's interest consists in. Moral autonomy, by contrast, is associated specifically with the relation between one person's pursuit of his own ends *and the others' pursuit of theirs*.

Although individualism may be the result of both autonomies, when the clauses emphasised are combined these components that apparently separate the two concepts, may indeed be indicative of reflective decision making which sublimates substantive independence in preference to the other person's pursuits. However, the choice still requires sufficient knowledge for the decision to be an informed choice. Otherwise, autonomous decisions are denied and the favour towards another for the common good is coerced. Whether individually or collectively people choose to surrender their autonomy, the decision must not be made by proxy against their will[19] as doing so removes the possibility of choice.

It may be useful to make a comparison with automated number plate recognition (ANPR) technology. That technology includes the capability to identify vehicle owners or individuals, the former by ANPR software and the latter by face recognition software. Number plate recognition is arguably impersonal and well understood by citizens and is not therefore a breach of second-order autonomy because its use is publicly understood by motorists as a means of justifiably penalising them, for instance when they exceed the speed limit. Such disobedience might be motivated by the need to be substantively independent and unconcerned about the consequences. Although hypothetical, such nonchalant behaviour is likely to be predicated by second-order preferences. Putting aside the use of ANPR the uncertainty or ignorance of how facial recognition software is used generally affects second-order autonomy, because although cameras can be seen, their operational frameworks

[17]Heteronomy: the opposite of autonomy.

[18]Waldron (2005), p. 307 (my italics).

[19]Lawrence (2005), p. 136.

are unknown and subsequently individuals are objectified—turned into a set of numbers—by the system's data protocols which can be understood by no-one except technical experts. By objectification I also mean the lack of agency and subjectivity that disallows opposition or individuals their value[20]; consequently, individuals are bodies to be observed and identified[21] whenever they behave 'incorrectly' or inadvertently antagonise the system. 'Operational frameworks' are the policies, goals, standards, modus operandi, procedures, safeguards and training that form an organisation's administrative infrastructure. Arguably an individual only becomes a subject when their information is collated with other personal data, and further reduces autonomy in the process of identification. The objectification highlights Dworkin's concept of autonomy because the effect of objectification stimulates second-order preferences and responses. This occurs when an individual's awareness of interference or violation of autonomy conflicts with their personal goals; or when second-order desires conflict with first-order desires which may stimulate an unarticulated (because of uncertainty or restraint) dissonant reaction to the secondary, unknown, uses of the data.

I now turn to a consideration of positive and negative liberty which are closely connected with questions of autonomy.

5.4 Autonomy and Freedom

Autonomy is clearly connected with freedom (which I use synonymously with 'liberty') but analytic philosophers are careful to make a conceptual distinction between the two. Freedom is said to be essentially a matter of the power or capacity to act,[22] conversely without freedom the capacity to act is denied. The emphasis is on the individual's *activity* (see below). 'Autonomy' will sometimes cover these in the way it is ordinarily used, but often the word is a drawing of attention to something deeper, namely, the 'personhood' or 'humanity' of an individual, or their values, life-meanings, creativity or—in religious terminology—their very soul or spirit. In this conceptual framework freedom is of value because autonomy is of fundamental value. Autonomy is the baseline of all human values because it affects human interaction and relationships, and figures in many policy debates from education to legal freedoms. Admittedly, this may also be regarded as a substantive ideological position or outlook that not everyone would share, which is a debate in political philosophy due to the centrality of the concept.[23]

[20]Nussbaum (1995), p. 257.

[21]Garfinkel (2001), p. 65.

[22]Pink (2011), pp. 541–563.

[23]Christman (2018).

5.5 Negative and Positive Liberty

In *Two Concepts of Liberty* Isaiah Berlin[24] delineated the boundaries of liberty by categorising the limits of power or interference by external agents on individuals. The effect, impact or influence of an agent's delegated authority delineates the difference between the boundaries. Berlin defined these boundaries in terms of negative or positive liberty. Negative liberty relates to interference. Simply put it is freedom *from X*, such as freedom from arbitrary arrest. It asks the question "how far or how much?" can agencies (including governments) legitimately interfere with an individual's movements, family life, speaking, sexuality, etc.? The lesser the interference the greater the degree of negative liberty. It focuses on the individual's personal agency that society allows. Positive liberty is concerned with the freedom *to have or do Y,* for example, to have health or education. It implies the question "what does, the government do for me?" or rather "am I free or empowered?" to pursue my values or potential. For instance, Berlin's description of a musician who interprets the composer's score and plays the music creatively within the bounds of the composition; it is not played robotically to any laws, which are barriers to liberty, but rather plays freely and unhindered. Such musical expression is most commonly exercised in jazz improvisation, where the central theme, melody or chord progression is enhanced and embellished. Or by concert soloists who are recognised by their individualistic playing style.

Therefore, the freedom of creativity, of personal flourishing, of interpretation or self-realisation that the musician experiences, the greater the self-governance and the greater the positive liberty.[25] Berlin describes positive liberty in terms of facilitating or supporting the ability, the enhancement of ability to act and not just the opportunity to do so.[26] He sees the latter as grounded in autonomy or self-governance. According to received wisdom, Berlin summarises, that true freedom is predicated by critical reason, the thoughtful consideration of what is required and what is helpful. This received wisdom is reflected in Dworkin's hierarchical concept of second-order autonomy. This is because Berlin's distinction of liberty, like Dworkin's hierarchy of autonomies, is relevant to my ethical critique of the major contemporary drift of FRT. Inasmuch that, under conditions of secretive control (whether government or private-corporate) surveillance and intrusion into privacy threaten us with the curtailment of positive liberty i.e. the freedom to flourish by positively defining and narrowing down our range of choices, and in feeling confident, trusting, honest, creative and challenging. In short, for the most part and increasingly we do not know who is in control of our images, or how that is done or why or when. Neither do we know how this technology can combine or converge with other technologies (such as telecommunications, social networks, nanoscale devices, drones, telemedicine, robotics and data-mining) or whether law and

---

[24]Berlin (1958).

[25]Lane (2007).

[26]*Ibid.*

regulations are keeping up or even whether there are such laws or regulations that citizens can appeal to.[27] The importance of Berlin's concept of the interplay of negative and positive liberty should be evident, because it helps to clarify the two related dimensions in the working of power and authority. We have to ask whether we are drifting towards a Kafkaesque society.

5.6 Kafka and Negative Liberty

Negative liberty in relation to ignorance and secrecy is illustrated (metaphorically) in Kafka's novel *The Trial*[28] by the impact that the faceless bureaucracy has on the character *Josef K,* after being arrested. He does not know the reasons and, at a higher or 'second-order' he does not even know if there are reasons or if there need to be. In a modern setting *Josef K* may have been wondering if his face had been spoofed by an FRT database hacker or there had been a face recognition 'false positive' (as mentioned earlier) or his facial image, stolen from a Facebook page, had been entered into a military intelligence database by someone who did not like him, this being further facilitated by a RFID enabled payment and his location pinpointed via his mobile phone, with smart (FRT enabled) CCTV confirming his identity.

The beginning of Chap. 1 sets the scene in which *Josef K* was expecting his breakfast, but his morning routine and self-assurance was changed when instead of the cook arriving an unknown man enters his room, "Who are you" *K* asks.[29] Ignoring this question, the man replies, "You rang". In this staccato interplay *K's* world is interrupted and diminished as the unknown man takes control; at the same time *K* questions why, the cook had not arrived with his breakfast. And still trying to take back control, yet not understanding what's happening *K* attempts to investigate his predicament but is told to stay in his room. This conversation continues with increasing exasperation as *K* tries to understand why this unknown man is interested in him. Eventually, *K* is ushered into the next room where another man is waiting. Subsequently the familiarity of the past is changed by the perception of the present moment as he strains to make sense of his predicament and although everything has the semblance of normality, *K* is unsettled by his changed situation that he wishes to leave, but cannot, having been arrested and told that he would discover the reason later.[30] *K* has no idea what crime he has committed, only that he is charged with an offence. At one level, his arrest is indicative of diminished negative liberty because

[27]For instance, GDPR. But, whether the GDPR alleviates these uncertainties, especially after, for example, the debacle over the Facebook app that Cambridge Analytica (the UK based data analytics consultancy) devised to unlawfully harvest the data from Facebook account holders, remains to be seen.

[28]Kafka (1925).

[29]*Ibid.*

[30]*Ibid*, pp. 1–3.

he is not free from arbitrary arrest, there appears to be nothing he can appeal to, to question the legitimacy of his arrest. He realises he is not free from capricious authority. On another level, his inability to obtain information about the alleged offence reduces his confidence, his sense of self: his freedom to exercise his intellect. It is humiliating; a threat to his very identity. In a word, it reduces his moral autonomy (and thus his positive liberty) which is his ability to remain the comprehender, interpreter and master of his circumstances. The intensity of his enquiry increases the interference and obduracy of the bureaucrats, and further reduces his liberty whereby the separate poles of Berlin's concept of liberty eventually converge when self-governance is interrupted and restrained. Whereby *Josef K*'s ability to manage who is, is curtailed[31] and his subsequent loss of identity, his selfhood, because self-management has been denied, and he has an identity (or non-identity) imposed upon him from which he cannot extricate himself. This further diminishes his independence that is predicated by negative liberty. Kafka's literary metaphor is potentially too conjectural, but nevertheless it serves to illustrate my contention that autonomy is especially affected where there is secrecy by authorities and ignorance on the part of citizens. This may already be partially true of FRT, and it may become more and more of a concern as the technology is refined and government becomes more authoritarian in the face of crises. We may re-interpret the Kafaesque scenario as one of rights and duties. From a rights perspective this scenario far exceeds the usual expectation of privacy; for the officers merely ignore *K's* protestation and requests for explanation. They are not concerned about his privacy in any regard, he was still in bed; they simply had the authority to enter his room and arrest him without warrant or warning.

5.7 Foucault's Police and Bentham's Prisoners

Although *The Trial* was published in the early twentieth century, it resonates with Michel Foucault's description of power assigned to the police that emerged from the state control of discipline in eighteenth century France:

> The organisation of a centralised police had long been regarded, even by contemporaries, as the most direct expression of royal absolutism; the sovereign had wished to have 'his own magistrate to whom he might directly entrust his orders, his commissions, intentions, and who was entrusted with the execution of orders and orders under the King's private seal'. In effect, taking over a number of pre-existing functions – the search for criminals, urban surveillance, economic and political supervision – the police magistratures and the magistrature-general that presided over them in Paris transposed them into a single, strict, administrative machine.[32]

[31] Hague (2011).

[32] Foucault (1977), p. 213. The King was Louis XIV who ruled France from 1643 to 1715.

The multiplicity of functions would have required numerous operational mechanisms to facilitate the depth of state control that sought to reach "the most elementary particle, the most passing phenomenon of the social body".[33] This exercise of power:

> [H]ad to be given the instrument of permanent, exhaustive, omnipresent surveillance, capable of making all visible, as long as it could itself remain invisible. It had to be like a faceless gaze that transformed the whole social body into a field of perception: thousands of eyes posted everywhere, mobile attentions ever on the alert, a long hierarchized net-work which, according to Le Maire, comprised for Paris *the forty-eight commissaires*, the twenty *inspecteurs,* then the 'observers' who were paid regularly, the *'basses mouches'*, or secret agents, who were paid by the day, then the informers, paid according to the job done, and finally the prostitutes.[34]

This secretive all-surveying and unaccountable state apparatus in Kafka's scenario subjected citizen *Josef K* to an uncertain present and future, detained without any apparent reason, not even a reason that was wrong—such as a case of mistaken identity. In some respects, this is dissimilar to Foucault's account, since *K* did not have an opportunity to modify his behaviour because he was unaware of being observed, as would have been the case had he been subjected to the 'compulsory visibility' that a panoptical (all-seeing) apparatus or architecture would facilitate.[35] The Panopticon penal technology envisioned by utilitarian reformer Jeremy Bentham enabled all prisoners to be watched all the time. The Panopticon prisoner knows that he is being watched all the time and has no freedom from surveillance (negative liberty) and no positive freedom to privacy, and being always a visible prisoner, he can only do what the system allows him to do, so has little or no provision for his flourishing (positive liberty). *K* does not know that he is being watched and may wrongly believe that he has at least got some privacy. Perhaps, this second condition may be closer to the current developing situation with FRT and related technologies. The extent, nature, operation and policies of FRT are hardly understood at all by the general public. Many do not know that there is something they ought to know.

Nevertheless, *Josef K*'s predicament illustrates the nature of personal autonomy and its value. *K* realises what he is about to lose and he tries to retain some authority. He does this not by justifying his actions, but by seeking answers to why the men have invaded his privacy. It is unclear in this opening scene what the pretext of the intrusion is and this remains an undercurrent throughout the novel, and illustrates the powerlessness of individuals when confronted by the mechanism of secretive state control. *The Trial* is a metaphor for the loss of personal autonomy when there is not only severe control of the information, but secretive control of information and its operation is given to unaccountable third parties or the state. Instead of the

---

[33] *Ibid*, p. 214.

[34] *Ibid*, p. 214.

[35] The Panopticon in the above ways can act as a laboratory that acts as a machine that "carries out experiments, to alter behaviour, to train or correct individuals" (Foucault 1977, p. 203). Thus, the Panopticon not only acts as a vehicle to carry out tasks but also as a disciplinary apparatus.

eighteenth century's panoply of agents, individuals release personal data or information which is managed by a Benthamite panopticon of data processors and analysts who are beyond the control of the data subject, subsequently this has the effect of diminishing positive liberty because of the data subject's loss of control. This loss is analogous to Dixon's[36] report *The One-Way-Mirror Society* which considers the burgeoning use of 'Big Data' and real-time analysis for commercial purposes.

5.8 Privacy and Autonomy

The concept of 'privacy' is as abstract, broad and consequently as fuzzy a concept as its family relations 'autonomy' and 'liberty'. Indeed, it is like those two tied up with the liberal tradition of thought. In some societies, such as Japan the concept of 'privacy' is defined as 'individual information', which is not to be known, and therefore will not be shared with others outside specific domains. It offers a contrast with *public* life, i.e. as relatively distinct domain of the life of family and friends. This contrast between the *public* and *private* alone offers us some insight into why a social media that trades in facial images largely intended for friends, family and community becomes a 'privacy concern' when those images are placed in or are leaked into the public space. FRT is not intended as a device for the private domain in that sense, but explicitly for the public domain. Again, the boundary between the two is not only conceptually fuzzy but practically impossible to maintain as a watertight boundary. Consequently, there are theoretical debates in ethics, philosophy and jurisprudence that attempt to ground and justify privacy as a moral, ethical and legal value. Generally, ethicists and legalists have been treating privacy as a *right*, moral or legal or both that it is important to respect and protect from 'violation' in a civilised democratic society.

Analyses of the meaning of privacy will generally refer to its value in defending 'human dignity' and/or 'human intimacy and the development of interpersonal relationships' and/or in maintaining our personal sense of identity and worth.[37]

Privacy is not necessarily regarded as a good thing. In the feminist critique of privacy, the argument is that the concept and practice of privacy serves in fact (at least some of the time) to dominate women, by isolating sexual domination as not a matter for public scrutiny or consideration. On the feminist argument one might infer that what is often regarded as intrusion into privacy should in fact be regarded as liberating for women's rights. One might imagine scenarios in which FRT might be deployed with that justification e.g. in recognising those engaged in wife abuse or who solicit prostitutes.[38]

[36] Dixon (2010). See Sect. 6.7.

[37] See Bloustein (1964), Fried (1970), Inness (1992) and Rachels (1975).

[38] See MacKinnon (1989).

Privacy then, is a multifaceted term which has been analysed, described and dissected by various commentators. The discourse focuses broadly on whether privacy is a value or an objective. Specifically, Ruth Gavison[39] observes that privacy must also be coherent in three contexts:

> First, we must have a neutral concept of privacy that will enable us to identify when a loss of privacy has occurred so that discussions of privacy and claims of privacy can be intelligible. Second, privacy must have coherence as a value, for claims of legal protection of privacy are compelling only if losses of privacy are sometimes undesirable and if those losses undesirable for similar reasons. Third, privacy must be a concept useful in legal contexts, a context that enables us to identify those occasions calling for protection, because the law does not interfere to protect every undesirable event.[40]

If it is a value, irrespective of the context and whether it can actually be legally protected, when privacy is breached it effectively challenges *a priori* personal desires; if it is an objective, the context will determine its purpose and indeed it is *a posteriori* value attributed by the individual. Each is a product of autonomy and a desire for independence or control. At this stage I am using ‘desire’ to describe that which motivates and initiates actions, which may not necessarily be formed from a hierarchy of choices. Yet, because privacy is multifaceted, Gavison[41] asks two questions about privacy in relation to its status and characteristics. In terms of status “is privacy a situation, a right, a claim, (or) a form of control or a value?” In terms of the characteristics of privacy “is it related to information, to autonomy, to personal identity, (or) to physical access?” These questions can be subdivided into *a priori* and *a posteriori* notions and suggest a hierarchy of choice that determines the level or degree of control. The former in terms of control and the latter in terms of claims when considered from the perspective of confidentiality and anonymity. Both confidentiality and anonymity correspond to Solove’s[42] depiction of an envelope and its contents, whereby the contents of an unopened envelope are confidential and until opened the sender remains anonymous[43]; the recipient although addressed by name, is also anonymous in terms of being potentially unknown by those handling the mail. Accordingly, the envelope and contents distinction merges Gavison’s dichotomy of privacy’s status and characteristics, because both apply to the envelope when it is opened without consent. This approach structures privacy in terms of information[44] and risks conflating confidentiality and privacy thereby inferring that loss of privacy occurs only when information is disclosed or obtained surreptitiously[45] and is illustrated by the case law discussed in Chap. 7.

[39] Gavison (1980), pp. 421, 471.

[40] *Ibid*, p. 423.

[41] *Ibid*, p. 424.

[42] Solove (2011).

[43] Assuming that is no return to sender address on the back of the envelope.

[44] Nissenbaum (2010).

[45] Berle (2011), pp. 43–44.

From an informational perspective, individuals cannot control how their information or data is handled and they rely on others who are responsible by statute to protect their informational privacy; this infers an extrinsic template on privacy whereby privacy is forcibly measured by its context rather than an intrinsic value that is predicated by and indicative of personal autonomy. The extrinsic nature of privacy and its contextualisation within an informational framework is evident when invasions of privacy occur, such as:

> the collection, storage, and computerization (*sic*) of information; the dissemination of information about individuals; peeping, following, watching, and photographing individuals; intruding or entering "private" places; eavesdropping, wiretapping, reading of letters; drawing attention to individuals; required testing of individuals and forced disclosure of information.[46]

Arguably, in 1980 the computerisation of data was in its infancy and Gavison's comments form the basis of Solove's later reflection and analysis. Putting aside the technological advances the privacy issues remain consistent and are central to the current discourse, and are amplified by the advances in technology and the subsequent capacity for surveillance and the concomitant legislative responses, for instance:

> The civil liberties committee of the European Parliament has voted to approve the EU Data Protection Regulation. Before voting, members of the committee inserted stronger safeguards for data transfers to non-EU countries, an explicit consent requirement, a right to erasure, and larger fines for non-complying businesses. The regulation is a comprehensive update of the 1995 EU Data Protection Directive that sets out new enforcement powers for privacy agencies. In 2012 and 2013, over twenty US consumer, privacy, and civil liberties groups sent letters to the European Parliament in support of the new data protection law. Until the U.S. passes comprehensive privacy legislation, the groups wrote, "the European Union offers the best prospect for the protection of Internet users around the globe."[47]

The EU's general data protection regulation classifies privacy within an informational framework and conflates privacy with confidentiality when individuals consent to the processing of their data. However, given the relationship between privacy and confidentiality they are inseparable when considered only from an informational perspective. But in spite of this, they are more representative of Gavison's second and third questions elicited above and therefore, whilst not being identical they cohere in what might be described as the 'privacy matrix'. Hence, for privacy to be meaningfully defined it requires an objective measure by which loss can be deduced and therefore, privacy is a value that requires contextual relevance to assess its validity. The flaw in this argument, if applied to face recognition technologies, is that the emphasis on information rather than privacy *per se* reinforces the secrecy paradigm and reverts back to the envelope and contents analogy and is indicative of the tension between whether privacy is a *'right'* or a *'condition'*.[48] Emphasising

---

[46]Gavison (1980), p. 436.

[47]Electronic Privacy Information Center (EPIC).

[48]Wacks (1989) (revised 1993), p. 20.

rights is problematic because 'rights' requires a normative statement about the need for privacy which according to Wacks is variously defined. Whilst Warren and Brandeis's[49] seminal essay on privacy noted that:

> Recent inventions and business methods call attention to the next step which must be taken for the protection of the person, and for securing to the individual what Judge Cooley calls the right "to be let alone" Instantaneous photographs and newspaper enterprise have invaded the sacred precincts of private and domestic life; and numerous mechanical devices threaten to make good the prediction that "what is whispered in the closet shall be proclaimed from the house-tops." For years there has been a feeling that the law must afford some remedy for the unauthorized circulation of portraits of private persons; and the evil of invasion of privacy by the newspapers...

Has raised:

> the question whether our law will recognize and protect the right to privacy in this and in other respects must soon come before our courts for consideration.

Which subsequently led:

> to the conclusion that the protection afforded to thoughts, sentiments, and emotions, expressed through the medium of writing or of the arts, so far as it consists in preventing publication, is merely an instance of the enforcement of the more general right of the individual to be let alone.

However, because 'rights' need a context Warren and Brandeis equate the breach of privacy to various assaults and regard 'rights' as a possession:

> In each of these rights, as indeed in all other rights recognized by the law, there inheres the quality of being owned or possessed -- and (as that is the distinguishing attribute of property) there may [be] some propriety in speaking of those rights as property.

Therefore, Warren and Brandeis presciently observed the impact of technology on privacy which is still contemporarily relevant and if 'rights' are property, like property they need protecting, and the level of protection against loss determined individually. From this perspective the European Union recognises the need for protection, which will be discussed in Chap. 8. Before discussing how legal measures protect privacy, Isaiah Berlin[50] provides the basis from which they are derived; and also provides the reason for the latitude of opinion that is evident on social media.

Typically, social media pages are wish list testimonies founded on personal choices, that reflect Berlin's description of autonomy by which individualism is paramount, where being a subject and not an object, being somebody and not a nobody is important; and deciding for oneself what is important enough for friends to see or know about. However, there is a downside to social media that is antithetical to Berlin's premise, inasmuch that some individuals are coerced and not independent, to the extent that they are persuaded to post inappropriate images or material that is demeaning and objectifying. Nevertheless, Berlin asserts that being

---

[49]Warren and Brandeis (1890).

[50]Berlin (1958).

conscious of oneself as a thinking, willingly responsible person is something to wish for and attain. Yet, even if that aspiration is entirely possible, there is the problem of choice; not all rights or indeed privacy are attainable. There may be the semblance of freedom, but the issue of compulsory visibility remains, and whilst the notions of negative and positive liberty are extant, they are only descriptions of governance and are the basis on which the validity of choice or prevention of harm can be evaluated. Moreover, Wacks suggests that 'privacy' is something we can autonomously control, and therefore we can choose to abandon privacy and reveal ourselves on social media if we choose to.[51]

From a human rights perspective this was emphasised in *Campbell v MGN* where in the House of Lords, Lord Hoffman said:

> [W]hat human rights law has done is to identify private information as something worth protecting as an aspect of human autonomy and dignity…the new approach…focuses upon the right to control the dissemination of information about one's private life.[52]

Accordingly, the range of personal details on social media or the degree to which celebrities reveal themselves in the public domain is taken as evidence of choice and *prima facie* the exercise of personal autonomy, which Hoffman perceived worthy of protection from intrusion or redress when intruded upon. From a hierarchical account of autonomy such as Dworkin's, choosing a course of action is dependent on the conditions of that choice and whether first and second-order preferences cohere. This does not need the law's protection unless the freedom of choice is circumvented by others accessing information without consent, or when technologies exceed the limits of the law or codes of practice, as is possible in the compulsorily visible public space. Subsequently, Wacks and Hoffman illustrate the first of two apparently contradictory rationales[53] of privacy: firstly, that privacy is defined spatially in terms of "seclusion or intimacy",[54] and secondly from Ziegler[55] (and Dworkin) as "freedom of action, self-determination and autonomy". These two concepts converge when they are contextualised in a framework that associates privacy as a means of protecting the "free development of personality".[56] This arguably evolves through free expression borne from coherent preferences that are the hallmarks of personal autonomy.

However, if freedom of expression, as the result of persuasion or education, predicates the loss of spatial privacy, it is no longer possible to be 'left alone' or unobserved. And if that loss is due to an overzealous, all-encompassing use of FRT enabled surveillance, then those that would wish to choose otherwise will have their freedom limited and constrained by the majority or even the prevailing political will.

[51]Wacks R *op cit,* p. 14.

[52]Campbell v MGN Ltd.

[53]Marshall (2009).

[54]*Ibid*, p. 52.

[55]*Ibid* cited by Marshall (2009).

[56]*Ibid*, p. 52.

References

Berle I (2011) Privacy and confidentiality: what's the difference? J Vis Commun 34(1):43–44. https://www.tandfonline.com/doi/abs/10.3109/17453054.2011.550845?journalCode=ijau20. Accessed 10 Aug 2019

Berlin I (1958) Two concepts of liberty in Isaiah Berlin 1969: four essays on liberty. OUP, Oxford

Bloustein E (1964) Privacy as an aspect of human dignity: an answer to Dean Prosser. N Y Univ Law Rev 39:962–1007

Campbell v MGN Ltd [2004] UKHL, 22 per Lord Hoffman paragraphs 50, 51. https://publications.parliament.uk/pa/ld200304/ldjudgmt/jd040506/campbe-2.htm. Accessed 10 Aug 2019

Chesterman S (2011) One nation under surveillance: a new social contract to defend freedom without sacrificing liberty. Oxford University Press, Oxford, p 145. Citing ICO and Parliamentary reports

Christman J (2018) Autonomy in moral and political philosophy. In: Zalta EN (ed) The Stanford encyclopedia of philosophy (Spring 2018 Edition). https://plato.stanford.edu/archives/spr2018/entries/autonomy-moral/. Accessed 10 Aug 2019

Dixon P (2010) The one-way-mirror-society: privacy implications of the new digital signage networks. http://www.worldprivacyforum.org/wp-content/uploads/2013/01/onewaymirrorsocietyfs.pdf. Accessed 10 Aug 2019

Dworkin G (1988, reprinted 1997) The theory and practice of autonomy. Cambridge University Press, Cambridge

Edgar TH (2017) Beyond Snowden: privacy, mass surveillance and the struggle to reform the NSA. The Brookings Institution

Electronic Frontier Foundation: FBI's Next Generation Identification Biometric Database. https://www.eff.org/foia/fbis-next-generation-identification-biometrics-database. Accessed 10 Aug 2019

Electronic Information Privacy Center: European Parliament Committee Approves Comprehensive Privacy Law. https://epic.org/2013/10/european-parliament-committee.html. Accessed 10 Aug 2019

Federal Bureau of Investigation CJIS Division: Next Generation Identification. https://www.fbi.gov/services/cjis/fingerprints-and-other-biometrics/ngi. Accessed 10 Aug 2019

Foucault M (1977) The birth of the prison (trans: Sheridan A) (First published as Surveiller et punir: Naissance de la prison. Éditions Gallimard, Paris, 1975; Penguin Books 1991)

Frankfurt HG (1971) Freedom of the will and the concept of a person. J Philos 68(1):5–20. Published by: Journal of Philosophy, Inc. http://www.jstor.org/stable/2024717. Accessed 10 Aug 2019

Fried C (1970) An anatomy of values. Harvard University Press, Cambridge

Garfinkel S (2001, pbk) Database nation: the death of privacy in the 21st century. O'Reilly & Associates Inc, Sebastopol

Gavison RE (1980) Privacy and the limits of law. Yale Law J 89(3):421–471. https://ssrn.com/abstract=2060957. Accessed 10 Aug 2019

Gill M, Spriggs A (2005) Accessing the impact of CCTV Home Office Research Study 292 Dev & Statistics Directorate, Home Office Research. www.homeoffice.gov.uk/rds/pdfs05/hors292.pdf via Google. Accessed 12 Aug 2019

Hague R (2011) Autonomy and identity, the politics of who we are. Routledge, Abingdon, Oxon

Inness J (1992) Privacy, intimacy and isolation. Oxford University Press, Oxford

Kafka F (1925) The Trial (trans: Parry I). Penguin Books 1994, Penguin Classics 2000

Kant I (1781) Critique of pure reason. http://www.gutenberg.org/files/4280/4280-h/4280-h.htm. Accessed 10 Aug 2019

Lane R (2007) Berlin on positive liberty. http://www.westga.edu/~rlane/law/lecture23_freedom2.html. Accessed 10 Aug 2019

Lawrence MA (2005) Reviving a natural right: the freedom of autonomy. Willamette Law Rev, June 2005; MSU Legal Studies Research Paper No. 02. http://ssrn.com/abstract=755564. Accessed 10 Aug 2019

MacKinnon C (1989) Toward a feminist theory of the state. Harvard University Press, Cambridge

Marshall J (2009) Personal freedom through human rights law? Autonomy, identity and integrity under the European Convention on Human Rights. Martinus Nijhoff, Leiden

Mill JS (1859) In: Gray J, Smith GW (eds) (1991) J. S. Mill on liberty in focus. Routledge, London & New York

Nissenbaum H (2010) Privacy in context: technology, policy and the integrity of social life. Stanford University Press, Stanford

Nussbaum MC (1995) Objectification. Philos Public Aff 24(4). http://www.mit.edu/~shaslang/mprg/nussbaumO.pdf. Accessed 10 Aug 2019

Pink T (2011) Thomas Hobbes and the ethics of freedom. Inquiry 54(5):541–563. https://doi.org/10.1080/0020174X.2011.608886. Accessed 10 Aug 2019

Rachels J (1975) Why privacy is important. Philos Public Aff 4:323–333

Solove DJ (2011) Nothing to hide: the false trade off between privacy and security. Yale University Press, New Haven and London, p 180

Wacks R (1989) (revised 1993) Personal information: privacy and the law. Clarendon Press, Oxford

Waldron J (2005) Moral autonomy and personal autonomy. In: Christman J, Anderson J (eds) Autonomy and the challenges to liberalism, new essays. Cambridge University Press. https://doi.org/10.1017/CBO9780511610325.015. Accessed 10 Aug 2019

Warren SD, Brandeis LD (1890) The right to privacy (the implicit made explicit). Harv Law Rev: 193–220. http://www.jstor.org/stable/1321160. Accessed 10 Aug 2019

Chapter 6
Compulsory Visibility?

Abstract The principle of compulsory visibility is an idea introduced by the philosopher Michel Foucault. This chapter considers how facial recognition technology magnifies visibility, whether by the use of body-worn cameras or by coercion or other means and has become panoptical in its reach. Unlike Bentham's panopticon FRT has replaced the physical structures and although not necessarily disciplinary, FRT imposes a compulsory visibility on persons subjected to its gaze, whenever they are exposed to its gaze whether for investigative or security purposes or on social networks.

6.1 Introduction

The principle of compulsory visibility is an idea introduced by the philosopher Michel Foucault. We need to ask whether FRT is a technology that lends itself to 'social disciplining', to the general acceptance and strengthening of this principle. Foucault says:

> Traditionally, power was what was seen, what was shown, and what was manifested ... Disciplinary power, on the other hand, is exercised through its invisibility; at the sametime it imposes on those whom it subjects a principle of compulsory visibility. In discipline, it is the subjects who have to be seen. Their visibility assures the hold of the power that is exercised over them. It is this fact of being constantly seen, of being able always to be seen, that maintains the disciplined individual in his subjection. And the examination is the technique by which power, instead of emitting the signs of its potency, instead of imposing its mark on its subjects, holds them in a mechanism of objectification. In this space of domination, disciplinary power manifests its potency, essentially by arranging objects. The examination is, as it were, the ceremony of this objectification.[1]

[1]Foucault (1977), p. 187.

I. Berle, *Face Recognition Technology*, Law, Governance and Technology Series 41,
https://doi.org/10.1007/978-3-030-36887-6_6

6.2 Body-Worn Cameras

We may get an impression of the meaning of 'compulsory visibility' if we first approach it, not from the angle of government and corporations, but from that of citizens as consumers of technology. There are already many live-streaming devices available such as dashboard cameras in private as well as public vehicles on the roads. We already know that Facebook is a popular global social network and it is called '*face* book' for a reason: it makes available by consumer choice the individual faces of family, friends and civil society groups. It has not been considered as particularly problematic in broad terms until recently.[2] Now imagine a society in which many or most people have a camera strapped to their body, clothing or headgear and can record individuals around them at will in everyday life.

In fact, the tiny 'body-worn camera' is becoming a popular fashion item to attach to one's clothing. Over-reacting police officers, dangerous drivers and people cruel to their pets are increasingly subject to images which can be provided in evidence against them. But this phenomenon is not restricted to criminal or unacceptable behaviour but to any behaviour whatsoever, anywhere and any or all the time. Facial images can be transmitted elsewhere in seconds, even to the other side of the world. In an article on 'on-body cameras' *New Scientist* magazine asks: "What happens when face recognition software and ubiquitous, always-on cameras meet? With a little know-how, they could easily be used unscrupulously".[3] The next step is the ubiquitous use by authorities, government agencies, public officials and powerful financial, industrial, marketing and media corporations of such cameras by the tens of thousands.

We must ask whether as the convergence of ubiquitous mini-camera and FRT develops, citizens would then be put in a position of 'compulsory visibility' to State authorities as well as private corporations.[4] The implications of this for social control and privacy are difficult to predict, yet, concern for their use is indicative of the cultural shift towards an increased reliance on cameras to record every human interaction.

6.3 Compulsory Visibility and Coercion

The loss of liberty implies constraint or limitation; it can also imply restraint which, depending on the context, can also be synonymous with punishment which is a secondary issue not connected to this discourse.

Constraint can be motivated by best interests, for instance, speed limits or licensing laws, or by society's response to anti-social or criminal behaviour. The

[2]EPIC 'Facebook Privacy' (n.d.).

[3]Rutkin (2015).

[4]For example, Sect. 3.1.1.

former is paternalistic and the latter a means of crime prevention that may result in confinement. The latter was of interest to Jeremy Bentham who devised a mechanism for keeping watch on constrained (and restrained) persons: in *The Panopticon Writings* Bentham[5] describes his *Panopticon* or *Inspection House* that is applicable to "any sort of establishment, in which persons of any description are to be kept under inspection and in particular to penitentiary-houses". The building that he envisaged had design features that would facilitate complete visibility:

> The building is circular. The apartments of the prisoners occupy the circumference. You may call them, if you please, the *cell.* The *cells* are divided from one another, and the prisoners by that means secluded from all communication with each other, by partitions in the form of *radii* issuing from the circumference towards the centre…The apartment of the inspector occupies the centre; you may call it if you please the *inspectors lodge.*[6]

In addition to penitentiaries, Bentham's design could be applied to work-houses, poor-houses and hospitals. In each application the persons were constrained for a variety of reasons. Whatever the reason they were compulsorily visible the panopticon was unyieldingly intrusive by design and freedom of choice virtually impossible. From Foucault's perspective, visibility was an intrinsic feature to maintain order and discipline but not all citizens were confined, and if inspection or vigilance was to be extended to those beyond the walls of the house another mechanism was necessary, hence the snoops and informants required in eighteenth century France. Each system or mechanism is essentially a political machine for keeping control; although Bentham's would arguably be more efficient and less labour intensive. Therefore, Bentham and Foucault are relevant to this discourse, inasmuch as the former is a prescription for mechanising control and the latter describes the method and mechanism of control. If their subjects lacked choice their capacity for self-governance was limited by that lacunae of opportunity and therefore, concomitantly need not be overtly coerced.

In each, whether eighteenth or twenty-first centuries the exercise of authority is evident in terms of disciplinary power. Hence, Neve Gordon[7] notes that:

> Foucault argues that the employment of visibility has changed over time. Indeed, the individuation and isolation of the subject occurred only with the introduction of disciplinary techniques, because these techniques *reversed the visibility of power*. Traditionally, power – which was embodied in the sovereign – was visible whereas the subject remained hidden. It was only the occasional reflection of sovereign power on the subject – e.g., when a subject was accused of some kind of offence and tortured in the town square – that positioned the individual under the limelight. Disciplinary power inverted this strategy. As opposed to sovereign power and judiciary power, which operate by virtue of the visibility, disciplinary power is exercised through its invisibility. The disciplinary techniques impose "on those whom it subjects a principle of compulsory visibility".[8] Thus, in contrast to sovereign

[5]Bentham (1789).

[6]*ibid* p. 35.

[7]Gordon (2002), pp. 131–132.

[8]Cited by Gordon (2002) *ibid.*

> power, the introduction of discipline forced subjects to come into view, since their visibility assures the hold of the power exercised over them.

Gordon's analysis describes the theoretical framework and reasoning for the panopticon. The ability to enforce discipline within a single building whatever its operational function or externally upon subjects at large would potentially create a controlled social environment that would maintain power over the subjects. The invisibility of disciplinary power is illustrated by Bentham's description of the panopticon's inspection lodge, as expounded by Scran.[9]

> [Not withstanding this], the Inspection lodge hall should be kept in darkness. Bentham suggests a number of means of achieving this. The aim is to prevent any view of the interior of the lodge or the inspectors by the prisoners under inspection. The methods include blinds on the outer windows to the lodge (those facing the cells across the Annular Area), and the division of the lodge into quarters on plan by partition wall.

The darkness confers the inspector's invisibility and whilst the residents may be aware of the inspector's attendance they would not be of his actual presence. Conversely, the residents would be aware of their constant surveillance and subsequent compulsory visibility that through Gordon's contemporary analysis:

> functions as a form of control in two distinct ways. On the one hand, the *actual* visibility of normative fiats is necessary for them to maintain their power over the subject. While on the other hand, the invariable *potential* visibility of the subject is sufficient to render him/her docile.[10]

Whether potential visibility is sufficient for controlling behaviour is contextually dependant on the environment and application. For instance, controlling an enclosed regulated population is feasible, such as prisoners.[11] However, controlling the behaviour of unregulated subjects with closed circuit television (CCTV) is not particularly effective in behaviour modification; although Gill and Spriggs[12] report that such generalisation is too simplistic and that evaluating the effectiveness of CCTV is more nuanced. Their report highlights the variety of factors that influence the effectiveness of CCTV and how it is adjunctive to crime prevention and detection.

These instances aside, the nature of the invisibility and visibility matrix is pertinent, because the applications of face recognition technologies are inherently analogous to Bentham's 'inspection lodge' and the concomitant Foucauldian and Gordonian analysis *vis-à-vis* surveillance. The technology makes visible individuals who previously would have been anonymous (invisible) but are now observed by hidden scrutineers or inspectors who are empowered to analyse, control or disseminate the data as required by the application's context. This cohesion of human resources and technology contemporises Bentham's panopticon, Foucault's

[9]Bentham (1791) Letter II.

[10]Gordon (2002), p. 132 *op cit.*

[11]Foucault (1977) *op cit.*

[12]Gill and Spriggs (2005).

description of visibility and consolidates Gordon's analysis of power and control which subsequently further erodes expectations of privacy as the boundary diminishes between the visible and invisible.

6.4 Compulsory Visibility and Face Recognition

Although not necessarily disciplinary, FRT imposes a compulsory visibility on persons subjected to its scrutiny whenever they are exposed to its gaze, whether for security purposes or on social networks. The compulsorily visible may have previously been enrolled into systems that are personally and socially beneficial; such systems may be architecturally autonomous, and thereby at some levels of functionality not require human intervention or operation, for instance, automated real-time bill payments and access control. Whilst these applications are seemingly benign they can potentially reduce autonomy and be coercive when systems do not allow choice or options that provide some selectivity. That is whenever enrolment is only a binary decision such as *'yes* or *no*', '*in* or *out*'. These binary modes use 'sweeteners' to encourage enrolment, for instance, sites or services that only allow access via a person's social network log-in, apparently for the sake of simplicity; or alternatively agreeing to the 'terms and conditions' as a condition of enrolment. Whilst these modes of access have a semblance of consent when users agree to the terms and conditions, in actuality users are often ignorant of the meaning or implications or are focussing on their pursuit to enrol at the expense of understanding the terms and conditions and the overall control that the service providers have on their content. Such control is pervasive on Facebook and is a motif for the casual approach to privacy that is symptomatic of say naivety or possibly even a *laissez faire* attitude. Another example of the social network site's control of the content is photo-tagging, which when used with the site's face recognition software identifies a tagged member wherever they appear on the site, and their description of tagging requires a fair level of competence and diligence to maintain control of personal content and site settings. Thus, according to Facebook, when tagging a friend in your status update, every person who sees that update can click on the photo for your friend's name and go to their timeline. Each time this happens they will be notified of that action. Additionally, if you or a friend tags someone in your post who is known by others, the visibility of the post is increased. However, "tags in photos and posts from people you aren't friends with may appear in timeline review where you can decide if you want to allow them on your timeline. You can also choose to review tags by anyone, including your friends".[13]

Herein is a default setting that requires the account holder to manage their tagged photographs after they have been posted on a Facebook timeline.[14] Managed or not

[13]Facebook 'Tagging photos'.

[14]Walker (2019).

photo-tagging is an example of compulsory visibility because any intervention occurs after the event and is beyond the immediate control of the tagged individual. Subsequent publication of the tagged photograph across the platform further increases visibility and exacerbates the privacy issues. Indeed, Facebook reported that as of September 2017 there were 2.07 billion monthly active users[15] who are required to use their real names on personal pages, which depending on privacy settings are made publicly available.[16] Each activation on Facebook is recorded and used to establish connections across the platform[17] which, when coupled with photo-tagging diminishes anonymity and reduces autonomy if an individual's Facebook timeline isn't monitored, or if their privacy settings carelessly or unknowingly allow tagging. Changes in data protection law may reverse this default and require users to 'opt-in' to tagging rather than 'opting-out' by customising their privacy settings.[18] But whether the shifting data landscape, inaugurated by the General Data Protection Regulation and Facebook's response affects photo-tagging remains to be seen.

6.5 Big Data

The current concept of 'Big Data' underpins compulsory visibility and exceeds Orwell's vision of the surveillance state depicted in his novel *Ninety Eighty-Four* which is ruled by a government called *Big Brother.* This government controls the population by monitoring their physical activities, which include the places visited, the social interactions and telephone calls made or received, all of which would require something similar to Foucault's description of the eighteenth century's monarch's rule. Instead of Big Brother's panoptic, the collection of information is gathered in computer databases and is described as Big Data. Hilbert et al.[19] calculated that in 2007 Big Data comprised a total storage capacity of 295 exabytes (or about 404 billion CDs) and that these capacities are growing exponentially: general-purpose computing capacity is 58% annually, telecommunications 28% annually and storage capacity 23% annually. Moreover, each new development requires more storage capacity or processing power which further diminishes control by both the consumer (data subject) and the retailer (data controller). The loss of control is associated by the potential need to contract out the data management to third parties, or to install systems that are managed by contractors. Furthermore, as an individual's personal details are repeatedly required by each database the need for

[15]Facebook Key Facts.

[16]Facebook Data Policy.

[17]*ibid.*

[18]Moreau (2019). Facebook's default allows tagged photographs to be posted unless users opt-out by selecting 'On', when asked to "review posts friends tag you in before they appear on your timeline".

[19]Rashid (2011).

interoperability maybe advocated or encouraged to either rationalise databases, or to verify identities across platforms and improve performance. Therefore, the need to regulate data processing to protect the data subject's information and to improve organisations' accountability is paramount especially when considered from the perspective of face recognition technology, and the concomitant expansion of Big Data that exceeds Dostoevsky's vision of tabulated actions and 'encyclopaedic lexicons'.[20]

6.6 Big Data and Face Recognition

The functionality that Big Data provides is illustrated in the context of face recognition, for instance, privacy researchers at Carnegie Mellon University (CMU) demonstrated "that it is possible to start from an anonymous face in the street and end up with very sensitive information about that person",[21] subsequently, this conforms with Solove's[22] description of the distinction in US law between an addressed envelope and its contents. The former equates to the anonymous face in the street and the latter to access to information. The potential intrusion reduces liberty and further supports the notion of privacy as a value and affirms the need for control.[23]

Without control autonomy is reduced, but what control is possible especially when remote intrusion is possible? Is this passive 'compulsory visibility' by default? Passive because it is unknown, and since it is unknown it is not accountable and is therefore not transparent.[24] This further predicates the loss of liberty and is synonymous with coercion because visibility is the default setting and the unknowns are arguably concealed when face recognition technology is used to manipulate choice *vis-à-vis* the benefits of access to services or activities, or when it is used as a surveillance tool. For instance, Facebook insist that enrolees "grant us a non-exclusive, transferable, sub-licensable, royalty-free and worldwide licence to host, use, distribute, modify, run, copy, publicly perform or display, translate and create derivative works of your content (consistent with your privacy and application settings)... You can end this licence at any time by deleting your content or account".[25] Although it is possible to nullify the impact of such wide-ranging rights it is impossible to fully mitigate against future unconsented use because the content is likely to be shared by others who have not deleted it, and is subsequently beyond the reach and control of the originator. Therefore, this increases visibility and also

[20]Dostoevsky (1864) (reprinted 2015), p. 471. See Sect. 1.7.

[21]Acquisti et al. (2014).

[22]Solove (2011).

[23]Wacks (1993), pp. 14–15.

[24]Brin (1998), p. 334.

[25]Facebook (2019).

adds to the overall content available that allowed the CMU researchers to identify anonymous pedestrians. Ultimately, Facebook or not, the inability to remain anonymous and invisible is demonstrative of the secrecy paradigm which is not feasible unless (at least technologically) a reclusive or secluded lifestyle is adopted. Given that either option poses its own problems, all those connected and online have become compulsorily visible and subject to coercive behaviours that are difficult to avoid. This results in a loss of liberty which affects behaviour, some of which is beneficial, some not.

6.7 Compulsory Visibility and Autonomy

The extent to which visibility is compulsory is determined by its context. The context also affects the voluntariness of the visibility and also autonomy or choice. Whether choice is voluntary is also context driven and determined by the conditions of access that are associated with compliance, or the location and environment. For instance, the ubiquity of Facebook has created a 'self-surveilling' social network which surpasses the mechanisms of state that Foucault or Kafka could have envisaged. Yet, social networks are not by design surveillance tools, but rather a platform for account holders to be *seen* and *heard*. They have become a means of communication for the invisible or anonymous to become visible. This exposure from a Foucauldian perspective is a component of power that relies on its ubiquity to generate activity and perpetuate itself. Similarly, Neve Gordon hints at the potential degree of visibility and the symbiotic relationship between the state and citizens:

> . . .since the subject's potential visibility is intricately tied to the actual visibility of normative fiats. In other words, the subject's potential visibility facilitates control only because a set of normative fiats is already circulating in society and the subject must, in some way, relate to these fiats. Along the same lines, the visibility of normative fiats necessarily affects the subject only because she/he is always visible.[26]

This visibility is not confined to social networks or potential state intrusion.

In *The One-Way-Mirror-Society*, a report prepared by The World Privacy Forum[27] for the US Federal Trade Commission, Pam Dixon describes the use of digital signage used in public and private spaces to gather information about consumers by recording their faces when passing the advertising signs and displays. Consumers are unaware of the activity yet information such as ethnicity, age and gender are obtained and analysed to target advertisements to individuals who gaze at the display. This form of marketing surveillance is unrelated to security cameras that pervade retail malls and department stores. Though in terms of the compulsorily visible citizen /consumer who is unaware of being categorised and targeted there are numerous policy questions which affect autonomy. Such that, Dixon asks, when will

[26]Gordon (2002), p. 132 *op cit.*

[27]Dixon (2010).

the signs differentiate their pricing based on gender, ethnicity, and other demographic characteristics? Are children under thirteen being recorded? And are police, private litigants, tax enforcers able to access the footage? Are consumers made aware of what is happening by the stores disclosing their signs usage? What is the proper role of consent in data collection and use?[28]

Whilst Dixon highlights the concerns associated with privacy the question of visibility remains unasked and unanswered. The issue highlights how anonymity is diminished when face recognition technology is used to identify individuals for secondary purposes as a means of increasing sales,[29] or adjunctively in the sweep of surveillance to identify and categorise,[30] such as occurred in the case of *California v Ciraolo* where the Court held "that while in public people lack a reasonable expectation of privacy from visual observation from above", and also the case of *United States v Dionisio* cited by Mallon[31] where the issue was whether a person's voice could be used for identification purposes. The Court held that, "No person can have a reasonable expectation that others will not know the sound of his voice, any more than he can reasonably expect that his face will be a mystery to the world".[32]

Therefore, if from these two cases the default or precedence in respect of loss of privacy in public is normalised in the US, UK and Europe, this amplifies visibility which becomes compulsorily non-optional and is analogous to the 'secrecy paradigm' whenever an individual is peripatetic and attending to ordinary activities. Although unlike the secrecy paradigm, the visibility paradigm has a greater impact on autonomy because of the pervasive unregulated uses of face recognition technology that Dixon describes. The secrecy paradigm relates to information and the expectation of privacy when it is shared.[33] The visibility paradigm is not related to the sharing of personal information *per se*, but functions in terms of 'sharing of presence' whereby walking past the display triggers the analysis. This subsequently raises the policy questions above, and potentially situates the activity within the scope of the secrecy paradigm. Yet, the Centre for Democracy and Technology reports that "most digital signage systems are not yet configured to identify individuals, but instead calculate a passer-by's age and gender",[34] and thereby the signage is used to advertise age and gender specific products and services, which may be inappropriate or unwarranted.

Therefore, the possibility of enhanced operability and functionality are grounds for contending that loss of privacy and liberty have a detrimental effect on autonomy, hitherto illustrated by Kafka's *Josef K.* This is not to advocate by precedent the shielding or protecting of those who perpetuate criminal acts. But rather to locate the

---

[28] *ibid* p. 5.

[29] Durrani (2013).

[30] Sternstein (2011).

[31] Mallon (2003), pp. 970–971.

[32] *Dionisio,* 410 U.S. at 14.

[33] Solove (2011), pp. 100–101 *op cit.*

[34] CDT (2012), p. 5.

pivotal points of the face recognition technology discourse within the context of privacy and liberty, and its effect on autonomy and social values such as trust and confidence.

References

Acquisti A, Gross R, Stutzman F (2014) Face recognition and privacy in the age of augmented reality. J Privacy Confidentiality 6(2):1. https://doi.org/10.29012/jpc.v6i2.638. http://www.heinz.cmu.edu/~acquisti/face-recognition-study-FAQ/. Accessed 12 Aug 2019

Bentham J (1789) In: Bozovic M (ed) The panopticon writings. Verso, London, pp 29–95, 1995

Bentham J (1791) Letter II Panopticon or inspection-house. http://www.scran.ac.uk/ada/documents/castle_style/bridewell/bridewell_jeremy_bentham_panoption_vol1.htm. Accessed 12 Aug 2019

Brin D (1998) The transparent society. Addison-Wesley, Reading

Center for Democracy and Technology (2012) Seeing is ID'ing: facial recognition & privacy. https://cdt.org/files/pdfs/Facial_Recognition_and_Privacy-Center_for_Democracy_and_Technology-January_2012.pdf. Accessed 12 Aug 2019

Dixon P (2010) The one-way-mirror-society: privacy: implications of the new digital signage networks. http://worldprivacyforum.org/2010/01/report-one-way-mirror-society/. Accessed 12 Aug 2019

Dostoevsky F (1864) (reprinted 2015) Notes from underground and other stories (trans: Garnett C). Wordsworth Classics, Hertfordshire, p 471

Durrani A (2013) JCDecaux to target shoppers with 400 digital screens outside Tesco. http://www.mediaweek.co.uk/article/1186211/jcdecaux-target-shoppers-400-digital-screens-outside-tesco. Accessed 12 Aug 2019

Electronic Privacy Information Center (EPIC) Facebook Privacy. https://epic.org/privacy/facebook/. Accessed 12 Aug 2019. Open culture: the problem with facebook: "It's Keeping Things From You". January 21st, 2014. http://www.openculture.com/2014/01/the-problem-with-facebook-its-keeping-things-from-you.html. Accessed 12 Aug 2019

Facebook 'Tagging photos'. http://www.facebook.com/help/www/463455293673370. Accessed 12 Aug 2019

Facebook Data Policy. https://www.facebook.com/policy.php. Accessed 12 Aug 2019

Facebook Key Facts. https://newsroom.fb.com/key-Facts. Accessed 12 Aug 2019

Facebook Terms of Service paragraph 3.3 The permissions you give us. https://www.facebook.com/legal/terms. Accessed 12 Aug 2019

Foucault M (1977) Discipline and punish: the birth of the prison (trans: Alan Sheridan A). First published as 'Surveiller et punir: Naissance de la prison' by Éditions Gallimard, Paris, 1975

Gill M, Spriggs A (2005) Accessing the impact of CCTV Home Office Research Study 292. Dev & Statistics Directorate, Home Office Research. www.homeoffice.gov.uk/rds/pdfs05/hors292.pdf. via.Google. Accessed 12 Aug 2019

Gordon N (2002) On visibility and power: an Arendtian corrective of foucault. Hum Stud 25 (2):125–145

Mallon B (2003) Every breath you take, every move you make, I'll be watching you: the use of face recognition technology. Villanova Law Rev 48:955. http://digitalcommons.law.villanova.edu/vlr/vol48/iss3/6. Accessed 12 Aug 2019

Moreau E (2019) What is 'Tagging' on Facebook? Lifewire, June 24 2019. https://www.lifewire.com/facebook-new-profile-and-timeline-privacy-settings-3486231. Accessed 12 Aug 2019

Rashid FY (2011) Global data storage capacity totals 295 Exabytes: USC Study. http://www.eweek.com/c/a/Data-Storage/Global-Data-Storage-Capacity-Totals-295-Exabytes-USC-Study-487733/. Accessed 12 Aug 2019

Rutkin A (2015) The rise of on-body cameras and how they will change how we live. New Scientist, vol 227, no 3031. https://www.newscientist.com/article/mg22730314-500-the-rise-of-on-body-cameras-and-how-they-will-change-how-we-live/. Accessed 12 Aug 2019

Solove DJ (2011) Nothing to hide: the false trade off between privacy and security. Yale University Press, New Haven

Sternstein A (2011) FBI to launch nationwide facial recognition service. http://www.nextgov.com/technology-news/2011/10/fbi-to-launch-nationwide-facial-recognition-service/49908. Accessed 12 Aug 2019

United States v. Dionisio, 410 U.S. 1 (1973) at 14. https://supreme.justia.com/cases/federal/us/410/1/case.html. Accessed 12 Aug 2019

Wacks R (1993) Personal information: privacy and the law. Clarendon Press Oxford, Oxford

Walker L (2019) Facebook privacy settings tutorial. Lifewire, June 20 2019. https://www.lifewire.com/what-is-tagging-on-facebook-3486369. Accessed 12 Aug 2019

Chapter 7
The Law and Data Protection

Abstract This chapter provides an overview of the range of legislation associated with the regulation of data management. Of special interest here is the status of personal images as 'data'. The issue of whether photographic or digital images are in fact data creates tensions that until recently did not exist. In other words, the technology has overtaken the legal discourse and has required either that the image data should be assimilated into existing law on a case-by-case basis, or for new laws to be drafted. Therefore, since face recognition is an imaging modality previous statutory instruments are inadequate, and this chapter provides the backdrop to the on-going legal discourse.

7.1 Introduction

The purpose of this chapter is to provide an overview of the range of legislation associated with the regulation of data management. Of special interest here is the status of personal images as 'data'. The issue of whether photographic or digital images are in fact data creates tensions that until recently did not exist. In other words, the technology has overtaken the legal discourse and has required either that the image data should be assimilated into existing law on a case-by-case basis, or for new laws to be drafted. Therefore, since face recognition is an imaging modality previous statutory instruments are inadequate, and this chapter provides the backdrop to the on-going legal discourse.

One should keep in mind that since 1998 the prohibition of unauthorised data acquisition and processing has been statutory law in the United Kingdom and has established the right to informational privacy.[1] This right to informational privacy has been variously described,[2] but essentially it is the right to have personal information kept undisclosed to third parties, and is defined by Raymond Wacks as:

---

[1]Manson and O'Neill (2007), pp. 97–121.

[2]Westin (1967) and Parent (1983).

I. Berle, *Face Recognition Technology*, Law, Governance and Technology Series 41,
https://doi.org/10.1007/978-3-030-36887-6_7

> ....those facts, communications, or opinions relating to an individual that it would be reasonable to expect him to regard as intimate or sensitive and therefore to want to withhold or at least to restrict their collection, use, or circulation[3]

It is reasonable to assume that Wacks' definition applies to images given that they meet his criteria of 'reasonableness'. Their content is such that they can be private and confidential. This was subsequently examined and contested later in UK and European courts.[4]

The due process of law is nuanced and subject to interpretation and contextual application, which differs in the United Kingdom, in European Union member states and the United States. For the purposes of this chapter, the UK/EU and US approaches to data protection will be compared. Furthermore, whilst there are significant differences, there are discussions leading towards the convergence of aspects of data protection procedures and information flows between the EU and the US, and these will be discussed below.

As noted in Chap. 4, before the referendum on 23rd June 2016 when the UK voted to leave the EU, the primacy of European law required the UK Parliament to incorporate and implement EU law into domestic law with the passing of the European Communities Act 1972. However, since the referendum the European Union (Notification of Withdrawal) Act 2017 confirms the UK's withdrawal (known as Brexit) and the implied repeal of the 1972 Act. Repealing the 1972 Act also transfers previous EU law into UK law. In the interim, before leaving the EU, newer legislation such as the GDPR has been implemented into UK law as the Data Protection Act 2018. Moreover, until the UK leaves, the European Court of Justice (ECJ) case law will be retained as law,[5] but eventually, it is expected that ECJ judgements will no longer be binding and the Supreme Court of the United Kingdom and Scotland's High Court of Justiciary will be the final courts of appeal.

Leaving aside the political complexities of Brexit, the following considers the various constituents related to data matrices and their intricacies. The contrasting approaches to data protection considered below illustrate some of the inconsistencies within the legislative approaches and also serve to highlight some apparent dichotomies. Moreover, Fig. 4.1 illustrated the inherent tensions between the state[6] and personal autonomy. These tensions are ameliorated in the EU by various directives and regulations that apply to member states, and also to non-EU countries.

---

[3]Wacks (1989, revised 1993), p. 26.

[4]To be considered below.

[5]The European Community Act 1972.

[6]The state can equally be a business corporation.

7.2 Data Protection and Privacy

The provisions of the UK's Data Protection Act 2018 (DPA) govern the processing of personal data of living individuals; processing includes holding, obtaining, recording, using and disclosing information. The Act applies to every type of media including *images* and paper. Data controllers are required to notify the Information Commissioner what information is held and be committed to protecting data quality and information security. The Act contains Six Data Protection Principles,[7] which describe the standards for data probity and security, and which apply to everyone who collects and stores data; and was drafted to implement the European Directive 2016/680 on data protection.[8]

However, the earlier UK Data Protection Act 1998 protected an individual's personal data from unlawful disclosure and processing at an institutional level it conceived the issue in terms of breach of confidentiality rather than for example, a human right. However, we find that the Human Rights Act 1998, Article 8(1) provides that everyone has the right to respect for their private and family life, their home and their correspondence; this redressed the 1998 Act's imbalance by protecting private information, so that "the holding, disclosure and refusal to allow access to such information may all constitute interferences with this right".[9] The EU Directive 2016/680[10] removes any dichotomy in UK law by incorporating that right without redress to Article 8(1) of the Charter of Fundamental Rights of the European Union[11] and which is incorporated into UK law by the 1998 Human Rights Act.

Then again, despite of Article 8, the earlier Data Protection Act (DPA1998) protected only the data and not the person. Subsequently, the loss of data (or poor data processing) is the principal issue here because no immediate interference of an individual's privacy was involved. Nevertheless, where lost data interferes with personal activities through fraudulent use of the information that is more likely to be a criminal activity not directly associated with Article 8(1) (of the Human Rights Act 1998) and privacy; even though interference with personal correspondence may be an outcome of the fraud. Putting aside the issues of fraud the Data Protection Act 1998 offered no real protection to individuals; it merely defined, within the context of data processing an organisation's responsibilities and duties towards its data subjects' information and not their privacy in terms of intrusion.

Therefore, from the UK perspective, both the DPA1998 and HRA Article 8(1) are essentially extended formulations of the common law duty of confidence which is defined by a threefold test such that: "the information must have the necessary quality of confidence; there must also be an obligation of confidence; and any disclosure of information is only a breach of confidence, if it is to the detriment of

[7]See Chap. 3, footnote 26.

[8]Council of the European Union Regulation (EU) 2016/680.

[9]Amos (2006), p. 346.

[10]The antecedent to the General Data Protection Regulation.

[11]Regulation (EU) 2016/680 para 1 *op cit.*

the confider [data subject]".[12] Hence, failure to comply with the DPA1998 was not a breach of a person's privacy but rather a breach of confidence, this was due to the complex nature of the interpretation of Article 8(1) and its juxtaposition to the DPA1998 because the implementation of Article 8 in "English law is fused to considerations of confidentiality which may conceivably prevent an expansive application of the right to privacy in respect of personal information".[13] This somewhat accords with Sir Brian Leveson's later assertion in 2015 that although individuals can cite the Convention's Article 8, UK courts are not tied to the ECHR Human Rights Convention, they only need to acknowledge it.[14] With the possible exception of *Mosley* (below), Leveson was just stating a fact and reflecting on past judgements. Whether the UK Supreme Court will do likewise in the future remains to be seen, given that the Data Protection Act 2018 is more prescriptive and cohesive than before.

Furthermore, Wicks' summary although correct in her analysis of the conflation of privacy and confidentiality, was somewhat contradicted in the case of *Mosley v News Group Newspapers Ltd.*[15] In *Mosley* what is confidential was also confirmed as private, which until Judge Eady's judgement in Mosley was not necessarily the case. Rather, UK courts have been unfavourable to suits of privacy principally because they have been brought by celebrities who are already in the public domain, and therefore, the courts have preferred to view such interference as the misuse of private information. Thus, by focussing on informational disclosure the courts have separated the two aspects of privacy: celebrities are not private persons in terms of anonymity, but unless already in the public domain, their personal information is confidential.[16]

The above examples are indicative of how since 1998 the data and juridical landscape has evolved and now includes digital capabilities such as mobile phones and surveillance modalities. Consequently, Directive 95/46/EC was repealed and has been superseded by Directive (EU) 2016/680 and formulated as the EU General Data Protection Regulation (GDPR).[17,18]

---

[12]Wicks (2007), p. 122.

[13]*ibid* p. 123.

[14]See Eglot (2015).

[15]Mosley v News Group Newspapers Ltd.

[16]*ibid* Mosley: Eady J at [133] and [134].

[17]*European Commission Memo, 27th January* 2014.

[18]Regulation (EU) 2016/680, *op cit*. See footnote 45 below.

7.3 Informational Privacy

In consideration of personal information, Nissenbaum[19] insists that the right to privacy needs to be contextualised within the information technology milieu before breaches of confidence can be determined, calling this the right to "contextual integrity". That is, we have a right to privacy, but it is not a right to control our personal information, such as restricting data sharing required within the financial or health sectors, nor is it a right to restrict access to this information where it is a statutory requirement such as for safeguarding purposes. Nevertheless, Nissenbaum adds that expectations of privacy that emanate from the flow of personal data are a right and should be shaped by a general confidence in the way that the principles of privacy operate and apply morally, and politically in social life.[20]

Expectations of informational privacy differ between the US and the EU. The US approach is 'sectoral' whereas the UK and EU have an 'omnibus' approach; her analysis[21] is complemented by Schwartz and Solove's[22] proposal for reconciling the differences between them (and is discussed below). Meanwhile, although Nissenbaum did not invent the terms, the omnibus approach is an overarching commitment to privacy that guides detailed legislation and rule-making. This approach recognises privacy as a fundamental human right which supersedes other moral and political rights, and therefore should not be treated as a commodity that can be traded against other interests; this right is formulated in ECHR Article 8. Conversely, the sectoral approach is so-called because there is no explicit right to privacy in the Constitution, which has led to legislation being developed independently 'sector by sector', for instance communications and law enforcement.[23] Without an overriding right to privacy, the US approach appears inconsistent, since it is possible that privacy protection in one sector will be inapplicable in another.

Moreover, the US Constitution's Fourth Amendment states that:

> [T]he right of the people to be secure in their persons, houses, papers, and effects, against unreasonable searches and seizures, shall not be violated, and no warrants shall issue, but upon probable cause, supported by oath or affirmation, and particularly describing the place to be searched, and the persons or things to be seized.[24]

At face value, the amendment appears to offer some privacy rights, but its nuanced conditions mitigate privacy because of the interpretative nature of reasonableness and probable cause. An example of this was the 1967 court case of *Katz v United States,* when the Supreme Court acknowledged that "the Fourth Amendment

[19]Nissenbaum (2010).

[20]*ibid* p. 231.

[21]*ibid* p. 237.

[22]Schwartz and Solove (2014).

[23]Nissenbaum (2010), pp. 237–238 *op cit.*

[24]US Constitution: Fourth Amendment.

cannot be translated into a general constitutional 'right to privacy'".[25] Moreover, Katz established a two-pronged test proposed by Justice Harlan for determining constitutionally protected searches, that is firstly whether there is an actual expectation of privacy; and secondly whether that expectation is one which society is willing to recognise as reasonable.[26]

Consequently, since Katz, the notion that no expectation of privacy exists whenever a person is in the public arena has been contested in US courts and was particularly addressed in *United States v Dionisio.*[27] In *Dionisio*[28] the issue was whether a person's voice could be used to identify them, this is relevant to face recognition because neither, from the US perspective qua *Dionisio*, affords an expectation of privacy in public. Moreover, the United States challenge to Katz's expectation of privacy was based on the notion that any activity in public is no longer private, and therefore to avail oneself of the full protection of the Fourth Amendment it is necessary not to venture into a public space. Therefore, both are indicative of Solove's 'secrecy paradigm',[29] which is derived from the narrow interpretation of the Fourth Amendment that confines privacy to the boundary of the internal home environment, but not beyond that boundary.[30]

This has been challenged in subsequent cases, and in *Human Rights: Civil Liberty, Privacy and the Law* below a further detailed discussion of civil liberty and the legal discourse follows. Without such discourse the prospect of a narrow interpretation of the Fourth Amendment being applied is likely, because any physical feature is subject to scrutiny and analysis and is only contestable in the courts. If such intrusion persists beyond what is reasonable this is arguably not too far removed from a state of exception. In extremis a state of exception implies a national unified response to perceived threats that necessitates the suspension of the rule of law or the constitution. The preventative is the various challenges to the breaches of the Fourth Amendment, without which liberty would be diminished but which also highlights the fragmented and sectoral approach to privacy that exists in the United States that also somewhat mitigates against a state of exception. However, given the ability (by government agencies) to monitor our activities by covert means of surveillance,[31] the likelihood of a state of exception being declared is remote because the rule of law on Whitehead's account is not suspended per se, but applied narrowly.

Yet in other contexts the need for data protection remains an essential aspect of privacy. Thus, if an individual's voice is not protected how much less someone's facial appearance? Keeping silent is possible in public, hiding one's appearance is

---

[25]See Mallon (2003). See fn 24 above.

[26]*Katz v. United States*, **389 U.S. 347** (1967). Cited by Mallon B *op cit.*

[27]United States v Dionisio 410 U.S. 1 (1973). Cited by Mallon B *ibid.*

[28]See Sect. 6.7.

[29]Solove (2011), pp. 100–101.

[30]See Sect. 4.4.

[31]See Whitehead (2013), p. 21.

generally not, and even a covered face attracts even more attention which in heightened times of anxiety about public safety can arouse suspicion. For instance, although anecdotal and based on personal observations whilst travelling on the London Underground shortly after the 7th July 2005 suicide incidents there was a tangible increase in anxiety whilst in the same carriage with anyone carrying a rucksack, this was exacerbated when that passenger also had some form of face covering. Furthermore, helmet clad motorcyclists must remove their helmets before entering a bank to avoid suspicion of criminal intent and be ordinarily subjected to CCTV monitoring. Whilst this is quite different to the after-effects of the 7th July, the principle can potentially incentivise the banning of face coverings to facilitate the use of face recognition technology to securitise identity.[32]

7.4 Data Protection and Privacy: The United States Sectoral Approach

Summarising data protection in the US, Jolly[33] writes that the US does not have any overarching federal law that regulates the collection and use of personal data. Alternatively, federal and state laws are fragmented, subsequently, policies overlap, merge, or potentially contradict one another. To avoid the difficulties of fragmentation, there are numerous guidelines created by government agencies and industrial corporations. These self-regulatory guidelines are not legally enforceable but are reasonably considered as "best practice".

This description of the fragmented approach to data protection in the United States stimulates the concern by US commentators and scholars such as Solove. This is because the fragmented and therefore sectoral approach is unregulated and decentralised. Moreover, this is influenced by conflicts of interest when the demands of business and concomitantly 'big data' pressurise 'best practice', which albeit conjecturally means "best practice for the business not the data subject / consumer". For example, in January 2012 Representative Edward Markey, a US lawmaker concerned with privacy issues had asked the US Federal Trade Commission (FTC) to investigate whether the changes in how Google handles consumer data had violated their agreement with the FTC. Markey and others were also concerned that Google's planned consolidation of user information would reduce consumers' privacy. Inasmuch that the planned unification of their privacy policies would "mean a simpler, more intuitive Google experience", and by treating information as a single repository of data, the company could further increase its advertising revenue and limit consumers ability to control how their data is shared.[34]

---

[32]See Chap. 11.

[33]See Jolly (n.d.), p. 2.

[34]Reuters (2012).

Subsequently, in March 2012, the US Federal Trade Commission (FTC) published their report *Protecting Consumer Privacy in an Era of Rapid Change: Recommendations for Business and Policymakers*,[35] to improve and arguably standardise self-regulation. Yet the legality of Google's action remained doubtful, to the extent that France's data protection authority, on behalf of the Article 29 group asked the EU data authority to investigate the matter. In the UK, the Information Commissioner's Office (ICO) also investigated whether Google's revised privacy policy complied with the current Data Protection Act.[36] The legislators and regulators reactions to the changed policy highlights the importance of centralised regulation that consolidates data protection law across Europe, which applies to all sectors, and is ultimately expressed in the GDPR. Contrariwise, the various US sectors privacy laws include: The Federal Trade Commission Act, The Financial Services Modernisation Act, The Health Insurance Portability and Accountability Act, The Electronic Communications Privacy Act.[37]

Additionally, the collection of personal data is also regulated by various state laws which when they provide greater protection, supersedes federal law.[38]

Given that the US sectoral approach is esoteric and complex, interactions or transfer of data between the US and EU has necessitated a means of reconciling the divergent approaches. Schwartz and Solove's[39] redefinition of personal identifiable information (PII) pre-empts the differences by establishing a standardised regulatory regime. Their proposal[40] divides data into three categories and places the data on a risk continuum:

[35]FTC (2012). The FTC performs a similar role to that of EU Information Commissioners though unlike the US, the European data protection laws apply universally to all data in every sector.

[36]Shear (2013).

[37]Jolly I *op cit* p.5. The Federal Trade Commission Act (15 U.S.C. s.41-58) (FTC Act) is a federal consumer protection law that prohibits unfair or deceptive practices and applies to offline and online privacy and data security policies. The Financial Services Modernisation Act (Gramm-Leach-Bliley Act (GLB)) (15 U.S.C. s.6801-6827) regulates the collection, use and disclosure of financial information. GLB limits the disclosure of non-public personal information and can require financial institutions to provide notice of their privacy practices and an opportunity for data subjects to opt out of having their information shared. The Health Insurance Portability and Accountability Act (HIPAA) (42 U.S.C. s.1301 et seq) regulates medical information.

The Electronic Communications Privacy Act (18 U.S.C. s.2510) and the Computer Fraud and Abuse Act (18 U.S.C. s.1030) regulates the interception of electronic communications and computer tampering respectively.

[38]HIPPA (2003). For instance the United States Department of Health and Human Services 'Summary of the HIPAA Privacy Rule [The HIPAA] "Privacy Rule provides exceptions to the general rule of federal pre-emption for contrary State laws that relate to the privacy of individually identifiable health information, [which] provide greater privacy protections or privacy rights with respect to such information".

[39]Schwartz and Solove (2014) *op cit.* See Sect. 4.6.

[40]*ibid.*

- *Identified Data:* Information refers to an identified person when it singles out a specific individual from others, and therefore poses a substantial risk of identification.
- *Identifiable Data*: Information in the middle of the risk continuum relates to an identifiable individual when there is some non-remote possibility of future identification. The risk level is low to moderate.
- *Non-identifiable Data*: Information that carries only a remote risk of identification. Such data cannot be said to relate to a person, taking account of the means reasonably likely to be used for identification.

Conversely, the UK and EU's approach to privacy and risk is homogenous, inasmuch as identification and identifiability are uniform[41]; nor is there any separation between sectors and compliance to the Data Protection Act 2018 is mandatory.

The various actions taken for commercial best interests challenge existing data and privacy law. The companies appear to 'push the envelope' to test the boundaries of legality, thereby attempting to change the law in their favour and homogenise American and European law. Yet, the burgeoning expansion of 'big data' that can potentially consolidate text and images requires due diligence. This diligence necessitates the need to acknowledge the notion of the 'secrecy paradigm', because the loss of anonymity that face recognition affords is a substantial threat to privacy and loss of personal autonomy described in the previous chapter. Since privacy and confidentiality are interrelated and are contractually supported by data protection law, any safeguards that fail to recognise the loss of anonymity when individuals are observed ultimately undermines the protection of the law and denies freedom of choice when the disclosure of information is coercive. It is coercive whenever the service terms and conditions insist on the forfeiture of privacy in exchange for access to the service.

The American sectoral approach weakens protection because the specificity of the law within one sector may not apply in another sector, which Schwartz and Solove's redefinition of personal identifiable information seeks to rectify. However laudable this is, their proposal does not address the issues of identification that face recognition creates and is not confined to any particular sector. Arguably therefore, because of the universality of identification that face recognition technology (FRT) affords, Schwartz and Solove's continuum of personal identifiable information should be homogenised in response to the characteristics of facial appearance that FRT relies upon. Moreover, the scope of the Data Protection Act and the GDPR[42] are potentially applicable to face recognition (see below) and are the benchmark for protecting homogenised personal identifiable information, because it includes physical characteristics used by FRT.

Although their redefinition addresses the issue of data security and is reminiscent of Nissenbaum's contention that privacy is context dependent, their proposal does

[41]Regulation (EU) 2016/680 §2, *op cit.*

[42]DPA 2018; GDPR Article 9.

not address the ‘secrecy paradigm’[43] where the risk of identification in public is increased, and where the Fourth Amendment ‘secrecy paradigm’ is amplified with face recognition technology. Given that both US and EU provisions for data protection concentrate on data per se, there is need to recognise that FRT is a form of electronic communication data capture that affects privacy and is discussed below.

7.5 Reconciling US and EU Provisions

An attempt to reconcile the divergent US and EU approaches to privacy, data-collection and confidentiality had been the introduction of ‘The Safe Harbour’ which created a voluntary self-certification programme for US companies to receive data from EU citizens. Since its introduction some companies had falsely claimed compliance[44] which is arguably a regulatory misdemeanour, and which has since been exacerbated by Edward Snowden’s revelations (Chap. 3) which had serious consequences for the continuation of the Safe Harbour programme.[45] Yet, because the scheme was self-regulated, from the European perspective it was a distrusted cosmetic exercise, such was the impact of Viviane Reding’s (the EU Justice Commissioner) call for rebuilding trust in an initiative that seeks to reconcile the differences between the US and EU, and satisfy the EU’s approach to data collection and privacy. From the American perspective there was a tendency to treat the programme as a ‘tick box’ exercise and subsequently a failure to comply with the programme. Reding stated that “safeguards should apply and citizens should have rights. . .we must make Safe Harbour safer. . .Let me put it simply: we kicked the tyres and saw that repairs are needed. For Safe Harbour to be fully roadworthy the U.S. will have to service it...Safe Harbour has to be strengthened or it will be suspended”.[46] It was subsequently suspended in late 2015 after the European Court of Justice (ECJ) ruled that the US had violated EU privacy law,[47] and has been replaced by the EU-US Privacy Shield Framework[48] that guarantees secure data flows from Europe and prohibits indiscriminate mass surveillance on Europeans’ personal data. Yet, this framework may still be found inadequate because the EU and US standards of privacy or what is private maybe irreconcilable; since the ECJ does not have any jurisdiction over US surveillance law.[49] Moreover,

---

[43] Solove (2011) *op cit.*

[44] FTC (2014).

[45] Viviane Reding V (2014).

[46] *ibid.*

[47] See Drozdiak and Sam Schechner (2015).

[48] EU—US Privacy Shield Framework (European Commission 2016).

[49] Edgar (2017), pp. 164–167.

the framework is administered by the International Trade Administration within the US Department of Commerce[50] and typifies the sectoral approach to privacy.

Nevertheless, even though the EU cannot impose its standards on American law, some principles are arguably universal and are the basis of the data protection reforms. In January 2014 Viviane Reding[51] defined the principles that would be used to reform and govern data processing. These included:

- Not distinguishing between the private and the public sector.
- [The] fourth principle relate(s) to surveillance. Data collection should be targeted and be limited to what is proportionate to the objectives that have been set. If this element of proportionality is lost, citizens' acceptance will be lost as well. Blanket surveillance of electronic communications data is not acceptable. It amounts to arbitrary interference with the private lives of citizens.
- [The] seventh, without a role for judicial authorities, there can be no real oversight. Executive oversight is good. Parliamentary oversight is necessary. Judicial oversight is key.

In parenthesis related to the fourth principle, Reding observed that:

- Data Protection rules should apply irrespective of the nationality of the person concerned. Applying different standards to nationals and non-nationals makes no sense in view of the open nature of the internet...distinguishing between the rights of individuals depending on their nationality and place of residence impedes the free flow of data.

Reding encapsulates Solove's and Agamben's[52] principal concerns that reflect the differences in the US and EU perspectives and have identified the fault-lines between the EU and the US. Considering Reding's fourth principle, the definition of 'surveillance of electronic communication data' is arguably open to interpretation and may not apply to face recognition unless images are universally defined as electronic communication data. The next section considers this possibility from the perspective of UK case law and European approaches to data collection and protection.

7.6 Data Protection and Face Recognition

Since data protection implies confidentiality does it apply to face recognition in public spaces where individuals have no expectation of privacy? We may begin by considering the image in the form of a photograph. In 2004 Naomi Campbell, the British super-model was photographed by a newspaper photographer leaving a

[50]Privacy Shield Framework (European Commission 2016).

[51]Reding V 2(014) *op cit.*

[52]Agamben (2005).

Narcotics Anonymous meeting; the subsequent court case examined her right to privacy qua Article 8 of the Human Rights Act 1998. The case eventually went to appeal at the House of Lords, where Baroness Hale,[53] in her concluding remarks noted that:

> 154...[W]e have not so far held that the mere fact of covert photography is sufficient to make the information contained in the photograph confidential. The activity photographed must be private. If this had been, and had been presented as, a picture of Naomi Campbell going about her business in a public street, there could have been no complaint. She makes a substantial part of her living out of being photographed looking stunning in designer clothing. Readers will obviously be interested to see how she looks if and when she pops out to the shops for a bottle of milk. There is nothing essentially private about that information nor can it be expected to damage her private life
>
> 155.[B]ut here the accompanying text made it plain that these photographs were different. They showed her coming either to or from the NA meeting.... They showed the place where the meeting was taking place, which will have been entirely recognisable to anyone who knew the locality. A picture is 'worth a thousand words' because it adds to the impact of what the words convey; but it also adds to the information given in those words. If nothing else, it tells the reader what everyone looked like; in this case it also told the reader what the place looked like. In context, it also added to the potential harm, by making her think that she was being followed or betrayed and deterring her from going back to the same place again.

Ultimately, in such cases celebrities are not anonymous, but their personal lives are private. This accords with Nissenbaum's contention that context is paramount when determining expectations of privacy. Had Campbell merely been shopping in "stunning designer clothing" her expectation of privacy would arguably have been less and likely be a publicist's idea or marketing ploy. In my view, Hale's judgement in this respect is correct; although the photograph was not taken of a private activity its use was contextualised by its intended purpose and was therefore private and confidential.[54] Under these circumstances Campbell illustrates the secrecy paradigm when photographs are contextualised. Campbell's desire to shield herself from unintended publication and protect her privacy is indicative of her second-order preferences for confidentiality.[55]

Returning to the question that FRT potentially combines the loss of anonymity and privacy whenever the data is aggregated during the process of identifying an individual. Whether this, as described in Chap. 2, is for specific purposes or in wider contexts such as social media is ultimately related to the purpose of the biometric data and its intended use. This further raises the question of whether biometric data is personal data. On one hand a stray finger-print is not easily identifiable personal data unless it can be matched to a known person, on the other hand someone's face can be matched and identified automatically on social network sites. The former requires expertise and access to an appropriate database, the latter as described above[56] is

[53]Campbell (Appellant) v. MGN Limited (Respondents).

[54]*ibid* as per para 155.

[55]Chapter 5 above.

[56]See Sect. 6.7.

readily available on social network sites. This is not to give the impression that the social use of face recognition is acceptable and beyond the scope of data protection, but rather that an examination of whether facial images are personal data (which therefore qualify for protection), is necessary to pre-empt any precedence to the contrary.

Personal data is defined in Directive 95/46/EC Article 2(a)[57] as:

> any information relating to an identified or identifiable natural person ('data subject'); an identifiable person is one who can be identified directly or indirectly, in particular by reference to identification number or to one or more factors specific to his physical, physiological, mental, economic, cultural or social identity

Although the definition remains sound[58] and includes physical characteristics or factors, personal data is variably interpreted by EU member states.[59] In the UK, the Directive was implemented as the Data Protection Act 1998 (DPA) which is principally concerned with informational confidentiality and data processing rather than privacy per se. However, the Directive's Article 2(a) includes physical factors which arguably includes facial images, but at the time of drafting would have referred only to photographs or similar media that could potentially be used for identification, (or confirm identification) when associated with other information as in the *Naomi Campbell v MGN* case.

Isolated from other information or personal data, an unconsented photograph such as occurred in the *von Hannover v Germany* case,[60] breached Princess Caroline of Monaco's privacy when she was photographed with her children whilst on holiday, and further illustrates the loss of privacy in public even when trying to maintain normal family life as a mother rather than a public figure. Upon this judgement Princess Caroline pursued several civil court actions to prevent further publication. In two *von Hannover* judgements since 2004, the Court did not uphold her Article 8 rights, favouring instead the balancing of privacy and freedom of expression (Article 10), where public interests were seen as overriding factors. Indeed, the Court's criteria reflected how context is paramount when assessing the claims and counter-claims[61]:

- Whether the information contributes to a debate of general interest
- The notoriety of the person concerned
- The prior conduct of the person concerned
- Content, form and consequences of the publication
- The circumstances in which the photograph was taken

Nevertheless, the balancing of Articles 8 and 10 will vary across Europe and although Baroness Hale's comments were appropriate; from the above criteria the

---

[57]EU Directive 95/46/EC.

[58]GDPR para (9).

[59]See Kindt (2013), p. 93 §189.

[60]von Hannover v. Germany.

[61]See Bedat (2013) and Callender Smith (2012).

moral argument against publishing Campbell's photograph can be upheld, because the attempt to hide the truth by not disclosing her addiction motivated the newspaper to obtain photographic evidence to prove she was lying.[62] Thereby breaching her Article 8 rights and exceeding the bounds of freedom of expression contained in Article 10.

However, is a photograph or facial image personal data, especially when Directive 95/46/EC states that personal data must be "adequate, relevant and not excessive" and processed "fairly and lawfully"?[63]

In *von Hannover*, the issue was unconsented publication of photographs and not unlawful disclosure of personal information as defined in the directive. Or rather a breach of privacy in terms of intrusion and not a breach of confidentiality which would reveal her identity; it was the intrusive paparazzi photography of her children that concerned Princess Caroline and not merely the fact that she was photographed. This was not data as such, but in conjunction with Campbell the two cases illustrate how privacy and confidentiality are associated and need to be respected regardless of them being public figures. Indeed, it is immaterial whether photographs are taken in public or not otherwise Article 8 would not apply to them, and their right to privacy would be superseded in favour of Article 10.

This was apparent in the case of *Murray v Express Newspapers*[64] when Dr. and Mrs. Murray's (better known as J. K. Rowling) infant son was photographed in public by a paparazzi photographer, and the picture was subsequently published without his parents' consent. The case focussed on the issue of whether there is an expectation of privacy in public, and if so:

> the law [would] give every adult or child a legitimate expectation of not being photographed without consent on any occasion on which they are not, so to speak, on public business then it will have created a right for most people to the protection of their image. If a simple walk down the street qualifies for protection, then it is difficult to see what would not. For most people who are not public figures in the sense of being politicians or the like, there will be virtually no aspect of their life which cannot be characterised as private.[65]

Citing von Hannover, Patten J added that:

> even after *von Hannover* there remains, I believe, an area of routine activity which when conducted in a public place carries no guarantee of privacy.[66]

Subsequently in his judgement, because there cannot be any expectation of privacy in public, the Murrays' claim was dismissed. Although this approach is identical to the narrow interpretation of the US Fourth Amendment Patten J dismissed the claim because of the dis-association privacy has with confidentiality.

---

[62]This was widely reported in the press with headlines declaring the Daily Mirror's lawyer had called her a liar. And was also contentiously considered as legislating privacy by the backdoor of medical confidentiality by Piers Morgan, editor of the Daily Mirror Newspaper at the time.

[63]Kindt (2013) *op cit*, p. 418 §241.

[64]Murray v Express Newspapers Plc & Anor [2007].

[65]*ibid* para 65.

[66]*ibid* para 66.

That is, rather than follow von Hannover, the authority for dismissal was taken from Campbell in terms of breach of confidence which in Patten's judgment did not occur or apply to the Murrays.[67] Consequently, the case went to the Appeal Court[68] and the judgement was reversed on the basis that the trial judge had not sufficiently considered the balancing of HRA Articles 8 and 10, and how they relate to the Data Protection Act 1998 in respect of confidence and data processing.[69] The three cases are seminally representative of my claim that photographs or images are personal data (while hitherto they were not), and although the courts may argue that individuals do not have rights to their images per se, they do have informational privacy rights which need protecting, especially when images increasingly acquire the status of personal data within face recognition modalities. Failure to observe or affirm this transformation reduces autonomy when second-order preferences are denied such as in situations of mandatory compliance; or unknowingly subsumed when systems do not obtain consent. Irrespective of the context, data protection rights guard against unlawful data processing (and handling) and are discussed below.

7.7 Biometric Data and the Development of the General Data Protection Regulation

Returning to the question about biometric data being personal data therefore requires a definition that acknowledges biometric data as personal data that complies with the Directive's and the new Regulation's criteria for protection, which also separates and recognises the differences evident in *von Hannover*. The issues of privacy and confidentiality in von Hannover and Campbell obscure the loss of anonymity and the subsequent increased visibility that biometric data affords. To that end Kindt (here and below) seminally provides a definition[70]:

> all personal data which (a) relate directly or indirectly to unique or distinctive biological or behavioural characteristics of human beings and (b) are used or are fit to be used by automated means (c) for purposes of identification, identity verification or verification of a claim of living natural persons

Since the inception of the Article 29 Working Party (which was established under Article 29 of Directive 95/46/EC), its task was to:

> advise the Commission on any proposed amendment of this Directive, on any additional or specific measures to safeguard the rights and freedoms of natural persons with regard to the processing of personal data and on any other proposed Community measures affecting such rights and freedoms.[71]

---

[67] *ibid* paras 18, 19,72 and 73.

[68] Murray v Big Pictures (UK) Ltd [2008].

[69] *ibid* paras 63 and 63.

[70] Kindt (2013) *op cit* p 149 §275.

[71] Directive 95/46/EC Article 30(c).

The Working Party did not in my view, adequately define the nature of biometric data when not expressing clearly its relationship to privacy and confidentiality. Stating in 2003 that "this kind of data is of a special nature, as it relates to the behavioural and physiological characteristics of an individual and may allow his or her unique identification".[72] In 2012 "such as facial images, or dactyloscopic (fingerprints) data" was added to the previous definition.[73] Subsequently, in later versions of the directive[74] facial images entered the personal data ambit, because the modalities that capture images can subsequently process them and append existing data. Thus, the Working Party noted in their 2012 Opinion that:

> [W]hen a digital image contains an individual's face which is clearly visible and allows for that individual to be identified it would be considered personal data...[75]
>
> Facial recognition relies on a number of automated processing stages....Therefore, facial recognition constitutes an automated form of personal data, including biometric data.[76]

Kindt is critical of the Working Party's descriptions above, because they do not provide any examples or reasons to support their formulation, although perhaps the Working Party were cognisant of the three UK cases described above. Nevertheless, Kindt responds by proposing the criteria for ascertaining whether facial images are biometric data[77] by assessing whether the aforementioned conditions are met:

- Face recognition images relate directly or indirectly to unique or distinctive biological or behavioural characteristics of a human being
- Face recognition images are used or are fit to be used by automated means, irrespective of where or how the images are captured[78]
- When face recognition images are used for purposes of identification, identity verification or verification of a claim of living natural persons. For example, comparing facial images with images stored in a database

Accordingly, applying Kindt's criteria, all the conditions are met, and facial images are by those criteria irrefutably personal data when added to data dossiers, and/or are used to connect an individual to their data. Given the diversity of applications and platforms that use facial images for identification and verification purposes the cursory acknowledgement by the Working Party obscures the issue of how facial images can be adequately protected by the subsequent Directive **(EU) 2016/680**[79] and is arguably the cause of Kindt's critique, which ultimately the new data regulation (GDPR) addresses.

---

[72] Cited by Kindt (2013) *op cit.*

[73] GDPR Article 4(1). Cited by Kindt (2013) *op cit.*

[74] Kindt (2013) *op cit.*

[75] Directive 95/46/EC Article 29.

[76] *ibid.*

[77] Kindt (2013) *op cit.*

[78] i.e. scanned photographs.

[79] Regulation (EU) 2016/680 *op cit.*

Criticism aside, since facial images challenge the efficacy of data protection measures initiatives such as Privacy Enhancing Technologies (PETs) which ameliorate the risks of privacy violation, and Privacy by Design (PbD)[80] which refers to establishing privacy measures and strategies before implementing systems have been promoted.[81] Generally PETs are the tools that assist reaching PbD, but they are not mandatory.[82] Nevertheless, the Privacy by Design principles are the benchmark for best practice. Kindt further comments that Privacy by Design complements appropriate legislation and legal enforcement, and "may be useful to solve various privacy and protection issues and to improve the privacy-compliance of systems but cannot replace the legislative framework".[83]

The legislative frameworks have their genesis in Directive 95/46/EC Article 17 (security of processing) which states that:

> Member States shall provide that the controller must implement appropriate technical and organizational measures to protect personal data *against accidental or unlawful destruction* or *accidental loss, alteration, unauthorised disclosure or access*, in particular where the processing involves the transmission of data over a network, *and against all other unlawful forms of processing*[84]

At face value, Article 17 appears to encompass most issues, but it is essentially only an advisory guideline[85] which Member States are encouraged to implement within their own data protection frameworks. However, since the adoption of the Directive in 1995 the data landscape has changed, and in response the new regulation[86] incorporates privacy by design principles[87] and extends the obligations of Directive Article 17 to processors[88]:

> 1. The controller and the processor shall implement appropriate technical and organisational measures to ensure a level of security appropriate to the risks represented by the processing and the nature of the personal data to be protected, having regard to the state of the art and the costs of their implementation.
> 2. The controller and the processor shall, following an evaluation of the risks, take the measures referred to in paragraph 1 to protect personal data against accidental or unlawful destruction or accidental loss and to prevent any unlawful forms of processing, in particular any unauthorised disclosure, dissemination or access, or alteration of personal data.

Although Directive 95/46/EC objectives and principles remain fit for purpose,

---

[80]Privacy by Design: 7 Foundational Principles.

[81]Kindt (2013) *op cit.*

[82]*ibid.*

[83]*ibid.*

[84]Directive 95/46/EC *op cit.* My italics.

[85]Kindt (2013) *op cit.*

[86]European Commission Regulation 2016/679 (proposed GDPR vis-à-vis Regulation 2016/680).

[87]*ibid* (Article 30) and implemented in GDPR Articles 25 and 30.

[88]*ibid* and implemented in GDPR Article 26.

> it has not prevented fragmentation in the way personal data protection is implemented across the Union, legal uncertainty and a widespread public perception that there are significant risks associated notably with online activity.[89]

Therefore, the new General Data Protection Regulation (GDPR)[90] creates a more coherent data protection framework that is more robust and standardised in order to develop the digital economy across all sectors and allow individuals to control their own data, for instance, when explicitly consenting to biometric data (Article 9).[91]

By advocating Privacy by Design principles, the EU and US approaches are seemingly converging as they respond to the expansion of the social networks use of photo-tagging, and the commercial use of cameras in digital signage that determine facial characteristics. To that end the US Federal Trade Commission (FTC) hosted a workshop in 2012 to explore the developments in facial recognition technology and to establish best practice principles. The FTC[92] recommended that:

- companies should maintain reasonable data security protections for consumers' images and the biometric information
- companies should establish and maintain appropriate retention and disposal practices for the consumer images and biometric data that they collect.
- companies should consider the sensitivity of information when developing their facial recognition products and services and avoid placing them in sensitive areas such as changing rooms or where children congregate

The report is only concerned with the uses of facial recognition in commercial and social networks, and does not include governmental uses of the technology, and is therefore unlike the EU Data Regulation discussed above. Nevertheless, although the FTC's best practice principles are not intended to serve as law enforcement templates the FTC does emphasise, apparently without reference to it, the Safe Harbour Agreement by reminding companies that:

> Under Section 5 of the FTC Act, the Commission is authorized to take action against unfair or deceptive acts or practices. 15 U.S.C. § 45(a). Unfair acts or practices are defined as those that cause or are likely to cause substantial injury to consumers which is not reasonably avoidable by consumers themselves and not outweighed by countervailing benefits to consumers or to competition. 15 U.S.C. § 45(n). If a company uses facial recognition technologies in a manner that is unfair under this definition, or that constitutes a deceptive act or practice, the Commission can bring an enforcement action under Section 5. In contrast, in other countries and jurisdictions, such as the European Union, in certain circumstances, consumers may need to be notified and give their consent before a company can legally use facial recognition technologies.[93]

Ultimately, the FTC report highlights the separation of commercial uses of face recognition from governmental surveillance uses presumably because any such

[89] *ibid* page 18(7).

[90] *ibid* page 18(6).

[91] *Regulation (EU) 2016/679 and 2016/680.*

[92] FTC Report (2012).

[93] *ibid.*

criticism or suggestions for best practice are beyond the Commission's jurisdiction and authority. The only authority for addressing the issues, and scrutinising government agencies use of communication surveillance which includes face recognition is the US Congress, and it is through the work of privacy campaigners, such as the Electronic Frontier Foundation (EFF),[94] that the same issues addressed by the FTC can be brought before the legislators. These campaigners have formulated the '13 Necessary and Proportionate Principles'[95] which outline how communications surveillance by governments and their agencies can be conducted and remain consistent with human rights, and which arguably cohere with the commercial controls that are FTC compliant. Moreover, the principles are akin to the new European Data Regulation, inasmuch that each applies to all sectors, thereby eliminating the dichotomy between them.

Although the 'Principles' are formulated to test the integrity of governments' surveillance communication modalities and the validity of their use, they can equally apply to commercial activities. For instance, the legality of a service provider's terms and conditions, for example Facebook, or for their intended purpose to prescribe the necessity for blanket surveillance of electronic communications metadata by authorised agencies. Additionally, they are a model for "reform of surveillance law and policy around the world"[96] and therefore they constitute a uniform approach that protects civil liberty and security. Regarding human rights the principles of 'necessity', 'proportionality', 'due process' and 'safeguards against illegitimate access', help locate the boundaries between civil liberty and security and will be discussed in Chap. 8. Meanwhile the contours of civil liberty, privacy and the law are discussed next.

7.8 Human Rights: Civil Liberty, Privacy and the Law

The potential power of face recognition technology to identify individuals and subsequently breach their privacy, was demonstrated in a study[97] by Acquisti et al. at Carnegie Mellon University (CMU).[98] In their third experiment they "illustrate [d] the ability of inferring strangers' personal or sensitive information (their interests and Social Security numbers) from their faces, by combining face recognition, data mining algorithms, and statistical re-identification techniques. The results highlight [ed] the implications of the convergence of face recognition technology and increasing online self-disclosure, and the emergence of "personally predictable"

[94] See Cohn et al. (2013) Electronic Frontier Foundation.

[95] Electronic Frontier Foundation.

[96] *ibid.*

[97] Cited by Welinder (2012).

[98] Acquisti et al. (2014).

information, or PPI. They raise questions about the future of privacy in an "augmented" reality world in which online and offline data will seamlessly blend".

In another offline experiment they took photographs of college students and matched them against Facebook photographs without logging on, and they were able to identify someone who had merely been tagged by another on Facebook.[99] The implications for privacy and civil liberty, depending on *who* or *how* this real function (that is available commercially) is used, presents, from the American perspective (but not necessarily uniquely), a legal conundrum.[100] If anonymity is no longer possible, and if the information is not used, is this a breach of privacy? On the other hand, where identity fraud is intended that is a criminal act and prosecutable. From the perspective of civil liberty, the United States Fourth Amendment[101] is significantly applied by American courts, for example, *United States v. Maynard.*[102] In this case a defendant on appeal had their conviction reversed because a GPS tracking device used for intelligence gathering was deemed unconstitutional and the evidence therefore inadmissible because its procurement had violated the Fourth Amendment. The nuanced legal argument rested upon whether the use of a tracking device constituted a search by emphasising the "reasonable expectation of privacy" expressed in the Fourth Amendment and concluded in *Maynard,* that "[I]n considering whether something is 'exposed' to the public....we ask not what another person can physically and may lawfully do but rather what a reasonable person expects another might actually do".[103] Applying this judgement to a potential review of state sponsored FRT, would the Court inquire whether "pedestrians expect their fellow travellers to discover their identities via FRT software".[104] Whilst this is hypothetical, the prospect of challenging the application of FRT described by Acquisti et al. has stimulated the debate to the degree that American case law appears to be developing against or in opposition to the political will for extending the use of FRT where it resembles an unreasonable seizure or where it is overzealous. For example, in *Nader v General Motors*[105] the court recognised that being observed in a public place is not a violation of privacy, but sometimes "surveillance may be so 'overzealous' as to render it actionable" because it could discover or reveal hidden details, which is the actionable harm, rather than the surveillance itself.[106]

Subsequent cases prior to *Maynard* divided opinion; for example, in *United States v Knotts*[107] the Supreme Court permitted the use of a tracking device without a warrant, consequently other courts have extended *Knotts* to situations where a

---

[99] *ibid.*

[100] Fretty (2011), p. 444.

[101] Fourth Amendment *op cit.*

[102] United States v. Maynard.

[103] *ibid* Maynard, 615F.3d at 559. Cited by Fretty (2011), p. 444.

[104] Fretty (2011) *op cit.*

[105] Nader v. General Motors Corp.

[106] See Solove (2008), p. 111.

[107] United States v. Knotts.

"device will track the person or object only in public places"[108] in these jurisdictions FRT would not violate privacy expectations because the action is similar to physically following a car on the road, or person in the street. Contrariwise, as in *Maynard* a warrant is necessary to comply with the Fourth Amendment. Otherwise, FRT if used on a massive scale and without reasonable suspicion would breach the Fourth Amendment.[109] Yet, the Fourth Amendment could be nullified if FRT were to become a risk management tool used by executive agencies and authorities for security purposes.

Citing *United States v. Mendenhall*[110] and *INS v. Delgado*[111] advocates of public FRT maintain that suspicion-less identification is not seizure unless the person is stopped or restrained.[112] The balance of opinion rests on the definition of seizure and whether or not FRT is a surveillance tool similar to other tracking devices or methods. From the *Mendenhall* and *Delgado* perspectives, the defendants claimed that their Fourth Amendment rights had been violated whilst being questioned by law enforcement officers.[113] The courts equated seizure with restraint or detention, neither which had occurred. Therefore, their constitutional rights could not have been violated and because FRT is likened to a tracking device, which in *Knotts* did not violate privacy; nor is it a means of restraint and therefore FRT is Fourth Amendment compliant.

These legal judgements were pronounced before it was possible to identify someone without first stopping them and FRT has changed that landscape. Unlike a tracking device which only locates the whereabouts of someone, FRT identifies that person remotely and when coupled with an enabled mobile (cell) phone tracking system has the capacity to 'seize' that person, which violates their Fourth Amendment rights. Any blanket use by government agencies or others raises civil liberties concerns and stimulates public debate; public disclosure and revelations from concerned insiders follows below. The concentration on the American landscape is borne from the literature and the public discourse related to Fourth Amendment rights. Furthermore, whilst the cases of *Knotts* and *Jones* appear contradictory they differ because in *Knotts* a warrant was not applied for and therefore could not expire, in *Jones* the warrant had expired. In each case the interpretation and application of the Fourth Amendment was subjective and nuanced.

In the UK, the Human Rights Act 1998[114] (HRA) and the Regulation of Investigatory Powers Act 2000[115] (RIPA) provide the legal framework for regulating

[108]Fretty (2011) *op cit* p. 450.

[109]*ibid* p 451; United States v. Garcia.

[110]United States v. Mendenhall.

[111]INS v. Delgado.

[112]Fretty D *op cit* p. 446.

[113]United States v. Mendenhall *op cit.*

[114]Human Rights Act (HRA) 1998.

[115]Regulation of Investigatory Powers Act 2000.

privacy rights and surveillance. Most notably the Regulation of Investigatory Powers Act is:

> An Act to make provision for and about the interception of communications, the acquisition and disclosure of data relating to communications, the carrying out of surveillance, the use of covert human intelligence sources and the acquisition of the means by which electronic data protected by encryption or passwords may be decrypted or accessed; to provide for Commissioners and a tribunal with functions and jurisdictions in relation to those matters, to entries on and interferences with property or with wireless telegraphy and to the carrying out of their functions by the Security Services and the Government Communications Headquarters; and for connected purposes.

In addition to the HRA and RIPA, the Police and Criminal Evidence Act 1984 (PACE)[116] regulates the powers and duties of the police. This legislation operates within the context of police investigations and is separate from RIPA. Both RIPA and PACE are subject, on appeal to Article 8 of the Human Rights Act 1998[117]:

> Right to respect for private and family life
>
> **1**. Everyone has the right to respect for his private and family life, his home and his correspondence.
>
> **2**. There shall be no interference by a public authority with the exercise of this right except such as is in accordance with the law and is necessary in a democratic society in the interests of national security, public safety or the economic well-being of the country, for the prevention of disorder or crime, for the protection of health or morals, or for the protection of the rights and freedoms of others.

Akin to the American cases referred to above, the following UK cases are instructive because they illustrate how an individual's rights are valued and how rights law on appeal at the European Court of Human Rights (ECtHR) on a case by case basis curtails or subjugates excessive authoritative power.

> *Perry v United Kingdom*[118]
>
> The applicant had been arrested in connection with a series of armed robberies of minicab drivers and released pending an identification parade. When he failed to attend that and several further identification parades, the police requested permission to video him covertly. He was taken to the police station to attend an identity parade, which he refused to do. Meanwhile, on his arrival, *he was filmed by the custody suite camera,* adjusted to ensure that it took clear pictures during his visit. The pictures were inserted in a montage of film of other persons and shown to witnesses. Two witnesses of the armed robberies subsequently identified him from the compilation tape.
>
> Neither Mr Perry nor his solicitor was informed that a tape had been made or used for identification purposes. He was convicted of robbery and sentenced to five years imprisonment. The Court assessed that the ploy adopted by the police had gone beyond the normal use of this type of camera and amounted to an *interference with the applicant's right to respect for his private life*. The interference had not been in accordance with the law because the police had failed to comply with the procedures set out in the applicable code (PACE): they had not obtained the applicant's consent or informed him that the tape was being made;

---

[116]Police and Criminal Evidence Act 1984 c. 60.

[117]HRA1998 *op cit.*

[118]Perry v. The United Kingdom. My italics.

neither had they informed him of his rights in that respect. It awarded the applicant 1,500 euros for non-pecuniary damage and certain sums for costs and expenses.

Similarly, *in R v Loveridge*[119] the police secretly filmed appellants by video camera in a magistrate's court. The Court of Appeal held that this effectively breached Article 8(1), as in *Campbell v MGN Ltd.*[120] Therefore, in each of these cases the appellants had their 'expectancy of privacy' violated and whilst Article 8 is not entirely comparable to the Fourth Amendment the expectation of privacy is the same test. *Perry v United Kingdom* and *R v Loveridge*, are indicative of how the expectation of privacy can be violated in the exercise of statutory powers. In both cases cameras were used covertly in official premises without consent and the judgements based on how this breaches police codes of practice.

However, when an individual is observed in public by the police or other agencies, can their expectation of privacy be the same as described above? From the American perspective, if filmed or photographed it is likely except that the argument for applying Article 8(1), irrespective of breaches in PACE or RIPA, would likely rest on the issue of an individual being in public view. This occurred in *Gilchrist v HM Advocate*[121] and *Kinloch [2012] UKSC*[122] where leave for appeal was not granted on that basis. Yet in *Campbell*, who was also in public view a different interpretation applied. The reason for the difference being that the former was a criminal investigation, and the latter a civil case.

References

Acquisti A, Gross R, Stutzman F (2014) Face recognition and privacy in the age of augmented reality. J Privacy Confidentiality 6(2):1. https://doi.org/10.29012/jpc.v6i2.638. Accessed 24 Aug 2019

Agamben G (2005) State of exception (trans: Attell K). The University of Chicago Press, Chicago

Amos M (2006) Human rights law. Hart Publishing, Oxford, p 346, an imprint of Bloomsbury Publishing Plc

Bedat A (2013) Case law, Strasbourg: Von Hannover v Germany (No.3), Glossing over Privacy. http://inforrm.wordpress.com/2013/10/13/case-law-strasbourg-von-hannover-v-germany-no-3-glossing-over-privacy-alexia-bedat/. Accessed 24 Aug 2019

Callender Smith R (2012) From Von Hannover to Von Hannover and Axel Springer AG: do competing ECHR proportionality factors ever add up to certainty? (October 25, 2012). Queen Mary J Intellect Property 2(4):388–392. https://ssrn.com/abstract=2037811. Accessed 24 Aug 2019

Campbell (Appellant) v. MGN Limited (Respondents) [2004] UKHL 22 on appeal from: [2002] EWCA Civ 1373. http://www.publications.parliament.uk/pa/ld200304/ldjudgmt/jd040506/campbe-1.htm. Accessed 24 Aug 2019

[119]R v. Loveridge.

[120]Campbell v. MGN Limited.

[121]The Law Society Gazette (2013).

[122]Kinloch [2012] UKSC 62.

Campbell v MGN Limited [2002] EWHC 499. http://www.bailii.org/ew/cases/EWHC/QB/2002/499.htm. Accessed 24 Aug 2019

Cohn C, Rodriguez K, Higgins P (2013) Increasing anti-surveillance momentum and the necessary and proportionate principles. Electronic Frontier Foundation, San Francisco. https://www.eff.org/deeplinks/2013/12/increasing-anti-surveillance-momentum-and-necessary-and-proportionate-principles. Accessed 24 Aug 2019

Council of the European Union Directive 95/46/EC of the European Parliament and of the Council of 24 October 1995 on the protection of individuals with regard to the processing of personal data and on the free movement of such data. http://eur-lex.europa.eu/LexUriServ/LexUriServ.do?uri=CELEX:31995L0046:en:HTML. Accessed 24 Aug 2019

Council of the European Union Regulation (EU) 2016/680 of the European Parliament and of the Council on the protection of natural persons with regard to the processing of personal data and on the free movement of such data and repealing Directive 95/46/EC (General Data Protection Regulation). (1). http://data.consilium.europa.eu/doc/document/ST-5419-2016-INIT/en/pdf. Accessed 23 Aug 2019

Council of the European Union Regulation 2016/679 of the European Parliament and of the Council on the protection of individuals with regard to the processing of personal data and on the free movement of such data (General Data Protection Regulation). https://eur-lex.europa.eu/legal-content/EN/TXT/?qid=1532348683434&uri=CELEX:02016R0679-20160504. Accessed 20 Sept 2019

Data Protection Act 2018, para 33. http://www.legislation.gov.uk/ukpga/2018/12/contents/enacted. Accessed 18 Sept 2019

Drozdiak N, Sam Schechner S (2015) EU court says data-transfer pact with U.S. violates privacy. The Wall Street Journal, October 6th 2015. http://www.wsj.com/articles/eu-court-strikes-down-trans-atlantic-safe-harbor-data-transfer-pact-1444121361. Accessed 24 Aug 2019

Edgar TH (2017) Beyond snowden: privacy, mass surveillance and the struggle to reform the NSA. The Brookings Institution, Washington, D.C., pp 164–167

Eglot J (2015) "British judges not bound by European court of human rights, says Leveson". The Guardian 24th May 2015. http://www.theguardian.com/law/2015/may/24/british-courts-echr-leveson. Accessed 23 Aug 2019

Electronic Frontier Foundation (Necessary and Proportionate.org) 13 International Principles on the Application of Human Rights to Communication Surveillance. https://necessaryandproportionate.org/principles. Accessed 24 Aug 2019. https://www.eff.org/document/13-international-principles-application-human-rights- communication-surveillance. Accessed 24 Aug 2019

EU – US Privacy Shield Framework. https://www.privacyshield.gov/Program-Overview. Accessed 24 Aug 2019

European Commission (2016) EU-US privacy shield. http://europa.eu/rapid/press-release_IP-16-216_en.htm. Accessed 24 Aug 2019

European Commission Memo, 27th January 2014. Data Protection Day 2014: Full speed on EU data protection reform. http://europa.eu/rapid/press-release_MEMO-14-60_en.htm. Accessed 24 Aug 2019

Federal Trade Commission (2014) FTC settles with twelve companies falsely claiming to comply with international safe harbor privacy framework. http://www.ftc.gov/news-events/press-releases/2014/01/ftc-settles-twelve-companies-falsely-claiming-comply. Accessed 24 Aug 2019

Fretty D (2011) Face-recognition surveillance: a moment of truth for fourth amendment rights in public places. Virginia J Law Technol 16(03):444. https://heinonline.org/HOL/LandingPage?handle=hein.journals/vjolt16&div=16&id=&page=. Accessed 24 Aug 2019

FTC (2012) Protecting consumer privacy in an era of rapid change: Recommendations for businesses and policymakers. http://www.ftc.gov/reports/protecting-consumer-privacy-era-rapid-change-recommendations-businesses-policymakers. Accessed 23 Aug 2019

FTC Report (October 2012) Facing facts: best practices for common uses of facial recognition technologies: executive summary. http://www.ftc.gov/reports/facing-facts-best-practices-common-uses-facial-recognition-technologies. Accessed 24 Aug 2019
Human Rights Act (HRA) 1998. http://www.opsi.gov.uk/acts/acts1998/ukpga_19980042_en_1. Accessed 24 Aug 2019
INS v. Delgado, 466 U.S. 210 (1084). https://supreme.justia.com/cases/federal/us/466/210/. Accessed 24 Aug 2019
Jolly I (n.d.) Data protection in the United States: overview, p 2 http://uk.practicallaw.com/6-502-0467#null. Accessed 23 Aug 2019
Katz v. United States, 389 U.S. 347 (1967) The warrantless wiretapping of a public pay phone violates the unreasonable search and seizure protections of the Fourth Amendment. https://supreme.justia.com/cases/federal/us/389/347/case.html. Accessed 23 Aug 2019
Kindt EJ (2013) Privacy and data protection issues of biometric applications. Springer, Dordrecht, p 93 §189
Kinloch [2012] UKSC 62. https://www.supremecourt.uk/decided-cases/#addsearch=kinloch%20[2012]%20uksc%2062,f=1. Accessed 24 Aug 2019
Law Society Gazette (2013) Admissibility- criminal proceedings – evidence obtained through covert surveillance. Re: Kinloch (AP) v Her Majesty's Advocate (Scotland) and Gilchrist v HM Advocate [2004] SSCR 595. https://www.lawgazette.co.uk/law/evidence/68897.article. Accessed 24 Aug 2019
Mallon B (2003) Every breath you take, every move you make, i'll be watching you: the use of face recognition technology. Villanova Law Rev 48:955. https://digitalcommons.law.villanova.edu/vlr/vol48/iss3/6/. Accessed 24 Aug 2019
Manson NC, O'Neill O (2007) Rethinking informed consent in bioethics. Cambridge University Press, Cambridge
Mosley v News Group Newspapers Ltd [2008] EWHC 1777 (QB), [2008] EMLR 20. http://www.bailii.org/ew/cases/EWHC/QB/2008/1777.html. Accessed 23 Aug 2019
Murray v Big Pictures (UK) Ltd [2008] 2008] UKHRR 736, [2008] 3 FCR 661, [2009] Ch 481, [2008] ECDR 12, [2008] Fam Law 732, [2008] 2 FLR 599, [2008] EMLR 12, [2008] HRLR 33, [2008] EWCA Civ 446, [2008] 3 WLR 1360. http://www.bailii.org/ew/cases/EWCA/Civ/2008/446.html. Accessed 24 Aug 2019
Murray v Express Newspapers Plc & Anor [2007] [2007] UKHRR 1322, [2007] HRLR 44, [2008] 1 FLR 704, [2007] ECDR 20, [2007] 3 FCR 331, [2007] EWHC 1908 (Ch), [2007] EMLR 22, [2007] Fam Law 1073. http://www.bailii.org/ew/cases/EWHC/Ch/2007/1908.html. Accessed 24 Aug 2019
Nader v. General Motors Corp., 25 N.Y.2d 560 (N.Y. 1970). https://casetext.com/case/nader-v-general-motors-corp-2. Accessed 24 Aug 2019
Nissenbaum H (2010) Privacy in context: technology, policy and the integrity of social life. Stanford University Press, Stanford
Parent WA (1983) Privacy, morality and the law. Philos Public Aff 12(4):269–288
Perry v. The United Kingdom. http://hudoc.echr.coe.int/sites/eng/pages/search.aspx?i=001-61228. Accessed 24 Aug 2019
Privacy by Design: 7 Foundational Principles. https://www.ryerson.ca/pbdce/certification/seven-foundational-principles-of-privacy-by-design/. Accessed 20 Sept 2019
R v Loveridge, EWCA Crim 1034, [2001] 2 Cr App R 29 (2002)
Regulation of Investigatory Powers Act 2000. http://www.legislation.gov.uk/ukpga/2000/23/pdfs/ukpga_20000023_en.pdf. Accessed 24 Aug 2019
Reuters (2012) January 27th 'Lawmakers press Google on privacy policy changes'. http://www.reuters.com/article/2012/01/27/us-google-privacy- idUSTRE80P1YC20120127. Accessed 23 Aug 2019
Schwartz PM, Solove DJ (2014) Reconciling personal information in the United States and European Union. Calif Law Rev 102:877. https://scholarship.law.gwu.edu/faculty_publications/956. Accessed 23 Aug 2019

Shear B (2013) When will the FTC follow the EU's lead in protecting digital privacy? https://www.shearlaw.com/when-will-the-ftc-follow-the-eus-lead-in-protecting-digital-privacy/. Accessed 23 Aug 2019

Solove DJ (2008) Understanding privacy. Harvard University Press, Cambridge, p 111

Solove DJ (2011) Nothing to hide: the false trade off between privacy and security. Yale University Press, New Haven, pp 100–101

The European Community Act 1972. https://www.instituteforgovernment.org.uk/explainers/1972-european-communities-act. Accessed 23 Aug 2019

United States Department of Health and Human Services. OCR privacy rule summary 2003:17. https://www.hhs.gov/sites/default/files/privacysummary.pdf. Accessed 23 Aug

United States v. Garcia, 474 F 3d 994, 998 (7th Cir. 2007). https://openjurist.org/474/f3d/994/united-states-v-garcia. Accessed 24 Aug 2019

United States v. Knotts, 460 U.S. 276 (1983). https://supreme.justia.com/cases/federal/us/460/276/case.html. Accessed 24 Aug 2019

United States v. Maynard, 651 F.3d 544, 555-56 (D.C.Cir.2010). https://casetext.com/case/united-states-v-maynard-5. Accessed 24 Aug 2019

United States v. Mendenhall, 446 U.S. 544 (1980). https://supreme.justia.com/cases/federal/us/446/544/case.html. Accessed 24 Aug

US Constitution: Fourth Amendment. http://www.law.cornell.edu/constitution/fourth_amendment. Accessed 23 Aug 2019

Viviane Reding, Vice-President of the European Commission, EU Justice Commissioner 'Data protection compact for Europe'. http://europa.eu/rapid/press-release_SPEECH-14-62_en.htm. Accessed 24 Aug 2019

von Hannover v. Germany (2005) 40 EHRR 1, [2005] 40 EHRR 1, 40 EHRR 1, [2004] EMLR 21, 16 BHRC 545, [2004] ECHR 294. http://www.worldlii.org/eu/cases/ECHR/2005/555.html. Accessed 24 Aug 2019

Wacks R (1989) (revised 1993) Personal information: privacy and the law. Clarendon Press, Oxford

Welinder Y (2012) A face tells more than a thousand posts: developing face recognition privacy in social networks. http://jolt.law.harvard.edu/articles/pdf/v26/26HarvJLTech165.pdf. Accessed 24 Aug 2019

Westin A (1967) Privacy and freedom. Atheneum, New York

Whitehead JW (2013) A Government of wolves: the emerging American Police State. Select Books Inc, New York, p 21

Wicks E (2007) Human rights in healthcare. Hart Publishing, Oxford, an imprint of Bloomsbury Publishing Plc, p 122

Chapter 8
The Law and Surveillance

Abstract This chapter considers the legalities of surveillance and the judicial powers that form the legal and regulatory frameworks associated with the constraints on liberty. The chapter uses case histories to describe the effect of surveillance and its potential harms, and the critical responses from privacy campaigners, and less frequently the differences of opinion that occurs between governments and their agencies when individuals in one jurisdiction are treated differently in another.

8.1 Surveillance, Regulatory Power and Rights

The cases in Chap. 7 illustrate how case law might evolve when FRT is used routinely in surveillance, especially if privacy is not sufficiently protected from intrusion or remedied when disclosure of confidential information occurs.

Whilst the US and UK responses differ the risk to civil liberty (in terms of freedom of movement or choice) is the same, when or if FRT is used as a 'risk management tool' (in terms of crime detection and prevention) in law enforcement or even as a marketing tool in commercial settings. Moreover, the differences between the US Fourth Amendment and UK legislation is significant; the Fourth Amendment "mandates strong judicial oversight and regulation when the government gathers information about people"[1] and requires that the government justifies its belief that any searches or seizures will provide evidence of crime. Whereas the UK legislation defines the limitations and duties of law enforcement agents and agencies in terms of rights and responsibilities which are scrutinised case by case and from which case law is derived.

The cases in Chap. 7 relate to criminal or civil actions, however, a further distinction is the separation between crime and espionage which are regulated in the US by the Electronic Communications Privacy Act (ECPA) and the Foreign Intelligence Surveillance Act (FISA),[2] and in the UK by the Police and Criminal

[1] Solove (2011), p. 1.
[2] *ibid* p. 73.

I. Berle, *Face Recognition Technology*, Law, Governance and Technology Series 41,
https://doi.org/10.1007/978-3-030-36887-6_8

Evidence Act (PACE), the Regulation of Investigatory Powers Act (RIPA) and the Intelligence Services Act (ISA).[3] Although the detailed subtleties between these are beyond the scope here, there is the risk of blurring the distinctions between them. Subsequently using the regulatory powers inappropriately stimulates, especially in the US, the most vocal pronouncements and debate from academic lawyers to whistleblowers.

More cogently though as noted above, is the general acceptance that the Fourth Amendment when narrowly interpreted only protects citizens' expectation of privacy when at home. Citing *California v Ciraolo*[4] Solove[5] notes that the Court held "that while in public people lack a reasonable expectation of privacy from visual observation from above" (and also whilst in public at street level). This is because the Fourth Amendment does not protect privacy in the public space, which arguably intensifies the public and political debate.[6] Indeed the public discourse is a vehicle that holds governments and their officers to account which depending on what is disclosed or how it is presented is the difference between treason and legitimate disclosure. Nevertheless, the Electronic Frontier Foundation's (EFF) '13 Principles'[7] are the benchmark for best practice, of which the following five stress how the State should legitimately conduct surveillance:

- *Necessity*
  The State has the obligation to prove that its communications surveillance activities are necessary to achieving a legitimate objective.
- *Proportionality*
  Communications surveillance should be regarded as a highly intrusive act that interferes with the rights to privacy and freedom of opinion and expression, threatening the foundations of a democratic society. Proportionate communications surveillance will typically require prior authorization from a competent judicial authority
- *Due Process*
  Due process requires that any interference with human rights is governed by lawful procedures which are publicly available and applied consistently in a fair and public hearing
- *Transparency*
  The government has an obligation to make enough information publicly available so that the general public can understand the scope and nature of its surveillance activities. The government should not generally prevent service providers from

[3]Intelligence Services Act 1994.

[4]California v. Ciraolo 476 U.S. 207.

[5]Solove (2011) *op cit* p.177.

[6]*vis a vis* UK HRA Article 8(1). Conversely, in the UK HRA Article 8(1) is regularly deployed by celebrities, politicians and royalty to protect their privacy when photographed or filmed surreptitiously.

[7]Electronic Frontiers Foundation.

publishing details on the scope and nature of their own surveillance-related dealings with State

- *Safeguards Against Illegitimate Access*
  There should be civil and criminal penalties imposed on any party responsible for illegal electronic surveillance and those affected by surveillance must have access to legal mechanisms necessary for effective redress. Strong protection should also be afforded to whistleblowers who expose surveillance activities that threaten human rights

Adopting these principles would obviate public disclosure and engender transparency and accountability. Given the US sectoral approach to informational privacy described above, from the US perspective the 'Principles' would need to be encapsulated in federal legislation for them to have any overarching effect in all sectors, including government agencies. Whether the US Legislature takes such action remains to be seen; yet the legislators overarching concern for security dominates the counter-argument against transparency, and regulatory power is exercised at the expense of due process.[8]

Conversely, EU case law has recognised the need to balance security, privacy and transparency thereby rehearsing the 'Principles' by modelling some of the dimensions pre-emptively, and by placing their decision within the scope of ECHR Article 8. For instance, in *Kadi*[9]: Kadi, a resident of Saudi Arabia was designated by the United Nations Security Council Sanctions Committee (UNSC) as an associate of Osama bin Laden and the Al-Qaeda network. Accordingly, in October 2001 Kadi was added to the Consolidation List of persons whose financial assets are frozen by UN Member States. However, to implement the Security Council's resolution within the EU, the European Council was required to introduce a regulation that permitted the implementation of the Security Council's resolution.[10]

Because the Security Council's resolution was deemed to have primacy over EU law it was challenged by the European Court of Justice (ECJ) since under European Union law the rights of defence and judicial protection are paramount, and the regulation was subsequently annulled. With that in view, the European Commission (EC) disclosed the reasons that had been provided by the UNSC Sanctions Committee to Mr. Kadi, and upon receipt of Kadi's comments the EC reinstated the restrictive measures by means of a further regulation. This was subsequently annulled by the Court because there was not enough evidence underpinning the measure and that indeed there was the possibility that the measure was unlawful.[11]

Whatever the merits or demerits of this case, the Court's ruling (within the purview of Article 8) echoed the Principles, by maintaining the balance between unaccountable decision makers and the need to test the veracity of the ruling, which

[8]Edgar (2017) discusses these issues in depth.

[9]ECJ: Kadi.

[10]European Council Regulation (EC) No 881/2002 of 27 May 2002.

[11]Kokott and Sobotta (2012), p. 1020.

was achieved by reviewing the quality of the narrative summary issued by the Security Council and subsequently concluding that the interference was unjustified. The nature of the Kadi case is somewhat reminiscent of Kafka's portrayal of *K* (Chap. 5), in that analogously Kadi was subject to restrictive measures which superseded his rights. From this perspective, it could, according to Dershowitz, arguably be said that the EU's response to the UNSC was borne from the need to correct past wrongs,[12] in response to the UNSC's utilitarian approach that appeased or appealed to a wider constituency. The former favours the rights of one person, the latter the greater good for the many. The balancing of these constituents should not be at the expense of liberty per se, because it disadvantages and limits the affected person's freedom to challenge the restrictions. Therefore, the ECJ ruling sets a precedent for testing whether surveillance is lawful when the grounds or evidence for identifying someone is doubtful.

The EU approach to balancing security and privacy is weighted by its adherence to transparency, because "the Union must be open to public scrutiny and be accountable for its work. This requires a high level of openness and transparency".[13] This is evident in Kadi and conflicts with the United States Legislators' approach that prefers to remain opaque. Whilst officially this is the stance taken by the United States, the issue of transparency remains within the American discourse as it applies to US citizens. Thus, the American Bar Association (ABA)[14] have usefully described and reflect upon the EU approach to transparency, whereby citizens have access to information about the structures and functions of the EU's government institutions and can participate in their processes. This participation is facilitated by having access to government documents, which is specific to the EU's approach to the complex issue of data protection and privacy that is absent in the US, and subsequently can conflict with attaining transparency.

Furthermore, the complexities of data protection and privacy are most evident when personal data is transmitted to the United States from the EU and its Member States,[15] to overcome this the Safe Harbour Agreement was established. The agreement, prior to its suspension, only applied to trading partners and companies for them to transfer data from the EU and had no effect on government authorised data surveillance. Before considering how Kadi and foregoing applies to face recognition, attention is drawn to the EU Directive 2006/24/EC which regulates "the retention of data generated or processed in connection with the provision of publicly available electronic communications services or of public communications networks..."[16] This directive applies to all internet service providers, social network

[12]Dershowitz (2004), pp. 115–116.

[13]European Commission, 'Strategic Objectives 2005-2009'.

[14]American Bar Association 'Transparency 3/10/08 Version' p. 1.

[15]*ibid* p. 6.

[16]European Council Directive 2006/24/EC.

sites and telephony services that are required to retain data generated by their users. The many categories of data include phone number and user ID.[17]

The two paragraphs below place this directive into the context of this book and are arguably the basis for the lawful surveillance of metadata by government agencies in the EU and UK; albeit challenged by the public disclosure discussed in Chap. 3.

Nevertheless, the fact that for the EU to comply, initially, with the UNSC required a regulatory instrument to do so that was challenged by the ECJ, and thus sits rather peculiarly against the backdrop of Directive 2006/24/EC. Although the balance for finding in Kadi's favour is likely found in the interpretation of paragraph nine of the directive:

> [U]nder Article 8 of the European Convention for the Protection of Human Rights and Fundamental Freedoms (ECHR), everyone has the right to respect for his private life and his correspondence. Public authorities may interfere with the exercise of that right only in accordance with the law and where necessary in a democratic society, *inter alia*, in the interests of national security or public safety, for the prevention of disorder or crime, or for the protection of the rights and freedoms of others. Because retention of data has proved to be such a necessary and effective investigative tool for law enforcement in several Member States, and in particular concerning serious matters such as organised crime and terrorism, it is necessary to ensure that retained data are made available to law enforcement authorities for a certain period, subject to the conditions provided for in this Directive. The adoption of an instrument on data retention that complies with the requirements of Article 8 of the ECHR is therefore a necessary measure.[18]

Presumably the second clause was not proven and Article 8 prevailed when Kadi challenged his inclusion on the Consolidated List. The directive continues at paragraph eleven that:

> [G]iven the importance of traffic and location data for the investigation, detection, and prosecution of criminal offences, as demonstrated by research and the practical experience of several Member States, there is a need to ensure at European level that data that are generated or processed, in the course of the supply of communications services, by providers of publicly available electronic communications services or of a public communications network are retained for a certain period, subject to the conditions provided for in this Directive.[19]

Whether Kadi's communications data was surveilled is a matter of conjecture. What is not conjectural is the notion that photographs are a form of communications data when images are transmitted by the means defined in EC/2006/24 and are subject to surveillance when processed by face recognition software. Therefore, Kadi is relevant, albeit paradigmatically, because the penalty was the proof of his exclusion. Similarly, if a person's appearance is captured and processed qua directive, whatever the impact or effect, their expectation of privacy is lost, whether, or not they are guilty of the offences the directive describes this constitutes an

---

[17] *ibid*, Article 5.

[18] *ibid* para 9.

[19] *ibid* para 11.

interference of their article 8 rights. Moreover, the volume of electronic communications coupled with the need to maintain security has driven politically motivated surveillance agendas, to that end the US 'Clarifying Overseas Use of Data (CLOUD) Act' requires all electronic communication service providers to preserve and disclose communications and records. The disclosure, when requested by law enforcement agencies will be compulsory and warrantless.[20] Privacy campaigners such as the Electronic Frontier Foundation (EFF) have opposed this act, because it weakens the privacy of all service users in the United States and elsewhere.[21] Consequently, the need to minimise or eliminate security risks has been at the expense of privacy, which analogously is evident in Kadi, because no information or evidence to substantiate the allegations was presented to the Court. This was either because, on one hand, the search to establish cause revealed nothing, or on the other hand, the intelligence agencies would have compromised their position if they had.

Whatever the failure to present evidence, Kadi illustrates in microcosm that mass surveillance is the means by which potential threats are identified and subsequently responded to. The means may justify a narrow application of the legal instruments described above, and the ensuing jurisprudence is influenced by the need for protection, and response to individual cases. Yet, mass surveillance challenges human rights and is harmful when it is unregulated or uncontested; the following considers the impact on human rights and discusses the adjunctive use of photography in the context of face recognition.

8.2 Human Rights, Mass Surveillance and UK Case Law

The UK's Regulation of Investigatory Powers Act 2000 (RIPA) defines "surveillance" as the:

(a) monitoring, observing or listening to persons, their movements, their conversations or their other activities or communications;
(b) recording anything monitored, observed or listened to in the course of surveillance; and
(c) surveillance by or with the assistance of a surveillance device.[22]

RIPA permits these activities in the investigation of suspicious behaviour or activities to gather evidence. To initiate the surveillance requires sufficient grounds for enquiries to begin, which in the case of individuals is arguably justifiable if the purpose is reasonable and the suspected criminality is intelligently acted upon.

Yet, when the only grounds are based on the need to survey large groups of people for the purposes of prevention and interruption of crime, the lawfulness of

[20]McMeley and Seiver (2018).

[21]Fischer (2018).

[22]RIPA.

such surveillance is questionable and analogous to Kadi. The impact of mass surveillance, especially in the UK, raises the question of harm that flows from such intrusion and whether human rights law is the remedy. From the perspective of privacy, human rights law is unlikely to be effective because the social benefits of mass surveillance include the interruption of planned terrorist attacks.[23] Such benefit is obvious. However, protecting people from danger is at the expense of the harms, such as, the loss of autonomy, especially when the surveillance is covert; the change in behaviour[24] related to freedom of expression or association; the loss of personhood as individuals become merely the sum of their data; the potential emphasis on specific groups vis-à-vis social sorting; poor data processing resulting in penalties that restrict or discriminate individuals; and the normalisation and expansion of surveillance.[25] Hence the emphasis in Chap. 4 on the sociological impact of surveillance. The loss of personhood is evident when autonomy is reduced (Chap. 5) and the effect of poor data processing is referred to in Chap. 10.

Returning to the question of the efficacy of human rights law (ECHR), the success of any claim relates to specific actions (or acts) that are incompatible with ECHR rights.[26] In addition to the act of 'surveillance' per RIPA §48(2), other 'acts' include 'retention' and 'use' of the material obtained. The material includes DNA or a photograph that could be admissible evidence in criminal proceedings. Although the court would address these acts separately, the court may find that one or the other act is lawful or unlawful depending on the circumstances, and a verdict based on the proportionality of their three-part analysis, and whether the conditions of article 8 apply.[27]

Given that CCTV is ubiquitous and normalised in the UK, it is curious just how seemingly acceptable it has become and is not in itself regarded as intrusive, inasmuch that "its harms are not appreciated and it is often seen as a welcome and reassuring presence".[28] However, Honess and Charman[29] have observed that "public acceptance is based on limited and partly inaccurate knowledge of the functions and capabilities of CCTV systems in public places". And therefore, its ubiquity cannot be used as indicator of acceptance.

Though a more likely consensus is to be drawn from Lord Steyn's view "that law enforcement agencies should take full advantage of the available techniques of modern technology and forensic science" because it "has the inestimable value of cogency and objectivity" that enables the detection of the guilty and elimination of

---

[23] Amos (2014).

[24] This may be an oversimplification, but is generally the accepted perceived wisdom, However, some proscribed activity is potentially beyond the reach of surveillance when hidden on the 'dark web'.

[25] Amos (2014), pp. 154–155 *op cit.*

[26] Amos (2006), p. 15; Amos (2014) *op cit* p. 169 endnote18.

[27] Amos (2014) *op cit* pp. 155–156.

[28] *ibid* p. 165.

[29] Honess and Charman (1992).

the innocent, such as occurred in *R v Chief Constable of South Yorkshire Police; Ex parte Marper (Marper)*.[30] Notably the claimants in *Marper* challenged the retention of their biometric samples, but did not challenge the act of obtaining them given Steyn's observation that "the taking of fingerprints and samples from persons suspected of having committed relevant offences is a reasonable and proportionate response to the scourge of serious crime",[31] and again is therefore a lawful interference of the right to privacy.

Putting aside the details of the alleged offence, the use of un-consented photography and subsequent face recognition is analogous to *Marper* wherein the retention and use of photographs is identical to other biometric samples and therefore challengeable; especially as the suspects were dismissed but their samples were retained.[32] Until 2012 the retention of DNA and fingerprints contained in the UK's unregulated national database comprised of samples taken during the investigation of crime. Yet, irrespective of the outcome all the samples were retained indefinitely. However, since 2012 keeping samples of those not charged is now unlawful and must be deleted from the database.[33] Deleting what could be described as 'close contact' physiological biometric samples create a distinction between those samples and other samples that are obtained remotely, such as photographs. For example, in *Wood v Commissioner of Police of the Metropolis (Wood)* the Court of Appeal held that retained photographs taken of the claimant, when leaving an arms trade fair company's annual general meeting, and which were later used to identify him from other publicly available records after he declined to reveal his name to the police had breached his HRA (ECHR) article 8 rights.[34]

8.2.1 Human Rights: Interference

Neither *Wood* nor *Marper* were charged with any offence, yet the justification for retaining their biometric samples was that in the event of any future offence they could be quickly identified and apprehended irrespective of whether they may be involved in any future activities that would necessitate any police action.[35] The most striking aspect in *Wood* is the notion that photographs can be taken and retained in an image database without due regard to the interference of a person's article 8 rights,

[30]Cited by Amos (2014), p. 156.

[31]*ibid* § I(3).

[32]S and Marper v UK 2008.

[33]Amos (2014), p. 159; p. 170 endnote 41: Police and Criminal Evidence Act 1984 (UK) (Police and Criminal Evidence Act) §§27, 61, 63. This database is now regulated by the Protection of Freedoms Act 2012 (UK).

[34]Cited by Amos (2014), p. 158.

[35]These cases are arguably emblematic given the volume of biometric data retained by the police.

especially when the photographs are taken covertly. Lord Justice Collins closing remarks summarise this issue:

> . . .that the last word has yet to be said on the implications for civil liberties of the taking and retention of images in the modern surveillance society. This is not the case for the exploration of the wider, and very serious, human rights issues which arise when the state obtains and retains the images of persons who have committed no offence and are not suspected of having committed any offence.[36]

Collins' summary analogously applies to face recognition and the concomitant impact on civil liberty when in a climate of pre-emptive suspicion, where personal autonomy is reduced and the expectation of privacy diminished. That is not to suggest that government agencies adopt a laissez-faire approach, but rather that agencies pay more attention to the social and ethical implications that are the consequences of poorly defined policy or unregulated procedures. In response to the overarching culture that Collins infers, the deletion of biometric samples has started (as noted above) but there remained the issue of photographs. This was further considered in *R (RMC) Commissioner of Police of the Metropolis (RMC)*, when similar to *Marper* and *Wood,* photographs were taken of the arrested persons who were not subsequently convicted of any offence. But although the case did not proceed the photographs were retained, which initiated a challenge under the Human Rights Act (HRA). Relying on the previous judgement in *Marper* the court found that:

> [I]n the light of the [previous] court's conclusion that the retention of the fingerprints constitutes an interference with the right to respect of private life, it is difficult to see how any different conclusion could apply to the retention of photographs.[37]

Since Steyn's observations the collection of data from mass surveillance has become normative and expansive; for instance, the use of surveillance tools to combine disparate data is a reality in traffic management schemes [see Chap. 9]. Nevertheless, the foregoing has concentrated on UK cases that are emblematic of risk aversion; that is although the evidence gathering arguably complied with RIPA, the retention of samples 'just-in-case' was until it became unlawful, is demonstrative of a lack of accountability and the public's loss of trust in government authorities. Moreover, the various regulatory acts described above codify practice and support the standardisation of procedures, and are the mechanism by which government agencies, organisations and individuals are held accountable by the judiciary and Parliament. Such challenges, given *R (RMC) Commissioner of Police of the Metropolis (RMC)*, would be within the scope of article 8, and the ostensibly applicable article 8(2) interference would not apply.[38]

---

[36]Wood *op cit* at [100].

[37]R (RMC) Commissioner of Police of the Metropolis (RMC).

[38]Human Rights Act 1998, Article 8: Everyone has the right to respect for his private and family life, his home and his correspondence. 8(2). There shall be no interference by a public authority with the exercise of this right except such as is in accordance with the law and is necessary in a democratic society in the interests of national security, public safety or the economic wellbeing

8.3 Face Recognition: Accountability and Trust

The cases discussed above illustrate how personal data is acquired and used. These cases are a microcosm of the actual use of data that is available, either by harvesting existing information or by gathering new data. They further illustrate how, until action is taken, the individuals were unaware of any scrutiny. Since Snowden's revelations the anxiety generated by the knowledge that all social network users' metadata is surveilled has reduced trust in the service providers and has shown that government agencies are unaccountable. Yet, from the legislation described the foregoing discussion suggests otherwise, inasmuch that the courts have held government agencies to account, and in so doing have tested the legitimacy of the law. This question's the purpose of the law if any expectation of privacy is lost, and whether the state is justified in the pretence that privacy is protected by rights legislation given the responses by the ECJ referred to above. The following chapter will discuss this.

Meanwhile, to partially conclude here: face recognition begins with a digitalised photographic image that is reified as data. As data it is subject to the service providers' terms and conditions, which in an era of mass surveillance requires greater accountability and trust. The burgeoning jurisprudence is evidence of change, but the tension between the European Court of Justice and the UK and US, coupled with the need for compatible data protection legislation requires due diligence, and the recognition that personal autonomy is diminished and threatened by the loss of choice (discussed in Chaps. 3 and 5).

8.4 Face Recognition: Privacy and Image Ownership

Since face recognition begins with a digitalised photographic image, disparate interpretations of Article 8 ECHR occur when considering the status of the image within the rights discourse. In some jurisdictions, privacy is the determinate and in others it is the right to one's own image. For instance, the right to one's own image exists in Belgium and France.[39] In her summary Baroness Hale in *Campbell v MGN* stated that "we do not recognise a right to one's own image"[40]; instead in the UK images are articulated in terms of physical and informational privacy which thus invokes article 8 especially when images are published. Moreover, not bestowing the right to one's image allows for the consideration of public interests, such as crime prevention or disorder.[41] Aside from public interests the implications of privacy,

---

of the country, for the prevention of disorder or crime, for the protection of health or morals, or for the protection of the rights and freedoms of others.

[39]Kindt (2013), pp. 193 §348.

[40]Campbell (Appellant) v. MGN Limited (Respondents).

[41]Kindt (2013) *op cit* p. 195 §351.

rights and image ownership are further discussed in Chap. 11 where regulatory issues are considered. Though to presage these regulatory issues, since the General Data Protection Regulation enhances earlier data law, and the subsequent UK's adoption of the wider European approach to data and image ownership may eventually necessitate recognising the right to one's own image (in the UK) to balance privacy against public interests.[42]

References

American Bar Association: Transparency 3/10/08 Version, p 1 http://www.americanbar.org/content/dam/aba/migrated/adminlaw/eu/TransparencyFinal31808.authcheckdam.pdf. Accessed 26 Aug 2019

Amos M (2006) Human rights law. Hart Publishing, Oxford, p 15

Amos M (2014) The impact of human rights law on measures of mass surveillance in the United Kingdom. In: Davis F, McGarrity N, Williams G (eds) Surveillance, counter-terrorism and comparative constitutionalism. Routledge, London

California v. Ciraolo 476 U.S. 207. https://www.law.cornell.edu/supremecourt/text/476/207. Accessed 26 Aug 2019

Campbell (Appellant) v. MGN Limited (Respondents)[2004] UKHL 22 on appeal from: [2002] EWCA Civ 1373 at para 154 https://publications.parliament.uk/pa/ld200304/ldjudgmt/jd040506/campbe-1.htm. Accessed 26 Aug 2019

Council of the European Union Directive 2006/24/EC of The European Parliament and of The Council of 15 March 2006 on the retention of data generated or processed in connection with the provision of publicly available electronic communications services or of public communications networks and amending Directive 2002/58/EC. http://eur-lex.europa.eu/legal-content/EN/TXT/?uri=CELEX:32006L0024. Accessed 26 Aug 2019

Council of the European Union Regulation (EC) No 881/2002 of 27 May 2002. http://eur-lex.europa.eu/legal-content/EN/TXT/?uri=celex%3A32002R0881. Accessed 26 Aug 2019

Dershowitz A (2004) Rights from wrongs: a secular theory of the origins of rights. Basic Books, New York, pp 115–116

Edgar TH (2017) Beyond snowden: privacy, mass surveillance, and the struggle to reform the NSA. Brookings Institution Press, Washington DC

Electronic Frontier Foundation (Necessary and Proportionate.org) 13 International Principles on the Application of Human Rights to Communication Surveillance. https://necessaryandproportionate.org/principles. Accessed 24 Aug 2019. https://www.eff.org/document/13-international-principles-application-human-rights-communication-surveillance. Accessed 24 Aug 2019

European Commission Strategic Objectives 2005-2009; Europe 2010: A Partnership for European Renewal; Prosperity, Solidarity and Security. Communication No 12 (2005) 5). https://eur-lex.europa.eu/legal-content/EN/TXT/?qid=1563193762276&uri=CELEX:52005DC0012. Accessed 26 Aug 2019

European Court of Justice: Kadi The Court dismisses the appeals against the General Court's 'Kadi II' judgement. Court of Justice of the European Union, Press Release No 93/13, Luxembourg 18 July 2013 Judgement in Joined Cases C-584/10 P, C-593/10 P and C-595/10 P Commission, Council, United Kingdom v. Yassin Abdullah Kadi. http://www.statewatch.org/news/2013/jun/ecj-kadi-ms-appeal-prel.pdf. Accessed 26 Aug 2019

[42]*ibid* p. 195 §351.

Fischer C (2018) The CLOUD Act: a dangerous expansion of police snooping on cross-border data. Electronic Frontiers Foundation. https://www.eff.org/deeplinks/2018/02/cloud-act-dangerous-expansion-police-snooping-cross-border-data#_ftnref1. Accessed 26 Aug 2019

Honess T, Charman E (1992) Closed circuit television in public places: Its acceptability and perceived effectiveness. http://webarchive.nationalarchives.gov.uk/20090410010408/http://www.crimereduction.homeoffice.gov.uk/cctv/cctv3.htm. Accessed 26 Aug 2019

Human Rights Act 1998 Article 8 'Right to respect for private and family life'. http://www.opsi.gov.uk/acts/acts1998/ukpga_19980042_en_1. Accessed 26 Aug 2019

Intelligence Services Act 1994 c.13. http://www.legislation.gov.uk/ukpga/1994/13/contents. Accessed 26 Aug 2019

Kindt EJ (2013) Privacy and data protection issues of biometric applications. Springer, Dordrecht, p 193 §348

Kokott J, Sobotta C (2012) The Kadi case – constitutional core values and international law – finding the balance? Eur J Int Law 23(4):1015–1024; p 1020. http://www.ejil.org/pdfs/23/4/2343.pdf. Accessed 26 Aug 2019

McMeley C, Seiver J (2018) The CLOUD Act — A needed fix for U.S. and foreign law enforcement or threat to civil liberties? The International Association of Privacy Professionals (IAPP). https://iapp.org/news/a/the-cloud-act-a-needed-fix-for-u-s-and-foreign-law-enforcement-or-threat-to-civil-liberties/. Accessed 26 Aug 2019

R (RMC) Commissioner of Police of the Metropolis (RMC) [2012] EWHC 1681 (Admin) [33]. https://www.judiciary.gov.uk/wp-content/uploads/JCO/Documents/Judgments/r-rmc-fj-metropolitan-police-commissioner-22062012.pdf. Accessed 26 Aug 2019

R v. Chief Constable of South Yorkshire Police (Respondent) ex parte LS (by his mother and litigation friend JB) (FC) (Appellant); R v. Chief Constable of South Yorkshire Police (Respondent) ex parte Marper (FC)(Appellant) Consolidated Appeals [2004] UKHL 39 on appeal from: [2002] EWCA Civ 1275 [2002] 1 WLR 3223. http://www.publications.parliament.uk/pa/ld200304/ldjudgmt/jd040722/york-1.htm. Accessed 26 Aug 2019

Regulation of Investigatory Powers Act 2000, §48(2) http://www.legislation.gov.uk/ukpga/2000/23/pdfs/ukpga_20000023_en.pdf. Accessed 26 Aug 2019

S and Marper v UK 2008. https://justice.org.uk/s-marper-v-uk-2008/. Accessed 26 Aug 2019

Solove DJ (2011) Nothing to hide: the false trade off between privacy and security. Yale University Press, New Haven, p 1

Wood v. Commissioner of Police for the Metropolis (CA) [2010] WLR 123, [2010] 1 WLR 123, [2009] ACD 75, [2009] EWCA Civ 414, [2010] EMLR 1, [2009] HRLR 25, [2009] 4 All ER 951, [2009] UKHRR 1254. http://www.bailii.org/ew/cases/EWCA/Civ/2009/414.html. Accessed 26 Aug 2019

Chapter 9
State Paternalism and Autonomy

Abstract This chapter examines how state paternalism affects autonomy. Paternalism is described as active and passive, both of which affect personal liberty but can be regarded as beneficial. The ethico-legal issues associated with paternalism are considered in detail and how the state might claim the right to use face recognition technology without consent is examined.

9.1 State Paternalism: Active and Passive

Our discussion of FRT in the framework of autonomy (first-order, second-order) and liberty (negative, positive) leads us deeper into the ethico-legal issue of state paternalism.

'State paternalism' is the term usually used to describe any situation in which the state intervenes in citizen activity within its jurisdiction to promote, modify, hinder or abolish that activity with the justification that such intervention is for the benefit of the individuals or groups or even the whole society that is involved in that activity even when there is substantial resistance to that intervention. Put simply, a State may claim the social rightness of a policy on the basis that it is good for people *even when* those people either say it is not good for them or claim they have a right to do things that are not good for them, that is, take certain risks. Such as riding a motorcycle without a helmet or driving under the influence of alcohol or drugs.

Since we are speaking here of actions of the State, we are speaking of matters of law rather than ethics although it is true to say that State paternalism may have moral perceptions underlying its justification for intervening, as is the case with preventing head injuries or harming others by irresponsible driving. To be clear: state interventions which are not based on any claim of ethical or moral rightness but are simply self-interested or wanton—such as genocide—cannot be described as 'paternalistic'. State paternalism is a highly controversial area precisely because there are differing perceptions of what constitutes moral rightness in certain circumstances. No doubt this is also the case with the growing State interest in and implementation of FRT in relation to those citizens who have sufficient understanding of FRT's potential applications.

I. Berle, *Face Recognition Technology*, Law, Governance and Technology Series 41,
https://doi.org/10.1007/978-3-030-36887-6_9

State paternalism usually refers to interventions which are against the will of those concerned (active paternalism); but could include those which are not against the will but nevertheless are not *with* the will of those concerned (passive paternalism). In this latter case that would most likely be because of the citizens' ignorance of the intervention or of its nature. For example, if a State agency puts fluoride into citizens' water supplies on the recommendation of experts because it believes it has a duty to protect them from dental decay (and from the taxation required to provide State dental care); while for the sake of argument most citizens know nothing about fluoride, then that could be described as passive paternalism. However, in that case, should a citizen ask for a justification it would doubtless be claimed by the State agency to be a benefit for that citizen or any citizen or all citizens.

Since State paternalism operates at the collective level of policy it is often embedded in some form of utilitarian ethical theory. That is, the justification for the intervention is said to be for the greater or common good even if a minority of individuals or groups do not benefit or are consequently disadvantaged. By contrast, a state may be dictatorial or authoritarian, but not 'paternalistic', if in its policies and actions it systematically acts against the will of the people without any concern for justifying that action in terms of benefits for the citizens. So, the criterion for state action being 'paternalistic' is that it is based on and supported by a strong claim to be an action that is for the benefit of the majority (or even everyone) even though many, or most, do not accept there is such a benefit or are willing to take the risks involved in the State's non-intervention.

FRT can now be added to many cases where there is or there is claimed to be State paternalism, including such legal restrictions as the wearing of seat-belts, wearing of motorcycle helmets, taking certain health and safety precautions at work, anti-drug legislation, medical confidentiality, public health measures, bans on smoking in public places and speed cameras. For FRT the question is whether government implementation of FRT in specific contexts can reasonably be justified by the State even if a) most or many citizens are against it or b) most or many citizens are ignorant of it but could reasonably be against it if they were not ignorant of it. It seems to me that our contemporary societal situation accords more with b), which is why I have already linked it with a lack of second-order autonomy. One may also link passive state paternalism with a lack of positive liberty i.e. a right to be educated about a new technology and, more so, a right to participate at some level in decision-making about the development and deployment of such a technology, and if required waive the right to privacy.

As is often the case with any state intervention, except those that are clearly dictatorial, the controversy is not simply a matter 'for or against' FRT. It is probable that many people would accept that State-sanctioned and operated FRT is acceptable in *some* circumstances (even a State duty) but not in others. One suspects that the widespread public scepticism about State uses of FRT (among those who know what it is) would be about,

(a) the distinction between the acceptable and unacceptable uses
(b) on what criteria such a distinction is made, and
(c) who makes these distinctions.

This scepticism of the well-informed leads to a range of other questions. The last of these may be reformulated as a question about the democratisation of technology development. While there can be any doubt that current technology development is undemocratic,[1] one should also ask what kind and what level of democratic involvement is justified and feasible? This is a question which is very inadequately addressed in society at present, and where it is addressed opinions may be polarised if decisions are made by referendum.

It raises the issue of government and corporate technology policy in relation to the question of human irrationality. That is, if a significant number of people—let us say a majority—have an irrational fear of FRT or some significant aspects of it, does the State have a right to proceed anyway? What is considered to be rational and irrational and who decides on that? There is also a question of jurisdiction. For example, does the USA have the right to use FRT images of British citizens and to use them for any purpose it chooses? This could occur if say the USA acts paternally in order to identify potential threats, which raises the question of how paternalism is interpreted.

In one interpretation paternalism is connotative of a claim to greater wisdom, knowledge and protection. This concept is derived from the Ancient Roman term *paterfamilias*, where the eldest male family member was responsible for the welfare of their family.[2] Since then, modern paternalism is exercised and justified in terms of best interests of another who (it is thought) lacks either the capacity to act on their own behalf, or the authority to act where capacity exists. In the former this is evident in medicine and in the latter, government agencies in their exercise of delegated authority that controls, constrains and restrains the actions of citizens. It is this latter exercise of paternalism by the State which assists or intrudes into citizen activity that could affect autonomy, because it potentially interferes with (or is perceived to interfere with) civil liberties and freedom of choice.

9.2 Ethics and State Power

The state according to Michael Mann is a "messy concept"[3] and can be defined and analysed from an "institutional" and "functional" perspective. The former defines the state by what it looks like and the latter by what it does. Following Weber, Mann notes[4] that the state contains four main elements:

1. a *differentiated* set of institutions and personnel, embodying
2. *centrality*, in the sense that political relations radiate outwards from a centre to cover a

[1]Collingridge (1981), Veak (2006) and von Hippel (2005).

[2]Pomeroy (1994).

[3]Mann (1984).

[4]*ibid* pp. 187–188.

3. *territorially demarcated area*, over which it exercises
4. a monopoly of *authoritative, binding rule making*, backed up by a monopoly of the means of physical violence

Mann's principal interest is in the government bureaucracies known as 'state elites' and the delegated powers of their staff. Whatever the rank, whether elite or plebeian, the state cannot survive without some form of organisational function, or facility that is operated by those employed to organise or perform the tasks that sustain state power. But what is meant by 'the power of the state?' and how is 'state power' exercised? In considering these questions, Mann describes state power as either 'despotic' or 'infrastructural'.[5] The former accords with Foucault's description of sovereign power that required a variety of acolytes empowered to fulfil the sovereign's authoritative control. Arguably, this form of power was limited by the span of control and access to citizens, for instance: before the reunification of Germany, the Stasi in East Germany employed two and half (and possibly fifteen) percent of the population to keep watch on everyone.[6] Employing human resources to physically keep watch arguably coerced the population to comply because of the immediate threat of force or harm otherwise.

With the rise of infrastructural power, that is "the ability to penetrate civil society"[7] the capacity to keep watch has changed from physical surveillance to the burgeoning use of technology to gather information. Citizens are no longer out of sight and beyond the gaze of the 'watchers', but rather because of the centralisation of information and self-disclosure citizens are exposed to the gaze of unseen domains. Thereby, the territorially demarcated area expands into the personal and private, and consequently creates tension between citizens' rights and the function of state power; the tension stimulates the public disclosure described in Chap. 3 and polarises public opinion by dichotomising the issues of privacy and security.

9.2.1 Liberty and State Power

Liberty in its broadest sense implies freedom from interference by another. Berlin modulated this by defining liberty as either negative or positive, as described above; his and other concepts of liberty are responses to the characteristics of power that affect liberty.[8] Moreover, to interfere with a person's liberty infers authority and

[5] *ibid* p. 188.
[6] Wikipedia (n.d.).
[7] Mann (1984), p. 188.
[8] Petit (1996), pp. 578–604.

capacity that are the hallmarks of power within the relationship between the actors; Pettit[9] distinguishes these hallmarks noting that:

> someone dominates or subjugates another, to the extent that (1) they have the capacity to interfere (2) with impunity and at will (3) in certain choices that the other is in position to make.

These aspects of power are universal and are evident in all kinds of relationships. From the perspective of choice, number three implies manipulation or coercion; this may be very subtle, and I contend that it is evident when agreeing to the terms and conditions to access the services of a variety of agencies. By agreeing to the terms and conditions, the individual relinquishes control and predicates further interference. This interference can take many forms, from intrusive 'pop-up' targeted advertising to data-mining, all are indicative of Pettit's analysis. The 'with-impunity' condition predicates interference and objectifies the individual by removing any form of redress[10]; such was *Josef K's* predicament. Kafka aside, herein is the exercise of State Power that without adequate controls or transparency interferes with liberty without limit.[11]

Conversely, can liberty be defined in terms of non-interference when it is not possible to discern whether interference has occurred? The concept of liberty as non-interference, probably derives from Hobbes assertion that "a free-man is he, that in those things, which by his strength and wit he is able to do, is not hindred to doe what he has a will to".[12] In other words, liberty is only possible in the absence of physical coercion or threat. However, the rule of law according to Pettit is coercive[13] and 'liberty', writes John Rawls, isn't without limitations when it needs safeguarding.[14] It is possible therefore, for the ends to justify the means if the limiting of liberty is for the greater good. Yet, non-interference is a feature of liberty, such that writes Pettit "while it represents even non-subjugating interference as a deprivation of liberty, it finds nothing hostile to liberty in a form of subjugation that does not involve any actual interference".[15]

Applying Pettit's formula to the secondary and tertiary uses of face recognition software implies no loss of liberty, because the individuals remain un-subjugated inasmuch they are unaware of the surveillance. However, due to the loss of autonomy in such scenarios (hypothetical or real) non-interference is probably an inadequate conception of liberty or freedom. In this context, autonomy is integrative of personhood and the maintenance of subjectivity, which when lost subjugates the person, even though no physical or coercive interference occurs. This concurs with

---

[9]*ibid* p. 578.

[10]*ibid* p. 580.

[11]See Chaps. 7 and 8.

[12]Hobbes (1651).

[13]Petit (1996), p. 596.

[14]Rawls (1971, rev 1999). Cited by Petit (1996).

[15]Petit (1996) p. 596.

Jeremy Bentham's view summarised by Pettit "that all government is in some measure an invasion of liberty".[16] This and the further observation "that those in power should not be able to interfere at will and with impunity in the affairs of citizens"[17] is encapsulated in the Fourth Amendment and ECHR Article 8, and arguably balances the tension between the two. Moreover, the General Data Protection Regulation regulates state and corporate interference by giving citizens the right to consent to data acquisition.

9.2.2 *Ethical State Power*

Since the exercise of State Power implies authority and control, it invariably provokes dissent. In Chaps. 3 and 4 above, a variety of dissenting views which focus on the issues of equality and justice are discussed. Generally, parliamentary and congressional democracies, such as those in the UK and US, encourage open debate and free elections are indicative of this. Yet, unless for instance, freedom of movement, expression and association are protected by law the legitimacy of State Power is suspect. Curtailing or constraining these freedoms further stimulates dissent, however, it is by debate and the drafting of regulations that the structures for ethical state power evolve. In the context of face recognition technology and its applications, the lack of transparency as revealed by Edward Snowden[18] is alarming because it instils distrust, which in turn stimulates anxieties that cannot easily be ameliorated. The anxieties are multi-faceted: the government cannot disclose how its surveillance agencies operate because of the risk of counter-measures against them, and indeed it might even be considered unreasonable to expect such disclosures. On the other hand, by not reassuring citizens that the measures are regulated and subject to the rule of law, consent flounders. Similarly, the issue of consent applies also in the relationship between the social network user and the network's operator, if there is insufficient regulation.

Moreover, consent is an essential component of democratic agency and governance, albeit within the constraints to liberty which is necessary for the rule of law to function. Yet, when government agencies monitor data flows on the social networks, consent is devalued as scrutiny is prioritised, and Statism expands. The purpose of this statist relationship may be based on the need to protect citizens, to pre-empt illegal activities and to apprehend potential threats to security. But to secure citizens' consent, the government should be accountable when the actions that support these reasonable purposes exceed the rule of law. Otherwise, a state of exception emerges and State Power becomes unethical and instead of liberal democracies "protecting

[16] *ibid* p. 599.

[17] *ibid* p. 600.

[18] See Chap. 3.

privacy for individuals and rejecting it for government...[there is] an erosion of privacy for individuals [and] governments have become ever more secretive".[19]

A counter-balance to either excessive Statism or over-reaching commercial interests is the establishment of regulatory controls which are supported by appropriate law. The following chapter surveys the legislative instruments and case law associated with data management and control that engender accountability, which seemingly protect individuals and their data. However, at face value although the law does 'seemingly' provide protection navigating the nuances and variations of the legislation is fraught with legal argument and conflicts of interest which affect accountability.

9.3 Paternalism and FRT

Paternalism arises in the case of biometric technology—where particularly face recognition technology exceeds consent—which arguably is justified when the best interests of the majority is greater than the interests of individuals. In the United States biometric technology has become "a touchstone for many public policy debates involving concerns of individual liberty, increased presence of governmental surveillance, legitimate paternalistic intervention in the name of harm and trust and confidence in institutions".[20] Additionally, Doyal and Gough,[21] reflecting the political philosophy of Hegel in the context of healthcare provision and distributive justice, succinctly express the justification for state intervention:

> [A] 'state' is required which through its normative structure and the power it commands, ensures that the rules which underpin survival and success of the collective as a whole are both taught and enforced. The material manifestation of political authority in this sense will always be some form of government, a system of justice and mechanisms for law enforcement.

The state founded upon plebiscite has the authority to act in the best interests of the majority, especially when the need to protect citizens arises which, for example, is summarised in the preamble to the American Constitution.[22] Therefore, the focus on State Power and whether the paternalistic use of face recognition technology is justified when high expectations of its protective efficacy are presented as a political goal and a technological objective. Taking this as the starting point, what might be the reason for adopting the technology?

In the previous chapter, the issues of privacy and the juridical approaches were discussed. The cases described how existing law was applied when the paradigms of face recognition technology (FRT) challenged privacy legislation. Beyond the

---

[19]Chesterman (2011), p. 9.

[20]Nelson (2011), p. 66.

[21]Doyal and Gough (1991), p. 89.

[22]American Constitution.

juridical, arguably the technology development goes beyond the current jurisprudence, and therefore creates tensions between society and the government as debated in the current discourse. Broadly the discourse centres on the balance between liberty and control. Liberty was discussed theoretically in Chap. 5 and the issue of control follows here. My intention is to frame this aspect within the political context of government control by initially further considering J. S. Mill's contribution to the issue of liberty, and its application to the normalisation of face recognition technology and control exerted by government agencies that challenge second-order autonomy.

9.4 Control, Paternalism and Autonomy

Mill defined freedom as the pursuit of our own good and being the guardian of one's own well-being[23]:

> The only freedom which deserves the name is that of pursuing our own good in our own way so long as *we do not attempt to deprive others of theirs or impede their efforts to obtain it.* Each is the proper guardian of his own health, whether bodily or mental and spiritual

Herein is the conditional nature of freedom as a societal good. That is when in the pursuit of 'our own good' it should not be at the expense of another's freedom. Furthermore:

> [T]he only purpose for which power can be rightfully exercised over any member of a civilised community, against his will, is to prevent harm to others[24]

In other words, without some constraint freedom can be abused. For instance, shouting 'fire' in a crowded theatre when there is no 'fire' abuses freedom of speech and impedes the freedom of the theatre audience. This is obviously clear-cut, but in many or most cases the justified application of constraint is open to disagreement or even indeterminate. Where freedom of speech is valued the tension between what is permissible (irrespective of acceptability) and what is proscribed (by loss of franchise) is dependent on current societal norms. For instance, language considered to be offensive is subject to scrutiny, and penalties or sanctions exist for using certain words that are derogatory, within certain cultural norms.

Thus, to reasonably limit freedom so that all may enjoy it, some norms are necessary to prevent abuse and herein lies the need for control i.e. limiting autonomy. 'Autonomy' cannot mean freedom to do *whatever* one wishes without restraint. These controls are framed through legislation and the judiciary. Some of these controls are aspects of soft power[25] that are unacceptably paternalistic by deploying secrecy, deviousness, strong persuasion or fear which may not *prima facie*

---

[23] Mill (1859) in Gray J, Smith GW (1991), p. 33. My italics.

[24] *ibid* p. 30.

[25] McClory (2010).

obstruct autonomy, but nevertheless ultimately impose ends that curtail freedom. The subtleties of the power of persuasion (as in advertising) may act at the second-order level by shaping or influencing behaviour to achieve compliance with regulations and alter behaviour. For example, the purpose of traffic management by means of signs that remind and warn is generally accepted and tacitly consented to, and whilst it can impede freedom by curtailing irresponsible behaviour, it does so justifiably to maintain freedom of movement on public roads and city centres.

However, there are controls on freedom and autonomy which are objected to (if only passively) by significant proportions of society in the West.[26] Entry visas sometimes fit that category. Traffic management and visa regulations illustrate the difference between non-coercive and coercive control, the former is a means to an end that aids traffic flows; the latter is complicated by the screening that occurs during the visa application process, and the subsequent data gathering when submitting to fingerprinting and iris scanning at points of entry that occurs, for instance in the United States. It could be regarded as coercive inasmuch as there is 'no choice' and there are strict penalties for non-compliance. Although for some individuals the process may not generate any sense of coercion and visa regulations would appear to them to meet the above Millian definition of freedom. They may be regarded as a reflection of their second-order desires having considered the necessity for the entry procedures. Or alternatively a pragmatic response to the status quo when they "act unreflectively on standards and principles which [they have] taken over from [their] social and cultural environment without ever subjecting them to critical evaluation".[27] This observation is important in considering a similar public un-reflectiveness about choice-restriction concerning face recognition.

Mill observes that choice is aided and abetted by perception, judgement and moral preference, which when absent "weaken reason" and render character "inert and torpid instead of active and energetic".[28] These 'character flaws' seem to suggest Mill's frustration with his contemporaries who probably found his notion of liberty incomprehensible. When such character flaws do not prevail (especially in the current discourse) the potential for individualist pluralism increases and resistance to political or social mores becomes evident when liberty is perceived as threatened. This gives rise to lobby organisations such as 'Big Brother Watch' and 'Liberty' who monitor and critique excessive government power.

Ultimately, since the government's claimed role is to protect its citizens it will probably act paternalistically in order to achieve the necessary objectives, which the next chapter discusses. Meanwhile, the boundaries of liberty and freedom are delineated and nuanced between 'freedom from interference (liberty)' and 'freedom to act' (or flourish), which were discussed in Chap. 5 in terms of negative and positive liberty. Delineating between them separates personal autonomy and empowerment (e.g. by education and health); the former is characteristic of an

---

[26]See Chesterman (2011), Nelson (2011), Solove (2011), Whitehead (2013).

[27]Gray (1991), p. 197.

[28]Mill (1859), pp. 74–75.

individual's personal agency and the latter is indicative of devolved authority to act within set parameters. Consequently, the degree of liberty and limits of freedom are the boundaries of the two sovereignties.

9.5 Citizen and State

The debate increasingly impacts on the role of biometrics, and face recognition in particular. Can it be argued that the invasion of privacy and possible intrusions facilitated by FRT are in fact a version of *positive* liberty, in so far as they socially empower individuals to flourish by safeguarding a field in which freedoms of creativity, confidence, and personal growth are potentiated; such as, the freedom of expression that Facebook facilitates, in spite of the excesses of echo chambers[29] or unconsented images; or the uses of FRT in criminal investigations to protect citizens. Or is the framework by which that safeguarding occurs taking away the second-order liberties of, most importantly, privacy, and thereby potentiating fear and distrust? We recall that a second-order liberty is a social or collective one—one that delineates a *range of possible* choices, while allowing single or individual choices.

Mill[30] delineates the boundaries of the sovereignties (autonomy) by asking a series of questions:

> [W]hat, then, is the rightful limit to the sovereignty of the individual over himself? Where does the authority of society begin? How much of human life should be assigned to individuality, and how much to society? Each will receive its proper share, if each has that which more particularly concerns it. To individuality should belong the part of life which is chiefly the individual that is interested; to society the part which chiefly interests society.

Dworkin imposes a more proactive interaction between the individual and the State, and observes that the individual may want to exceed Mill's limitations and for which criticism of the individual can be detected, inasmuch as the exercising of autonomy is blamed for igniting conflict or dissent:

> [A]s a political ideal, autonomy is used as the basis to argue against the design and functioning of political institutions that attempt to impose a set of ends . . .upon the citizens of a society.[31]

However, is it reasonable to assume that sometimes or even often the purpose of the 'ends' are for the good of society that includes the protection and security of citizens? One answer may be that the decision to impose such 'good' is paternalistic and is possibly evident when legislators impose a set of ends that homogenise values without consultation or debate, for instance to establish the mechanisms that secure and protect citizens. To that end the reasoning for such action is apparently

[29]See Quattrociocchi et al. (2016).

[30]Mill (1859), p. 90.

[31]Dworkin (1988) (reprinted 1997), p. 10.

utilitarian. A well-established difficulty with utilitarianism, simply formulated, is that the minority may suffer the aggregated decisions of the majority, and that this has everything to do with mere calculation and nothing to do with morality or ethics.[32] If mere calculation is the only determinate, from a Kantian perspective such action could be deemed heteronomous and not autonomous, because of the external influence of the majority, or of the law-makers.

From a Marxist perspective the 'good' may be generated by an 'automatic' process of 'commodity fetishism' or even manipulated by an over-emphasis of the perceived benefits by the powers-that-be, so inducing a 'false consciousness' whereby citizens fail to see or develop their awareness of the deeper foundations of an inegalitarian political economy that the 'good' represents on the surface. According to Marx's analysis it is characteristic of capitalism to mask a systemic exploitation with an ideological veneer of 'freedom of choice'.[33] In this analysis FRT could be understood as a 'natural' development of control which appears to leave freedom of choice untouched. Put crudely, citizens either do not know about or do not care enough about FRT developments so long as they continue to have choices about holidays, shopping and entertainment. If, however FRT were to intrude too obviously into that arena of commodities then the illusory freedom of citizens could be eroded. There is evidence that FRT may be moving into that arena e.g. in large retail stores.[34] The foregoing may be somewhat speculative, and no doubt has some important truths within it, but then, I am largely following the classical model of liberalism. At the sametime it is hard to fully accept, because it limits choices that may be at odds with personal morality.

Yet it is unlikely that citizens are empowered to alter or influence the status quo, and therefore any disposition towards second-order autonomy is denied because of constrained or even restrained choice. Eventually, the status quo is accepted and "socialisation into the norms and values of society will take place".[35] Dworkin adds at a "young age", but arguably (after Dworkin) the 'good' could be represented in such a way that mature citizens nonchalantly acquiesce without complaint or critique. From this perspective, such as it infers a line of least resistance, Mill's version of happiness or utility is excluded because the least resistant approach does not comply with Mill's composition of liberty. That is, the action is not associated with "liberty of conscience. . .thought and feeling (or) absolute freedom of opinion and sentiment. . .".[36] This diminishes a citizen's capacity to identify with the reasons for either rejecting or accepting the status quo; they may also be unaware of the loss of identification. Thus, if autonomy has some relationship to an individual's ability to scrutinise their first and second-order preferences and critically choose to act when this is denied autonomy is no longer effective because action and subsequent

[32]See Smart and Williams (1973).

[33]See Fine (1984), pp. 20–26.

[34]BBC News (2013). See Sect. 6.7 Compulsory visibility and autonomy.

[35]Dworkin (1988), p. 11.

[36]Mill (1859), p. 33.

ownership predicated by evaluation and reflection is not possible.[37] Consequently, when an individual loses control or choice by prohibition or statute, paternalism in a variety of degrees prevails; especially when according to Mill paternalism is interventional[38]:

> [A]ny part of a person's conduct affects prejudicially the interests of others, society has jurisdiction over it; and the question whether the general welfare will or will not be promoted by interfering with it, becomes open to discussion.

This ratifies Mill's principle of harm and justifies governmental interference, which when combined conforms to utility. For example, the seemingly random baggage inspections and 'pat-downs' at airport security check-points.[39] These actions are now a regular aspect of air travel and have been accepted by many travellers as a (sometimes unpleasant) necessity; indeed, without cooperation travel would not be possible and therefore submitting to a 'pat-down' or a body scan is second-order compliant if the desired objective is to fly somewhere. Yet is this cooperation an assertion of autonomy or merely acquiescence to the status quo? Given that without this form of consent the objective fails, it is arguably the latter and is a paradigm of face recognition because to acquiesce is a reduction of freedom due to loss of control and second-order preferences. Yet, quid pro quo on one hand, such loss is a protective measure which enhances freedom on the premise of securing safe transit, and on the other hand, it is a means of identifying persons of interest. From this perspective, Nelson[40] observes that:

> [T]he individual can know neither the range of future choices nor the harms to be avoided, making paternalistic intervention an attractive option that has the effect of preserving the common good and individual liberty because it enhances the currency of personal information by protecting against threats even though individual choice is overridden.

Yet the overall effect of such wide-ranging intervention that Nelson implies requires the sublimation of individualism across a spectrum of activities. That is, since it is generally accepted that surveillance modifies behaviour inasmuch as it may deter crime,[41] it also normalises acceptance and a laissez-faire attitude towards the authorities and powers that may or may not use surveillance for the greater good. From this perspective the nature of face recognition technology and its effect on second-order preferences, and the concomitant tension between liberty and control form the boundaries of this discourse; principally because biometric identifiers provide the means of identity assurance that paternalistic protection purports to defend.[42] Therefore, for the purposes of law enforcement the New York Police

---

[37]Dworkin (1988), pp. 16–17.

[38]Mill (1859), p. 90.

[39]The random checks are indicative of the political will not to attribute social typologies and avoid social sorting. Further discussion of this phenomena is beyond the scope of this book.

[40]Nelson (2011), p. 165.

[41]CCTV & Surveillance Cameras. For example, crime prevention on London buses.

[42]Nelson (2011), p. 167.

Department's (NYPD) Domain Awareness System (DAWS) potentially allows the police to efficiently collect and collate large amounts of information from a variety of data sources such as cameras, phone calls and licence plate readers.[43] This capacity to collect, collate and annotate information accords with Nelson's assertion that individuals are oblivious to potential harms of excessive surveillance, yet, the protection provided by DAWS is arguably paternalistic.

9.6 Face Recognition and Second-Order Preferences

Since Mill and Dworkin claim that liberty, power and control are necessary conditions for individuals to exercise their autonomy how practical or realistic is such a broad claim when applied to surveillance systems that use face recognition modalities? The short answer: it is not practical or realistic and second-order preferences are denied. But before considering why, and how indeed autonomy may be limited, Mill's 'Principle of Harm'[44] is of assistance and reiterated here:

> [That] the only purpose for which power can be rightfully exercised over any member of a civilised community, against his will, is to prevent harm to others...

Mill recognises that individualism is conditional and subject to constraint of personal liberty, power and control. Clearly where harm is indicated or suspected, society will take an interest, such as on those occasions described in Chap. 7. However, a precursor to the overt prevention of harm is the modifying effect on behaviour that surveillance has on citizenry whereby prevention is pre-emptive and behaviour subsequently self-limited. This after Bentham and Foucault, is the effect of "bureaucratic power [which imposes] regimentation and self-discipline on the subjectivity of modern individuals"[45]; this is akin to Berlin's concept of positive liberty, inasmuch as society sets the boundaries of autonomous behaviour by permitting or even tolerating what is acceptable individualism. Furthermore, individualism is also limited by the context of permissibility that is paternally prescribed, for instance: prohibiting how long a child may work or access certain types of work; or the legal requirement for motorcyclists to wear helmets. Both of these are examples of altered behaviour and practice each of which create spheres of restraint: the former by prevention and proscription of employment of minors, and the latter by personal restraint and the requirement in law to reduce the risk of head injury. Both are expressions of paternalism in which their prohibitionist nature is protectionist: the child from exploitation and the motorcyclist from the severe consequences of serious injury. Whilst these examples are simple depictions of paternalism, they do

---

[43] See Whitehead (2013), p. 86.

[44] Mill (1859), pp. 30–31.

[45] Nelson (2011), p. 106.

not represent the scope of protection (Chaps. 5 and 7) that governments have exercised since September 11th 2001.

9.7 Preventing Harm and the Effect on Second-Order Preferences

On these accounts, paternalistic interventions are deemed necessary to prevent harm, and can be described as 'managerialist' in terms of regulation and function.[46] For the *paterfamilias* this required advising and controlling domestic affairs and was arguably a mentoring and coaching role that equipped the next in line. Since then, modern expressions of paternalism have generated debate around the limit of intervention and its permissibility and moreover, the question of permissibility, asking if the 'should / ought' equation is related to whether intervention is a duty or not especially when knowledge or suspicion of impending harm requires a response. This is not a problem for a parent restraining a child who is about to run into the road, but it is a problem in our context when the 'what is the harm' question is challenged by competent individuals who may resist intervention. The relative uncertainty of safe air travel is an example of paternalistic protectionism engendered by the duty to interrupt and prevent harmful acts. Van de Veer[47] asserts that:

> Our central question in this inquiry is whether certain types of paternalistic acts or particular paternalistic acts are morally permissible. Those claiming that a paternalistic act is wrong deny its permissibility. If it can be established that an act is permissible, there is always the further question of whether it is impermissible not to do it. If and only it is true that both an act is permissible, and it is impressible not do it is there a duty to do it. So "the" question of justification of paternalism can be understood as two questions: (1) whether paternalism is permissible or (2) whether paternalism is a duty.

In certain circumstances permissibility and duty converge once the need for intervention has been established in law. For instance, The US Transportation Security Administration (TSA) is permitted to search checked baggage, and if searched the owner is notified by the TSA's 'Notice of Inspection' that is added to the baggage.[48]

In this instance, since the TSA "is required by law to inspect all checked baggage", any failure is a derogation of duty, but the number of bags searched is probably limited by the volume of bags passing through the scanning machinery. Therefore, whatever the protocols that exist regarding the apparent random selection of bags inspected, there are presumably features that the contents of the bags exhibit which cause them to be selected and which infer randomness by suspicion in adherence to legal necessity. Arguably it is suspicion (whether biased or otherwise)

---

[46]Kremer (2014), p. 128.

[47]Van de Veer (1986), p. 41.

[48]TSA-OSO Form 1000 (Rev. 1-13-2010).

that initiates the inspection and the purpose of intervention rather than random selection, which is demonstrative of government power. Unlike the parent and child scenario above where the moral imperative is not authorised by law per se, but for concern for the child's safety and parental responsibility, the TSA requires the legal imperative to act; otherwise as was illustrated in Chap. 7, any inspection or search would be unconstitutional. Although these inspections are less invasive another modality of pre-flight screening requires a random selection of travellers to submit to a full-body scan that are invasive and have raised concerns about safety and privacy. Accardo and Chaudhry[49] report:

> The public concern regarding privacy invasion from backscatter units has been an issue for years. In 2012 the Electronic Privacy Invasion Center (EPIC; Washington, DC) sued the Department of Homeland Security (DHS) with allegations that the new passenger screening program was unlawful, invasive, and ineffective… The court ruled that the backscatter units could be used in airports as long as passengers were offered alternative choices to the backscatter scan. Measures have been taken by the manufacturing companies to assuage some of the privacy concerns. Implementation of technology to obscure the passenger's face on the image, technology that makes the images less graphic, and using separate rooms to analyse the images are a few of the measures taken by the TSA to reduce privacy concerns. The computer programs were modified so that the images could not be stored, printed, saved, or transmitted. Despite these various measures to ensure the privacy of each passenger, passengers are still concerned about the detail and privacy of their images.

Arguably in an attempt to secure trust, Accardo and Chaudhry also reported[50] that manufacturers were adding Automated Target Recognition software to scanners to alleviate the privacy issues by only displaying a generic outline of the human body, rather than the more detailed images obtained by the backscatter machines and simultaneously locate areas that a TSA agent can investigate if necessary. But the question of dignity remains vis-à-vis the need to pass through the scanner when selected. Thus, it appears that the need not to associate ethnicity or nationality requires an emphasis on random selection which becomes a form of theatre; those not selected are the audience and the security personnel the stage managers. Hence the dignity question: those who are not selected feel relieved, and those that are, probably feel embarrassed by the attention. Though conjectural, this probability remains a feature of air travel which is impossible to reject before boarding an aircraft. Given this fact, and the fact that flight safety is of paramount importance, the theatrical nature of the process could be eliminated by scanning everyone; after-all, ordinarily everyone passes through a metal detection scan and potentially can be searched. Since the basic principle is to prevent harm, the universal application of whole body scanning needs considering for the following reasons: firstly, it would eliminate the avoidance of social sorting and secondly, it would instil communitarian paternalism in terms of personal altruism and trustworthiness. Consequently,

[49] Accardo and Chaudhry Ahmed (2014), pp. 198–200.

[50] *ibid* p. 199.

government power is legitimised[51] and synergises with personal responsibility which is second-order compliant and consensual; furthermore, by energising both autonomies each is the antidote to the overbearing influences that beset paternalism which Mill and Dworkin are critical of.

The recognition of trustworthiness is not data dependent but rather a real-time event that can be recorded and stored for future verification. Any data supplied at the time of booking flights is used to authenticate passengers, and anyone on an exclusion or watch-list is prevented from travel.[52] Therefore, no-one at the stage of being scanned has been excluded; and each person has divulged information and has consented to authentication of their status that legitimises their place in the security line. This accords with Samuelson's[53] moral rights approach to data interests, inasmuch that since individuals have an interest in deciding what information to divulge, decisional autonomy and ownership are evident in the pursuit of personal goals and are features of personal paternalism when security is paramount as in the example above. Thus, individual liberty is enhanced when "paternalistic intervention, in the form of policy or technology"[54] coheres with personal interest and choice. This resonates with Beauchamp and Childress's[55] bioethical principles of autonomy, non-maleficence, beneficence and justice: when individuals provide information and cooperate with government policy by submitting to the scan, and this is reciprocated by government policy when justice, instead of the apparent arbitrariness of random selection is replaced by equality. To that end, paternalistic intervention is indicative of the need to prevent harm by screening for the 'unknown knowns'; thus, when those screened are cleared to travel the uncertainties prior to boarding a flight are relieved.

Nonetheless, I contend this only applies in narrowly defined specificities such as air travel, and not the more generalised uses of surveillance that have adopted face recognition modalities. Unlike the consensual paternalism illustrated, other specificities may not cohere with personal choice because the overall objective or outcome is not readily identifiable yet is justified by the need for vigilance and the prevention of harm. In some applications[56] the lack of clarity is evident when the uses of

---

[51]Nelson (2011), p. 171 reflecting on Hart HLA 'Paternalism "the protection of people against themselves" according to Hart, is necessary to the preservation of society, but the enforcement of morality requires justification that society finds acceptable lest the exercise of power be viewed as illegitimate'.

[52]For example, the United States 'Secure Flight Program'.

[53]Samuelson (1999), pp. 1146–1151. See Chap. 11.

[54]Nelson (2011), p. 192.

[55]Beauchamp and Childress (2001).

[56]For instance, social networks and the interoperability of multiple data dossiers that contain identity photographs. The potential aggregation of data is not second-order compliant because consenting to one use may leverage unconsented use elsewhere.

information gathering are obscured by incomprehensible terms and conditions,[57] and the concomitant lack of transparency that disables the data subject. Since I contend that face recognition technology reifies images into data which is then subject to data protection provisions (Chap. 7) that maybe inadequate. Moreover, this infringes second-order preferences because of the inherent loss of control experienced by data subjects and the uncertainties of data security, especially after Snowden's revelations and the mistrust that ensued.[58] Consequently, any loss of trust that is not addressed by adopting appropriate ethical standards which begin with transparency and include adequate redress or design when necessary, such as those outlined in Chap. 7, further undermine autonomy and decisional freedom.

Indeed, Rule[59] has argued that there is a paucity of ethical justification for information gathering which undermines consensual paternalism, whereby what the provisions:

> [D]o not do is address the central ethical issue implicated in the extension of surveillance: the tension between an essentially utilitarian logic of efficiency and Kantian logic of rights. There can be no doubt that widening surveillance is efficient for all sorts of institutional purposes – that it helps allocate credit, collect taxes more productively, track would-be terrorists and other wrongdoers, crack down on unlicensed and uninsured drivers, direct advertising to just the most susceptible consumers, and on and on. Were it not for these attractive efficiencies, government and private organisations would never bother to invest vast sums needed to create systems. *But whether the growth of these systems is compatible with values of individual autonomy and choice over "one's own" information is another matter entirely.*

Rule's criticism highlights a utilitarian and unitary paternalism that is expressed by the purpose of data protection that requires organisations to securely process information and protect it from unlawful disclosure. But, expectations of confidence are not universal: a US national survey comprising 9154 respondents reported that "about 59% of respondents do not have confidence in U.S. state or federal regulations to protect the public from data security breaches by organisations".[60] And therefore, on one hand paternalistic intervention designed to protect data is hampered by poor compliance on the other. Rule includes tracking would-be terrorists and other wrongdoers; and valuing their autonomy as being incompatible with the need for protection against their activities. However, the potential for coalescing the purposes of protection irrespective of risk enhances utility at the expense of individual autonomy, which could be justified when tracking would-be wrongdoers who have arguably relinquished their rights to data protection.

---

[57]The often dense and incomprehensible terms and conditions (T&Cs) may eventually disappear as the GDPR takes effect. However, if the T&Cs are not entirely clear and understandable, then they cannot be said to be providing information that allows consent to be informed.

[58]See Sect. 3.3.1 Public Disclosure.

[59]Rule (2007). Cited by Nelson (2011), p. 192.

[60]Ponemon Institute.

For law-abiding citizens when choice is denied the boundaries become personal and devalue individual worthiness. In one such case,[61] an employee was forced to retire when the company he worked for introduced palm scans (a biometric identifier) for security, and for time and attendance purposes, which he refused to provide because of his religious beliefs. The company did not accommodate his beliefs which led to his constructive dismissal, which subsequently violated US federal law when they refused to consider an alternative to their new time and attendance system.[62] This case illustrates how administrative and economic objectives override autonomy and stimulates dissent. By demanding that all employees submit to scanning when clocking-in is indicative of a loss of trust and is typical of the surveillance modalities referred to above; although not illustrative of a loss of privacy per se, it rather illustrates how informatising physical features offends second-order choices and denies abstention when conscientious objection is not allowed. From this perspective, abstention becomes disobedience which is punishable by loss of liberty, such as the financial freedom that employment rewards.

9.8 Threats to Privacy

Yet within the wider discourse of face recognition, the above arguments suggest some loss of liberty is to be expected as a trade-off for the security that face recognition modalities purport to achieve. Which shows, when the benefits of efficiency and security are added to the reasons for the adoption of biometric identifiers whether by companies or governments, the less opportunity there is to opt-out; especially when access by identity verification, monitoring and / or surveillance are the principal reasons for their adoption. In the context of surveillance this is reasonably at the expense of privacy, which in the nascency of the digital individual became a matter of concern, for instance:

> It is in private that people have the opportunity to become individuals in the sense that we think of the term. People, after all, become individuals in the public realm just by selectively making public certain things about themselves. Whether this is a matter of being selective about one's religious or political views, work history, education, income, or complexion, the important point is this: in a complex society, people adjust their public identities in ways that they believe best, and they develop those identities in more private settings.[63]

Since Currey's observation, face recognition technology has widened the scope of surveillance whereby its prevalence diminishes an individual's ability to adjust their public identity which when coupled to the potential monetisation of the individual's data by commercial enterprise further reduces autonomy. Indeed, with the increasing amount of discrete pieces of information being assembled across a

[61]EEOC v. CONSOL Energy, Inc. and Consolidation Coal Company.

[62]EEOC sues Consol Energy and Consolidation Coal Company for religious discrimination.

[63]Curry (1997), p. 688.

wide range of databases, individuals lose control of their privacy and data; and this results in the demand for data protection and information governance. These needs are framed in data protection law and regulation that are in essence paternalistic, that is quid pro quo the reward for disclosing information.

However, face recognition applications potentially harvest information without consent or knowledge which further reduces any reasonable expectation of privacy in public, and unless this harvesting of information falls within the parameters of data regulation, there is no guarantee of appropriate governance, and therefore Mitchell Gray's observation remains increasingly relevant:

> As surveillance proliferates and urbanites become accustomed to encountering new levels of observation in their daily lives, their recourse to claims of facial privacy in specific situations slips away. As soon as society becomes accustomed to a type of surveillance, the reasonable expectation of privacy has disappeared. Urbanites have gradually seen many aspects of privacy disappear. Unlike twenty years ago, the watchful eye of the video camera at stores, casinos and many other businesses and government agencies goes almost unnoticed, and drivers submit readily to being photographed while breaking driving laws.[64]

Gray's comments are supported by the 2018 Legatum Institute Prosperity Index which among its indices ranks personal freedom in Canada (1st), United Kingdom (18th) and the United States (23rd).[65] Personal freedom includes civil liberties and the freedom of choice. Each of these rankings, which fluctuate from year to year, represent the growing challenge to civil liberties for the sake of security that in all probability are (or have been) exacerbated by Snowden's disclosure of excessive surveillance.

The Index quantitatively illustrates the threats to privacy that were reported in 2007 by The Royal Academy of Engineering, whereby:

> [C]itizens are in no position to agree or reject surveillance. This limits the extent of the freedom of citizens to go about their lawful business without being observed and monitored. It also extends the capacity for agencies and institutions to subject a section of the public realm to surveillance for their own purposes.[66]

Preceding the above statement, the Academy noted that the effect of surveillance technology may require trading some aspects of privacy in exchange for the benefits. And that the effect on privacy may differ, because privacy is multifaceted and comprises of various elements, for instance[67]:

- privacy as anonymity: we might want some of our actions (even those done in public) not to be traceable to us as specific individuals;
- similarly, we might wish for privacy of identity: the right to keep one's identity unknown for any reason, including keeping one's individual identity separate from a public persona or official role;

---

[64]Gray (2003), p. 317.

[65]Legatum Institute Prosperity Index 2018.

[66]Royal Academy of Engineering (2007), p. 33.

[67]*ibid*, p. 11.

- privacy as self-determination: we might consider some of our behaviour private in that it is 'up to us' and no business of others (where those 'others' may range from the state to our employers);
- privacy as control of personal data: we might desire the right to control information about us—where it is recorded, who sees it, who ensures that it is correct, and so on

These reservations are in response to an over-arching paternalism by the State, and its sponsoring of technologies that effectively diminish or deny control. Control is relinquished and replaced by data protection legislation that ultimately only addresses the lawfulness of data processing and handling.[68] Although control of personal data is an acknowledged principle, taking control can be bureaucratic and requires knowledge of the information held across multiple platforms, and the means of access to each data controller.

The freedom to control personal information is an example of Dworkin's dichotomy of liberty and autonomy[69]:

> [l]iberty, power, control over important aspects of one's life are not the same as autonomy, but are necessary conditions for individuals to develop their own aims and interests and to make their values effective in the living of their lives

Liberty according to Dworkin is the principal condition that permits control, and the subsequent authority (power) to request access is exercised in terms of decisional freedom that are features of second-order preferences that are borne from the capacity for self-governance discussed in Chap. 5. These conditions do not apply when the paternalistic uses of surveillance supersede personal preferences, and from which the secrecy paradigm is deduced. Yet, due to the ubiquity of surveillance there is no relationship between the observed data subject and the data controller. Therefore, neither the secrecy paradigm, that is the loss of privacy in public nor the permissibility of information access are connected, because other than for limited verification purposes (i.e. traffic violations) access to the surveillance data is denied. This resonates with Foucault's[70] description of state control in eighteenth century France (Chap. 5) where the citizenry is observed by the monarch's acolytes but remained disconnected from the king. In modern democracies the monarchy has deferred to parliament or has been superseded by congress, each of these exercise power by plebiscite and whose accountability structures are supported by the rule of law. Therefore, a significant benefit of the GDPR, is that, data controllers and processors must seek their data subjects' consent, which is predicated by Dworkin's observation.

[68]Berle (2011).

[69]Dworkin (1988), p. 18.

[70]Foucault (1977).

References

Accardo J, Chaudhry Ahmed M (2014) Radiation exposure and privacy concerns surrounding full-body scanners in airports. J Radiat Res Appl Sci 7:198–200. http://www.sciencedirect.com/science/article/pii/S1687850714000168. Accessed 26 Aug 2019

American Constitution, https://www.law.cornell.edu/constitution/preamble. Accessed 26 August 2019

BBC News, 04-11-2013 'Tesco petrol stations use face-scan tech to target ads' http://www.bbc.co.uk/news/technology-24803378. Accessed 26 Aug 2019

Beauchamp TL, Childress JF (2001) Principles of biomedical ethics, 5th edn. Oxford University Press, New York

Berle I (2011) Privacy and confidentiality: what's the difference? J Visual Commun 34(1):43–44. https://www.tandfonline.com/doi/abs/10.3109/17453054.2011.550845?journalCode=ijau20. Accessed 26 Aug 2019

CCTV & Surveillance Cameras, https://www.tfl.gov.uk/corporate/privacy-and-cookies/cctv. Accessed 22 Sept 2019

Chesterman S (2011) One nation under surveillance: a new social contract to defend freedom without sacrificing liberty. Oxford University Press, Oxford, p 9

Collingridge D (1981) The social control of technology. Palgrave Macmillan

Curry MR (1997) The digital individual and the private realm. Ann Assoc Am Geogr 87 (4):681–699. http://onlinelibrary.wiley.com/doi/10.1111/1467-8306.00073/abstract. Accessed 26 Aug 2019

Doyal L, Gough I (1991) A theory of human need. MacMillan Press Limited, Basingstoke, p 89

Dworkin G (1988) (reprinted 1997) The theory and practice of autonomy. Cambridge University Press, p 10

EEOC sues Consol Energy and Consolidation Coal Company for religious discrimination. http://www.eeoc.gov/eeoc/newsroom/release/9-25-13d.cfm; and https://www.eeoc.gov/eeoc/newsroom/release/8-27-15a.cfm. Accessed 26 Aug 2019

Fine B (1984) Marx's capital: 'commodity production. Palgrave, London, pp 20–26

Foucault M (1977) Discipline and Punish, Birth of the Prison, translated by Alan Sheridan. (First published as 'Surveiller et punir: Naissance de la prison' by Éditions Gallimard, Paris, 1975; Penguin Books 1991)

Gray J (1991) Mill's conception of happiness. In: Gray J, Smith GW (eds) On liberty in focus. Routledge, London, p 197

Gray M (2003) Urban surveillance and panopticism: will we recognize the facial recognition society? Surveill Soc 1(3):314–330. https://ojs.library.queensu.ca/index.php/surveillance-and-society/article/view/3343. Accessed 26 Aug 2019

Hobbes T (1651) Leviathan. http://www.gutenberg.org/files/3207/3207-h/3207-h.htm. Accessed 26 Aug 2019

Kremer J (2014) On the end of freedom in public spaces: legal challenges of wide-area and multiple-sensor surveillance systems. In: Davis F, Mcgarrity N, Williams G (eds) Surveillance, counter-terrorism and comparative constitutionalism. Routledge, Oxford, p 128

Legatum Institute Prosperity Index 2018. http://prosperity.com/#!/ranking. Accessed 26 Aug 2019

Mann M (1984) The autonomous power of the state: its origins, mechanisms and results. Eur J Sociol 25(2):185–213 Archives européennes de sociologie 1984, published by Cambridge University Press. www.jstor.org/stable/23999270. Accessed 22 Sept 2019

McClory J (2010) The new persuaders: an international ranking of soft power. Institute of Government. http://www.instituteforgovernment.org.uk/sites/default/files/publications/The%20new%20persuaders_0.pdf. Accessed 26 Aug 2019

Mill JS (1859) In: Gray J, Smith GW (eds) (1991) On liberty in focus. Routledge, London, 1991, p 33

Nelson LS (2011) American identified: biometric technology and society. Massachusetts Institute of Technology, published by the MIT Press, p 66

Petit P (1996) Freedom as antipower. Ethics 106(3):578–604. University of Chicago Press. https://www.jstor.org/stable/2382272?seq=1#page_scan_tab_contents. Accessed 26 August
Pomeroy SB (1975) Goddesses, whores, wives, & slaves: women in classical antiquity. Pimlico 1994
Ponemon Institute National Survey on Data Security Breach Notification 2005. Cached on Google
Quattrociocchi W, Scala A, Sunstein CR (2016) Echo Chambers on Facebook (June 13, 2016). https://papers.ssrn.com/sol3/papers.cfm?abstract_id=2795110. Accessed 26 Aug 2019
Rawls J (1971) (Rev 1999) A theory of justice. Revised Edition 1999. The Belknap Press of Harvard University Press, Cambridge
Royal Academy of Engineering (2007) Dilemmas of Privacy and Surveillance Challenges of Technological Change. https://www.raeng.org.uk/publications/reports?q=Dilemmas%20of%20Privacy%20and%20Surveillance%20Challenges%20of%20Technological%20Change. Accessed 26 Aug 2019
Rule JB (2007) Privacy in peril. Oxford University Press, Oxford
Samuelson P (1999) Property as intellectual property. Stanf Law Rev 1126–1173. Stan Law Rev 52:1125, p 1146–1151. https://scholarship.law.berkeley.edu/facpubs/2137/. Accessed 26 Aug 2019
Smart JJC, Williams B (1973) Utilitarianism: for and against. Cambridge University Press, Cambridge
Solove DJ (2011) Nothing to hide: the false trade off between privacy and security. Yale University Press, New Haven
TSA-OSO Form 1000 (Rev. 1-13-2010) Section 110(b) of the Aviation and Transportation Security Act of 2001, 49 U.S.C. 44901(c)-(e)
(United States Equal Employment Opportunity Commission) EEOC v. CONSOL Energy, Inc. and Consolidation Coal Company, Civil Action No. 1:13-cv-00215-IMK
United States 'Secure Flight Program'. http://www.tsa.gov/stakeholders/secure-flight-program. Accessed 26 Aug 2019
Van de Veer D (1986) Paternalistic intervention: the moral bounds of benevolence. Princeton University Press, Princeton, p 41
Veak TJ (ed) (2006) Democratizing technology. State University of New York Press
von Hippel E (2005) Democratizing innovation. MIT Press
Whitehead JW (2013) A government of wolves: the emerging American Police State. Select Books Inc, New York
Wikipedia (n.d.) Stasi. https://en.wikipedia.org/wiki/Stasi#Personnel_and_recruitment; Mass Surveillance in East Germany. https://en.wikipedia.org/wiki/Mass_surveillance_in_East_Germany. Accessed 26 Aug 2019

Chapter 10
State Paternalism and Data

Abstract This chapter discusses how the data is entrusted to data controllers. However, the disconnection between data subject and data controller requires the data subject to trust their information to the paternalistic actions and oversight of the data controller that are the operational aspects of adherence to data protection legislation. But depending on the purpose for which the data is obtained or information surveilled, necessitates judicial oversight to prevent excessive or disproportionate use of surveillance powers that include the covert interception of data. The chapter further discusses the issues surrounding the conflicting demands of State Paternalism and Data.

10.1 Protecting Privacy: Data Protection and the Political Dimension

The disconnection between data subject and data controller requires the data subject to trust their information to the paternalistic actions and oversight of the data controller that are the operational aspects of adherence to data protection legislation. In this instance, such benevolent paternalistic intervention is defined as "the attitude or actions of a person, or organization, that protects people and gives them what they need, but does not give them any responsibility or freedom of choice".[1]

Although the OECD[2] data protection principles are generally universal[3] their adoption and interpretation is influenced and subject to the legislative culture that differs between the UK/EU and US and will arguably be subject to the prevailing interpretation of fair practice principles. Whilst these differences were discussed in Chap. 7, they are in each jurisdiction responding to the perceived necessity for the free flow of information required for security purposes. From this perspective, how data is disseminated or not, is unknown and therefore not entirely second-order

[1]Merriam-Webster Online Dictionary.

[2]Organisation for Economic Co-operation and Development.

[3]OCED Privacy Framework (2013), p. 76.

I. Berle, *Face Recognition Technology*, Law, Governance and Technology Series 41,
https://doi.org/10.1007/978-3-030-36887-6_10

compliant, which in respect of security has become normalised and expected. In other circumstances and scenarios it is difficult for individuals to understand the complexity of personal data and for them to make informed choices related to how their personal data should be disclosed.[4] To ameliorate these difficulties the 'Fair Information Practice Principles' (FIPPS) of 'transparency, 'choice', 'information review and correction', 'information protection', and 'accountability'[5] are the basic requirements of data protection, that were, and are expected in the United States.[6] Yet, although the OECD further developed these principles, in practice they are somewhat optimistic, given that the data subject may be unaware of their existence, or that there is no *a priori* substantiation of compliance. Nevertheless, protecting data privacy is an essential and even an authoritarian response to the burgeoning need for data security whether the data subject is cognisant or not. Moreover, the growth and value of personal data intensifies the risk that data[7] will be used in unforeseen ways that exceed the original intention the organisation and individual expected after the data was collected. Inasmuch, that the various collection and processing methods make it possible for more detailed monitoring of an individual's activities. To alleviate the privacy risks, greater attention to the unauthorised monitoring and unexpected secondary uses is necessary, if the negative effects of Big Data[8] are to be curtailed.

Yet, the value of personal data is indeterminate and increasingly monetised by social media enterprises (SMEs) for marketing purposes, of which the unanticipated risks require greater adherence to fair practice, especially transparency and accountability. Such adherence to fair practice is now expected within the GDPR compliance frameworks, as data subjects' consent is now a feature of the data landscape. However, the mass monitoring of on-line activity demanded by parliament and congress when the threat to public safety heightens, challenges the purpose of data protection if transparency and accountability are the tenets to be observed. In each case, the notion of choice is non-existent if individuals wish to retain a digitised persona; and although Solove[9] argues that the notion of 'nothing to hide, nothing to fear' is a spurious justification for mass surveillance, it is not a reason for ignoring the need for vigilance in respect of security. Given the statutory demand for data protection, the monitoring of data by government agencies demands their greater governance if the principles of data protection are to be observed, because:

> Surveillance gives significant power to the watchers. Part of the harm is not simply in being watched but in the lack of control that people have over the watchers. Surveillance creates

[4]*ibid* p. 67.

[5]Fair Information Practice Principles (FIPPs).

[6]Dixon (n.d.).

[7]OECD (2013) *op cit* p. 390.

[8]See Sect. 6.5 'Big Data'.

[9]Solove (2011), p. 1.

> the need to worry about the judgement of the watchers. Will our confidential information be revealed? What will be done with the information gleaned from surveillance?[10]

The loss of control is unconsented and is therefore not autonomous; it is this loss of choice that creates the anxieties that are symptomatic of being watched, and which also demarcate the line between benevolent and non-benevolent paternalism when the rubric of security takes precedence over other considerations. Moreover, there is the risk of inducing mass paranoia if sufficient numbers become fearful of the consequences of the surveillance that Solove describes, and governance is one essential approach that can help to alleviate such fear. Such governance may be vested in a government ombudsman or commissioner who represents individuals and to whom the surveillance agencies are accountable.

However, when public safety is at risk the response by governments is to extend powers that demote data privacy to allow access to personal communications. To that end the UK's proposed Communications Data Bill 2012 and the Data and Investigatory Powers Act 2014 (the DRIP Act)[11] permitted the interception of communications data and consequently stimulated public debate. The UK government justified the necessity of communications data interception, stating that:

> The House will know that communications data – the 'who, where, when and how' of a communication but not its content – and interception – which provides the legal power to acquire the content of communication – are vital for combating crime and fighting terrorism. Without them, we would be unable to bring criminals and terrorists to justice and we would not be able to keep the public safe.[12]

Colloquially called 'the snooper's charter' the Communications Bill[13] and the Act undergirds the Regulation of Investigatory Powers Act 2000 stating that:

> The Secretary of State may by notice (a "retention notice") require a public telecommunications operator to retain relevant communications data if the Secretary of State considers that the requirement is necessary and proportionate for one or more of the purposes falling within paragraphs (a) to (h) of section 22(2) of the Regulation of Investigatory Powers Act 2000 (purposes for which communications data may be obtained).[14]

Whilst the Data and Investigatory Powers Act proscribed data disclosure[15] it also permitted the interception of data when necessary and extends the authority of agencies to access data, potentially without judicial oversight or review.[16] Although

---

[10] *ibid* p. 179.

[11] DRIP Act. Additionally, the later Investigatory Powers Bill superseded the Draft Communications Bill in 2016.

[12] Theresa May MP (2014), then Home Secretary.

[13] Johnston (2015).

[14] Data Retention and Investigatory Act 2014 paragraph 1(1).

[15] *ibid* Paragraph 1(6a).

[16] *ibid* at 6b.

the Act was rescinded in 2016,[17] the impact of the legislation prompted significant responses by opponents of such powers, for example, Liberty reported that:

> The Bill also fails to narrow the loose and lax communications data access regime for public authorities provided by Chapter 2 of RIPA and under the section 25(1) Regulation of Investigatory Powers (Communications Data) Order 2010. The law currently authorises the acquisition of communications data by hundreds of public authorities and most public bodies are able to authorise internally their access to communications data for the same broad range of purposes under which communications data is retained. Barring local authority access, there is no requirement for independent prior judicial authorisation when communications data is sought by public bodies.[18]

Nevertheless, the government claimed that "the proposed legislation is capable of being fully compliant with the Data Protection Principles and the Data Protection Act 1998".[19] Yet given the political and social responses to the Communications Bill and the DRIP Act, the claim that they complied with the Data Protection Act 1998 or even the General Data Protection Regulation (GDPR) remains uncertain[20] and seemingly optimistic, which adds credence to Solove's caution above. Conversely, Solove's and Liberty's cautions could be regarded as a confected counter-argument if overly applied in opposition to the draft Communications Bill and the Data and Investigatory Powers Act 2014 and their later iterations[21], because they have been variously publicised as not being about the 'what' of communication, but rather the 'where' and 'when'[22] that is of interest to the security services. Hence, by restricting the surveillance to the 'envelope' and not the content unless lawfully necessary, both legislative instruments are data protection compliant.

Yet given increasing use of encryption by individuals content may not be accessible even when warranted, and encrypted message or email service providers are likely to be beyond the reach of UK law or other jurisdictions. Such cybersecurity issues challenge the efficiency and efficacy of anti-terror powers, and although it might be reasonable to believe that there would be checks and balances against function creep the risk of the abuse of power is possible: either for paternalistic reasons or excessive interference by government agencies.

For example, until the European Court of Human Rights intervened in 2008[23] the reluctance to destroy DNA samples taken from innocent people and stored in the UK Police National DNA Database was cause for concern. Subsequently, Gene Watch UK reported that:

[17]Data Retention and Investigatory Act Explanatory Notes, para 110. See fn.11 above; the new bill was given Royal Assent on 29th November 2016 becoming the Investigatory Powers Act 2016.

[18]Liberty (n.d.).

[19]See fn.17 above: Paragraphs 100–102.

[20]Hill (2017).

[21]Investigatory Powers Act 2016.

[22]Cavendish (2015).

[23]The 'Marper' case.

> The Coalition Government [has] adopted the Protection of Freedoms Act on 1st May 2012. The Act entered into force on 31st October 2013. The National DNA Database Annual report for 2012/13 reports that over 1.7 million DNA profiles taken from innocent people and from children have been removed from the DNA database and 7,753,000 DNA samples have been destroyed.[24]

It is likely that the principal reason for the government's reluctance was the loss of a resource that could be used in future criminal investigations. Prior to the Protection of Freedoms Act[25] the police in England and Wales had been able to take samples without consent from anyone arrested on suspicion of any recordable offence which includes begging and taking part in an illegal demonstration. Although Gene Watch UK were not opposed to the DNA Database per se they opposed its use because[26]:

- it allowed the permanent retention of DNA samples and records from anyone arrested for virtually any offence, regardless of whether they are charged or convicted;
- uses of the Database were not adequately documented or controlled;
- legislation had been rushed through without adequate public or parliamentary debate, in a political context where there are increasing concerns about a growing police state or surveillance society;
- the uncontrolled expansion of the DNA database would not make a significant difference to the detection of serious crime.

The political will that initially ignored the demands for reform was probably based on the need to prevent harm, and in doing so failed to consider the consequences of the other harms delineated above.

10.2 Protecting Privacy: UK Data Protection and the Face Recognition Paradigm

The reduced DNA Database represents a seismic shift against the unwarranted retention of data; although paradoxically, the deletion of DNA data is inconsistent when compared to the need for data retention that is prescribed in the DRIP Act and the later Investigatory Powers Act that extended the previous Act's powers. This inconsistency when applied to face recognition is paradigmatic because both types of data are obtained without explicit consent whenever DNA is physically obtained during an investigation; and individuals' facial features are recorded, remotely or otherwise and stored in various databases that can be lawfully accessed. Therefore, since both Acts seek to monitor the 'where' and 'when' of communication, the

[24]Gene Watch UK (n.d.).

[25]Protection of Freedoms Act 2012.

[26]*ibid.*

potential for including 'association' is likely when individuals are identified and would be (arguably) a powerful tool in criminal investigations. DNA samples are physical entities which require careful handling and storage to maintain their evidential integrity before and after analysis.[27] The resultant DNA profiles are stored in the database or databases that are structured to contain information from different sources such as reference samples from known individuals or crime scenes. The efficacy of the database statistically supports its existence because many crime scene samples have matched individuals on the database.[28] Arguably, to counter opposition to the excessive data retention and its effect on privacy Syndercombe-Court claims that the database protects privacy because those not matched are excluded from police interest.[29] The veracity of this claim is seemingly correct given that the police retain control of the database and the fact that DNA samples are limited to specific events. These artefacts are the trace remains of activities and the submission of samples on demand; yet the submitted samples are taken for comparison purposes and are only deleted if no match is found. Moreover, the submission of samples does not equate to consent but is rather a form of coercion because not to comply may infer guilt. This could be described as 'un-consented consent' or 'passive voluntariness' which is not second-order compliant, due to the enforcement imposed and is also paradigmatic of the border controls described above (Chaps. 1 and 2). This type of voluntary submission also occurs when individuals are monitored when in public, by the coercive nature of surveillance that affects behaviour, and the loss of control experienced when the risk of function creep in a burgeoning surveillance society increases. Consequently, the DNA Database is representative of other personal information databases, and the concerns of civil liberty organisations equally apply to those databases that contain identifiable images of data subjects. Each is subject to data processing protocols, but specifically the ubiquity of images may exceed the capacity of the control protocols (and mechanisms) and reduce autonomy. Furthermore, in parenthesis the DNA Database is uniquely used in the detection of crime and its subjects are overtly connected to police interests.

Image databases are varied and multi-functional and can potentially be accessed by others without the subject's knowledge; data subjects may also be unaware of their inclusion in the image database, or via social networks in the cached data held in search engines. In each case, unless the subject is aware of their included image their right to access personal information is precluded. Yet, whilst many facial images may be voluntarily uploaded onto social networks their secondary unknown uses are paradigmatic of DNA when used as a resource or a repository. As such the voluntariness of images does not qualify as consent to legitimise function creep, and therefore without consent, burgeoning face image databases are comparable to the DNA Database because of their content and potentiality, and additionally the loss of personal control. The Protection of Freedoms Act does not include photographs and

---

[27]Syndercombe-Court (2011), p. 195.

[28]*ibid* p. 229.

[29]*ibid* p. 230.

some UK police forces are using face recognition software to search their image databases. The use of this technology is unregulated which led Mike Barton, national policing lead for the Police National Database, to admit that while fingerprints and DNA were covered by law there was no legislative necessity to manage custody images. Although Barton, interviewed on BBC Newsnight[30] cited the Data Protection Act and the Police and Criminal Evidence Act as the operational framework[31] his comments and justification for using the technology was rebutted by David Laws because its use lacked Parliamentary approval.[32] Commenting in 2014 on the unregulated image database, Alastair MacGregor QC, the Biometrics Commissioner stated that:

> Police forces in England and Wales continue to follow a policy of retaining almost all custody photographs for an indefinite period regardless of whether the individuals concerned have or have not been convicted of an offence.[33]

MacGregor's comment implied how the Protection of Freedoms Act, which authorises the removal of extraneous DNA samples, does not apply to custody photographs of those not convicted of any offence.[34] Nor does the Act include other biometric identifiers of which, given the issues of privacy, a photograph is the most contentious. Although Barton claimed that the retention of images was and is lawful, a court ruling[35] in 2012 contradicted him, and therefore, custody photographs of unconvicted persons must be deleted upon request. However, the quantity[36] of images are arguably unmanageable and would take an excessive amount of time to find and delete the images.

Although the image database is rightly criticised it will eventually need to be regulated because it serves the same purpose as its DNA counterpart, and not doing so is contradictory. However, if images from other databases, such as the Passport Office or DVLA,[37] are accessible by means of the police system the issues discussed in Chap. 4 will surface. The attraction for doing so is arguably for crime detection and the prevention of harm, such interoperability requires judicial oversight, if only to justify the retention of custody photographs; but the need to balance other harms against the justification for such a database, to avoid breaching human rights,[38] is paramount. Similarly,[39] the United States Government Audit Office (GAO)[40] has

[30]Hopkins and Morris (2015).

[31]BBC Newsnight 'UK police built secret face photo database (02Feb15)'.

[32]Stockley (2015) re David Laws.

[33]Ford (2014).

[34]For detail see Biometrics Commissioner Annual Report 2016.

[35]R (RMC and FJ) v Metropolitan Police Commissioner.

[36]Law and Lawyers (2015).

[37]Driver and Vehicle Licensing Authority.

[38]Re fn 35 above.

[39]Charette (2018).

[40]GAO (2016, 2017).

criticised the Department of Justice (DOJ) and the Federal Bureau of Investigation (FBI) for their extensive use of FRT and their disregard of privacy, especially when privacy breaches are the consequences of FRT inaccuracies. However, the GAO acknowledges that using face recognition systems is a valuable tool for FBI investigations. Yet, a coalition of American civil rights and liberties organisations[41] have expressed their concern about how Amazon's 'Rekognition'[42] automated face recognition product potentially threatens communities and harms social cohesion.

One consequence of balancing harms is the counter-narrative of tolerance associated with the acceptance of face coverings worn for cultural and religious reasons, and the effect that this has on the efficacy of data searches when a covered face is not visible to observers or data analysts. This raises the issue of authoritarianism if face coverings are banned to ameliorate risks. Although further discussion is beyond the scope of this book, the issue is nevertheless relevant here because accepting the practice acknowledges the human dignity of the wearers, but which also acknowledges the need for an inclusive consistent approach that maintains social cohesion.

10.3 Data Processing and Second-Order Preferences

Since individuals entrust their personal and private information to public and private sector organisations the importance of data integrity and processing cannot be understated or devalued, and therefore the obligation to protect information from unauthorised disclosure is arguably paternalistic for the prevention of harm. Hence in the UK (and discussed in Chaps. 2 and 4), data processing is regulated by the Data Protection Act 2018[43] containing Six Principles.[44] Principle 1 states that:

> The first data protection principle is that the processing of personal data for any purposes must be lawful, fair and transparent;

Chapter 3 of the Act gives data subjects the 'right to know' and the 'right to amend' what data is held[45] and although the data processor is responsible for the integrity and security of the data held, these rights are implicative of control by entitlement. However, the entitlement is only effective upon request or more likely only when the data user proactively informs their data subjects. Yet, control infers choice and choice is conditioned by autonomy the exercise of which would require data subjects to appropriate their Chap. 3 entitlement. Mill[46] succinctly observed that:

---

[41] ACLU (2018).

[42] Amazon 'Rekognition'.

[43] Data Protection Act 2018.

[44] *ibid* Chapter 2 §86.

[45] *ibid* Chapter 3 §§92-100.

[46] Mill (1859; 1991), p. 74.

> The human faculties of perception, judgement, discriminative feeling, mental activity, and even moral preference, are only in making a choice. He who does anything because it is the custom, makes no choice.

Mill presciently observed the loss of autonomy whenever any action or activity becomes customary and Mill's maxim remains relevant to this contemporary discourse and the genesis of second-order preferences can be discerned. Consequently, any loss or lack of control is evident whenever individuals cursorily agree to the terms and conditions of the organisations that gather personal information; and whenever the organisation becomes the custodian of personal information, irrespective of a data subject's rights and the value of their data.

In each case, individuals have either willingly provided, or have been persuaded to provide personal data in exchange for the benefits the organisations offer; subsequently organisations are permitted to "legitimately collect, transfer and process the information" and "individuals have also started to collect, manage and use personal data in similar ways, for example through social networking sites".[47] Moreover, the relationship between the submission of information and privacy is separated by the practical legal issue of data protection and civil liberties. Therefore, the right to informational privacy is constrained by its context and by any overarching legislation that nullifies the expectation of privacy or confidentiality. For instance, Robinson et al report that because of the multiplicity of legal frameworks data controllers can be unsure which rules take precedence and where this causes uncertainty confusion can ensue. The implications of this are evident when personal data is required or retrieved for litigation purposes and is retained longer than necessary, or when for national security purposes, companies are obliged to retain communication (personal) data to assist identifying suspects. Conflict can also occur regarding whistleblowers, whose anonymity is protected by one set of rules, but countermanded by another set of rules that require that the source should be revealed.[48] For example, the SWIFT case,[49] "where data could not be revealed under EU law but was required to be revealed under US law. In such cases, the data controller would face liability whatever they did, making responsibilities and liabilities difficult to determine in a fair and transparent manner". Hence, the dichotomy in HRA[50] Article 8 between the right to privacy and confidentiality [HRA 1998 Article 8(1)] but which is conditional and subject "in accordance to the law and necessary in a democratic society" [HRA 1998 Article 8(2)], to permissible interference and disclosure of information.

The tension described by Robinson et al typifies the American "third party doctrine" whereby any information held by a third party is no longer private and loses Fourth Amendment Protection. In 1976, in the case of the *United States v. Miller*, the US Supreme Court explained that "all [Miller's financial records] the

---

[47] Robinson et al. (2009), p. viii.

[48] *ibid* pp. 37–38.

[49] SWIFT case. Cited by Robinson et al. (2009).

[50] Human Rights Act (HRA) 1998.

documents obtained…contain only information voluntarily conveyed to the bank…in the ordinary course of business".[51]

Since the duty of confidentiality is predicated by trust; when organisations are conflicted between their duty to protect data, and their responsibility to disclose data to government officials, the promise or expectation of trust is untenable. This is a reversal of Edward Shils' comment during the 1950s McCarthy era, that in liberal democracies the values of privacy and confidentiality need to be respected in peoples' personal affairs and business, and conversely the affairs of government should be transparent and publicised.[52] The normalisation of this polar reversal has accelerated with the demands for security and control. Consequently, the relationship is no longer a mutual partnership because the individual data subject has no guarantee of confidentiality. Therefore, second-order preferences are especially undermined when the benefits are deemed essential, or the information is a statutory necessity and real choice impossible.

In respect of privacy concerns the 2010 UK Home Office's Code of Practice[53] cautiously observed that the escalation of data processing to data-mining can construct a mosaic of an individual's behaviour and thus scrutinise their private life. This scrutiny must be lawfully authorised to avoid breaching both the Human Rights Act 1998 article 8 and the Regulation of Investigatory Powers Act 2000 (RIPA). Furthermore, even if Barton (above) believes that "there is currently no legislative requirement for the management of custody images" the de facto police image database falls within this framework because photographs are included in the totality of information available, and any identifiable image not in the public domain is confidential and therefore private,[54] and only by Parliamentary review[55] will the matter of balancing security and privacy concerns be addressed. Additionally, the necessity to comply with European Court of Justice ruling in Kadi (Chap. 8) sets the precedent for regulating devolved powers.

10.4 The Data Subject and Face Recognition Systems [State Data-Mining Power]

Digital images of an individual's face are easily identifiable when the person is known and recognised and are an acceptable form of social interaction amongst social network users. These images, depending on the privacy protocols, are in the

[51] Solove (2011) *op cit*, p. 102;104;. fn. 1, p. 222. Citing United States v. Miller, 425 U.S. 435 (1976).

[52] Shils (1956), pp. 22–23.

[53] UK Home Office.

[54] Re: Mosley v News Group Newspapers Ltd.

[55] Such review will likely include judicial and ECHR compliance issues (and the future effect of the GDPR).

public domain, on private pages or in closed groups and when access is limited by the privacy protocols the images remain ostensibly private. Yet, social networks and other image databases negate the expectation of privacy because of the 'third party doctrine' noted above. Therefore, individuals are exposed to the harms of face recognition analysis that occurs without their knowledge. Nevertheless, I am not suggesting that the avoidance of harms should provide a cloak of anonymity at the expense of crime detection and prevention, but rather that there be sufficient independent oversight of the procedures and processes[56] that comply with the Fair Information Practice Principles (FIPPs) referred to above.

The complexities of data mining involve a process of searching through voluminous amounts of data to discover patterns, trends, and relationships.[57] This 'knowledge discovery in databases process' (KDD)[58] involves mining the collected data for pattern analysis, evaluation and verification. For example, previously scanned shopping items that initiate vouchers for discounts on the same product at the next shopping trip. Part of the process includes 'training data' that refers to the data portion used to fit a model,[59] such as the products bought. Aside from the data-mining technicalities, face recognition systems when used in commercial or border control applications[60] compare (in real-time) the machine-readable image contained in identity documents (such as passports or identity cards) with that of the individual presenting the document to verify identity.

In other applications individuals were unaware[61] of surveillance that was authorised by The Regulation of Investigatory Powers Act (RIPA). The Act authorised and regulated covert investigatory techniques which includes the acquisition and disclosure of communication data[62] of which, between 2005 and 2010 2.7 million requests were made from UK public authorities to private service providers for information.[63] Also, a wide range of government authorities, such as police forces, Customs and Excise, and various government ministries and departments are permitted to request information citing RIPA to justify their requests.[64]

These authorities have de jure State powers but amongst them the intelligence services are authorised to monitor communications data by the enhanced authority of the Data and Investigatory Powers Act (DRIPA and the later Investigatory Powers Act 2016), noted above. Whilst the State may only be interested in the 'where' and 'when' of communication data any identifiable image included may trigger the 'what', if the metadata indicates its availability. Although, this may only occur

[56]Cole (2014), pp. 112–113.

[57]Hernández-Aguilar et al. (2011), p. 130.

[58]Han and Kamber (2002). Cited by Hernández-Aguilar *op cit* (2011).

[59]Terminology and Notation.

[60]Chapter 2.

[61]Big Brother Watch Report (2012), p. 15.

[62]*ibid* p. 9.

[63]Cole (2014), p. 96 *op cit.*

[64]Big Brother Watch *op cit* p. 23.

when there is sufficient evidence to initiate further scrutiny resulting from the data-mining technique used; yet after Snowden's revelations about the excessive monitoring of data this approach and use of data-mining may be more akin to a dragnet than to specific persons of interest.

Nevertheless, the range of authorities and the scope of their power infers a reduction of freedom from intrusion especially when coupled with some apparently spurious use of RIPA powers, for instance, when tackling anti-social behaviour and the questions over proportionality[65] that it poses whenever investigations do not result in convictions, inasmuch that the number of uses and outcomes are indicative of the over-zealous use of the legislation from dog-fouling offences and parking misdemeanours. These unintended consequences and misuse of RIPA powers caused the 2010–2012 Coalition Government to establish a seriousness threshold. Henceforth, any investigation would require judicial approval for the deployment of covert surveillance, namely, (a) the acquisition and disclosure of communications data, (b) the use of directed surveillance and (c) covert human intelligence sources. This judicial oversight is a function of the Protection of Freedoms Act, that was part of the 2012 legislative programme "that would safeguard civil liberties and reduce the burden of government intrusion into the lives of individuals".[66]

Nonetheless, the restrictions placed upon local authorities do not change the landscape because a combination of communication data and face recognition software is still judicially justifiable. For example, Transport for London (TfL)[67] use "CCTV to capture and monitor images of events that take place in specific locations in real time". This information is shared with the police and local authorities when necessary and is DPA compliant. Apart from the scene recorded the transport system is likely to also have data from any prepaid card (an 'Oyster' card in London) and possibly access to photo-card data; any image held on an image database plus the captured image from the video footage will assist the identification of a possible perpetrator of a crime (or any other data subject) when the police use face recognition software.

This is not an entirely hypothetical scenario but is rather a synthesis of current practice and with judicial application and oversight, multi-agency collaboration is expected to be accountable and consistent across all sectors of devolved power. Consequently, by using all the available data, remaining anonymous is unlikely and a successful conviction is made possible. The practice is less than ideal and is subject to abuse and misapplication as reported by independent organisations such as Big Brother Watch. Nonetheless, the role of the legislation is the yardstick by which Parliament can measure due process and respond when due process exceeds the law. Hence the reaction to the unauthorised police image database. Moreover, in a landmark challenge brought by MPs David Davis and Tom Watson to Government

---

[65] *ibid* p. 17.

[66] Protection of Freedoms Bill.

[67] Transport for London.

surveillance law, the High Court ruled in 2015 that DRIPA[68] was unlawful. The Court found that sections 1 and 2 of DRIPA were incompatible "with the British public's right to respect for private life and communications and to protection of personal data under Articles 7 and 8 of the EU Charter of Fundamental Rights".[69] In March 2016 the unlawful sections of DRIPA ceased to have any effect. This is despite Leveson's[70] comments on ECHR rulings because of the overall primacy of the EU Charter of Fundamental Rights and the supremacy of the European Court of Justice. However, DRIPA was finally repealed in December 2016 and replaced by the Investigatory Powers Act.[71,72,73]

Similarly, the repealing of the Identity Cards Act 2006 (ICA) in 2010[74] and the subsequent destruction of the national identity register (NIR) that was implemented by the ICA is consistent with the revised DNA database vis-à-vis the quantity of information held and ineffectiveness of the scheme, and the loss of public support.[75] Whilst the purpose of the NIR may well have been well intentioned—a desire to create an inclusive society perhaps—it was a paternalistic over-reaction to the suicide bombings in London and Madrid in the preceding year which ultimately could not have been prevented with an identity card. Indeed, the London bombers were identified after the event from the CCTV footage and judicious searching through other data.

Combining these elements: CCTV, a DNA database, a national identity register and a police image database with face recognition technologies, would likely assist crime prevention and improve crime detection rates, but it would also create an overarching panopticism, whereby citizens become unified data subjects with basic freedoms lost, and the Kafkaesque scenario[76] would potentially be realised by the machinations of State power. Therefore, if the impetus for face recognition technologies is primarily for security and safety purposes at the expense, of not only privacy but also freedom, the greater the need for restraint and the robust balancing of harms, that does not rhetorically respond with Benjamin Franklin's statement that:

> Those who would give up essential Liberty, to purchase a little temporary Safety, deserve neither Liberty nor Safety.

---

[68] Data Retention and Investigatory Powers Act 2014.

[69] David Davis and others; EU Charter of Fundamental Rights.

[70] See Chap. 7.

[71] Investigatory Powers Bill Explanatory Notes.

[72] Investigatory Powers Act 2016.

[73] Eventually, the UK will be beyond the jurisdiction of the ECJ when (assuming) the country leaves the EU, but the UK will still need to comply with EU law governing personal data and privacy, which has necessitated the Data Protection Act 2018. It is further likely that future EU legislation will also require compliance, of which the GDPR is a precedent.

[74] Identity Documents Act 2010 c. 40 Repeal of Identity Cards Act 2006.

[75] Liberty 'ID Cards'.

[76] Chapter 4.

Nor does it conversely respond with the aggressive opposition that proponents of more surveillance exhibit which thereby polarises the debate.

According to one American legal scholar[77] Franklin's quotation has become a mantra for civil liberties, which was not Franklin's intention in 1755. However, the context has since changed and therefore the loss of anonymity that is made possible with the aggregation of data is a civil liberties issue that does need balancing against the extended powers vested in government agencies, and which the next chapter will consider.

References

ACLU (2018) American Civil Liberties Union Letter to Amazon. https://www.aclunc.org/docs/20180522_AR_Coalition_Letter.pdf. Accessed 27 Aug 2019

Also 'Davis and Watson DRIPA challenge: Government surveillance law is unlawful, High Court rules,'. Liberty 17th July 2015. https://www.liberty-human-rights.org.uk/news/press-releases-and-statements/davis-and-watson-dripa-challenge-government-surveillance-law. Accessed 27 Aug 2019

Amazon "Rekognition". https://aws.amazon.com/rekognition/. Accessed 27 Aug 2019

BBC Newsnight item 'UK police built secret face photo database (02Feb15)'. Was originally available from: https://www.youtube.com/watch?v=gmp7uk_sMlU. However, subsequently removed "UK police built secret fac... The YouTube account associated with this video has been terminated due to multiple third-party notifications of copyright infringement". Later amended to "This video is no longer available because the YouTube account associated with this video has been closed"

Big Brother Watch Report (2012) A legacy of suspicion: how RIPA has been used by local authorities and public bodies. http://www.bigbrotherwatch.org.uk/files/ripa/RIPA_Aug12_final.pdf. Accessed 27 Aug 2019

Biometrics Commissioner Annual Report 2016. https://www.gov.uk/government/publications/biometrics-commissioner-annual-report-2016

Cavendish C (2015) Let M15 spy on granny and her azaleas; a jihadist may be lurking behind them. The Sunday Times, 18th January 2015 http://www.thesundaytimes.co.uk/sto/comment/columns/CamillaCavendish/article1507963.ece. Accessed 27 Aug 2019

Charette RN (2018) Automated Facial Recognition: Menace, Farce, or Both? IEEE Spectrum, 29 May 2018. https://spectrum.ieee.org/riskfactor/computing/it/automated-facial-recognition-menace-farce-or-both. Accessed 27 Aug 2019

Cole D (2014) Preserving privacy in a digital age: lessons of comparative constitutionalism. In: Davis F, McGarrity N, Williams G (eds) Surveillance, counter-terrorism and comparative constitutionalism. Routledge, Oxford, pp 112–113

Data and Investigatory Powers Act 2014 (DRIP Act). http://www.legislation.gov.uk/ukpga/2014/27/contents/enacted. Accessed 27 Aug 2019

Data Protection Act 2018 (DPA). http://www.legislation.gov.uk/ukpga/2018/12/contents/enacted. Accessed 27 Aug 2019. See Chapter 3, footnote 26

Data Retention and Investigatory Act Explanatory Notes, para 110. http://www.publications.parliament.uk/pa/bills/lbill/2014-2015/0037/en/15037en.htm. Accessed 27 Aug 2019

David Davis and others judgement: https://www.judiciary.gov.uk/judgments/secretary-of-state-for-the-home-department-v-david-davis-mp-and-others/. Accessed 27 August 2019

[77]Cited by Wittes (2011), p. 1.

Dixon P (n.d.) A brief introduction to fair information practices. https://www.worldprivacyforum.org/2008/01/report-a-brief-introduction-to-fair-information-practices/. Accessed 27 Aug 2019

EU Charter of Fundamental Rights of the European Union (2000/C 364/01). (http://www.europarl.europa.eu/charter/pdf/text_en.pdf. Accessed 27 Aug 2019

Fair Information Practice Principles (FIPPs) privacy course. University of California, Berkeley. https://security.berkeley.edu/fipps. Accessed 27 Aug 2019

Ford R (2014) Photos of innocent kept by police despite court ruling. The Times, 19 December 2014. https://www.thetimes.co.uk/article/photos-of-innocent-kept-by-police-despite-court-ruling-3rh25pxwj59. Accessed 27 Aug 2019

GAO (2016) Face Recognition Technology: FBI Should Better Ensure Privacy and Accuracy. https://www.gao.gov/products/GAO-16-267

GAO (2017) Face Recognition Technology: DOJ and FBI Need to Take Additional Actions to Ensure Privacy and Accuracy. https://www.gao.gov/products/GAO-17-489T. Accessed 27 Aug 2019

Gene Watch UK 'The UK Police National DNA Database'. http://www.genewatch.org/sub-539478. Accessed 27 Aug 2019

Han J, Kamber M (2002) Data mining concepts and techniques. San Francisco. Morgan Kaufmann Publishers. Cited by Hernández-Aguilar et al (2011)

Hernández-Aguilar JA, Zavala C, Díaz O, Burlak G, Ochoa A, César Ponce J (2011) Biometric data mining applied to on-line recognition systems. In: Midori A (ed) Biometrics - unique and diverse applications in nature, science, and technology, p 130. https://www.intechopen.com. Accessed 2 Feb 2020

Hill R (2017) UK.gov admits investigatory powers act illegal under EU law: cops to be stripped of powers to OK access to comms data in tweaks to Snooper's Charter. The Register. https://www.theregister.co.uk/2017/11/30/investigatory_powers_act_illegal_under_eu_law/. Accessed 27 Aug 2019

Hopkins N, Morris J (2015) 'Innocent people' on police photos database' 3rd February 2015. http://www.bbc.co.uk/news/uk-31105678. Accessed 27 Aug 2019

Human Rights Act (HRA) 1998. http://www.opsi.gov.uk/acts/acts1998/ukpga_19980042_en_1. Accessed 27 Aug 2019

Identity Documents Act 2010 c. 40 Repeal of Identity Cards Act 2006. http://www.legislation.gov.uk/ukpga/2010/40/crossheading/repeal-of-identity-cards-act-2006. Accessed 27 Aug 2019

Investigatory Powers Act 2016. http://www.legislation.gov.uk/ukpga/2016/25/contents/enacted. Accessed 27 August 2019

Investigatory Powers Bill 2016. https://www.gov.uk/government/uploads/system/uploads/attachment_data/file/228824/8359.pdf. Accessed 27 Aug 2019

Investigatory Powers Bill Explanatory Notes. https://publications.parliament.uk/pa/bills/cbill/2016-2017/0002/en/17002en03.htm. Accessed 27 Aug 2019

Investigatory Powers Regulations: https://www.gov.uk/government/publications/investigatory-powers-regulations. Accessed 27 Aug 2019

Johnston I (2015) David Cameron pledges new 'snoopers' charter' if he wins general election. The Independent 12th January 2015. http://www.independent.co.uk/news/uk/politics/david-cameron-pledges-new-snoopers-charter-if-he-wins-election-9971379.html. Accessed 27 Aug 2019

Law and Lawyers (2015) '18 million images 'Facial recognition ~ Police database revealed'. http://obiterj.blogspot.co.uk/2015/02/facial-recognition-police-database.html. Accessed 27 Aug. 2019

Liberty: ID Cards. https://www.liberty-human-rights.org.uk/human-rights/privacy/id-cards. Accessed 27 Aug 2019

Liberty: Liberty, Privacy International, Open Rights Group, Big Brother Watch, Article 19 and English PEN briefing on the fast-track Data Retention and Investigatory Powers Bill. Liberty 80 para 13. https://www.liberty-human-rights.org.uk/sites/default/files/Briefing%20on%20the%20Data%20Retention%20and%20Investigatory%20Powers%20Bill.pdf. Accessed 27 Aug 2019

Merriam-Webster Online Dictionary, s.v. "paternalism" http://www.learnersdictionary.com/definition/paternalism. Accessed 27 Aug 2019

Mill JS (1859; 1991) In: Gray J, Smith GW (eds) On liberty in focus. Routledge, New York, p 74

Mosley v News Group Newspapers Ltd [2008] EWHC 1777 (QB). http://www.bailii.org/ew/cases/EWHC/QB/2008/1777.html. Accessed 27 Aug 2019

OCED Privacy Framework (2013) p 76 http://www.oecd.org/sti/ieconomy/oecd_privacy_framework.pdf. Accessed 27 Aug 2019

Protection of Freedoms Act 2012. http://www.legislation.gov.uk/ukpga/2012/9/contents/enacted. Accessed 27 Aug 2019

Protection of Freedoms Bill. https://www.gov.uk/government/publications/protection-of-freedoms-bill. Accessed 27 Aug 2019

R (on the application of) RMC and FJ -v- Commissioner of Police of the Metropolis and Secretary of State for the Home Department and Liberty and Equality and Human Rights Commission (RMC and FJ) v Metropolitan Police Commissioner [2012] EWHC 1681(Admin). https://www.judiciary.gov.uk/judgments/rmc-fj-police-commissioner-judgment-22062012/. Accessed 22 Sept 2019

Robinson N, Graux H, Botterman M, Valeri L (2009) Review of the European Data Protection Directive. p. viii. https://www.rand.org/pubs/technical_reports/TR710.html. Accessed 27 Aug 2019

Shils EA (1956) The torment of privacy: the background and consequences of American security policies. Free Press, Glencoe, pp 22–23

Solove DJ (2011) Nothing to hide: the false trade off between privacy and security. Yale University Press, New Haven, p 1

Stockley B (2015) Re David Laws (Member of Parliament from 2001–2015) letter to Lord Bates, Home Office Minister. https://www.thejusticegap.com/40-uk-adult-population-police-photos-database/. Accessed 27 Aug 2019

SWIFT case and the American Terrorist Finance Tracking Program. http://europa.eu/rapid/press-release_MEMO-07-266_en.htm?locale=en. Accessed 27 Aug 2019

Syndercombe-Court D (2011) DNA analysis: current practice and problems. In: Gall J, Payne-James J (eds) Current practice in forensic medicine. Wiley-Blackwell, Chichester, p 195

Terminology and Notation (for Predictive Analytics) 'Training Data'. http://www3.nd.edu/~busiforc/handouts/DataMining/dataminingdefinitions.html. Accessed 27 Aug 2019

'The Marper case' Gene Watch UK. http://www.genewatch.org/sub-563146 S. and Marper v. The United Kingdom [2008] ECHR 1581, (2009) 48 EHRR 50, 25 BHRC 557, 48 EHRR 50, [2009] Crim LR355 http://www.bailii.org/eu/cases/ECHR/2008/1581.html. Accessed 27 Aug 2019

Theresa May MP (2014) (Then UK Home Secretary) https://www.gov.uk/government/speeches/communications-data-and-interception. Accessed 27 Aug 2019

Transport for London "Surveillance Cameras" (CCTV). https://www.tfl.gov.uk/corporate/privacy-and-cookies/cctv. Accessed 27 Aug 2019

UK Home Office (2010) Covert Surveillance and Property Interference Revised Code of Practice (2010). Para 2.6 (Archived & withdrawn). https://www.gov.uk/government/uploads/system/uploads/attachment_data/file/97960/code-of-practice-covert.pdf. Replaced by: Covert surveillance and property interference code of practice (2018) https://www.gov.uk/government/publications/covert-surveillance-and-covert-human-intelligence-sources-codes-of-practice. Accessed 27 Aug 2019

United States v. Miller, 425 U.S. 435 (1976). https://supreme.justia.com/cases/federal/us/425/435/case.html. Accessed 27 Aug 2019

Wittes B (2011) Platform Security and the Hostile Symbiosis Between Liberty and Security. https://www.brookings.edu/research/against-a-crude-balance-platform-security-and-the-hostile-symbiosis-between-liberty-and-security/. Accessed 27 Aug 2019

Chapter 11
The Future of Face Recognition Technology and Ethico: Legal Issues

Abstract This chapter summarises the impact of face recognition technology on privacy and confidentiality and looks to the future of FRT in terms of its technical developments, and the main ethico-legal issues that may arise. Moreover, the use of FRT by commercial enterprises and governments is divergent when, opposing interests occur between the lawmakers and the public, and between the public and commercial enterprises. The future of FRT should, and to some extent shall, also be shaped by its ethical acceptability and legal regulation. Ultimately, an individual's identity is intimately tied up with their face, and direct technological recognition by the facial contours will be a continuing issue of social concern and sensitivity.

11.1 Face Recognition: The Future and Its Implications

The future of face recognition technology (FRT) will be determined by its performance and efficiency. Like many technological advances before FRT, for instance mobile phones, early adoption was limited by cost and infrastructure. Similarly, face recognition has advanced since its inception which Chap. 2 describes. The use of FRT by commercial enterprises and governments is divergent when, as in the foregoing chapters, opposing interests are evident between the lawmakers and the public, and between the public and commercial enterprises. This book emphasises that the future of FRT should, and to some extent shall, also be shaped by its ethical acceptability and legal regulation. An individual's identity is intimately tied up with their face, and direct technological recognition by the facial contours will be a continuing issue of social concern and sensitivity.

11.2 Threat Recognition and Securitising Identity

In Chap. 2, the development of face recognition technology was described and included examples of its commercial and government uses. The race to develop reliable systems coupled with the competitiveness of technology companies that was

I. Berle, *Face Recognition Technology*, Law, Governance and Technology Series 41,
https://doi.org/10.1007/978-3-030-36887-6_11

spawned by the events of ninth September 2001 in New York has resulted in some non-deliverable expectations. This occurs when the systems using face recognition either fail to provide efficient transit, such as airport e-gates, or when the systems are successfully spoofed or have an unacceptable 'false acceptance rate'. Nonetheless, given that face recognition utilisation requires initial enrolment to securitise identity for easier or automated access, or to assist government agencies detect persons of interest, it raises expectations of successful interventions and outcomes. Conversely without enrolment by whatever method identifying an unknown individual is impossible.

Therefore, at best, and assuming the efficiency and accuracy of FRT, identifying individuals is only possible either in 'real time' (airport e-gates for instance) or after an incident when FRT is a modality used in the data search. The former has become a regular feature at airports, but the latter has become a rather contentious issue because it may require advocating the pre-emptive use of face recognition enabled surveillance which is regarded as a threat to civil liberty. Lyon warned policy-makers of this, because "high technology surveillance systems. . .cannot achieve what their proponents claim but they may all too well curtail cherished and hard-won civil liberties",[1] rather than be a solution for the detection and prevention of crime and terrorism. Yet the ability to securitise identity is a powerful argument that is tangential to the other two apparently conflicting arguments (civil liberties and crime detection or prevention) that are also central to the discourse which the previous chapters have discussed and are summarised below.

The CCTV image[2] of Mohamed Atta who hijacked and flew one of the aircraft into the Twin Towers did not prevent the atrocity. The image was captured by a video surveillance-camera as he passed through airport security, before boarding the flight, was generally regarded as an intelligence and security failure due to the lack of the right technology. It was assumed that, had the airport used face recognition technology the attacks might have been prevented, because his image could have been checked against photographs of suspected terrorists held on FBI and other agencies files.[3]

The failure to intercept the hijackers was not the failure to immediately match their image but was rather the inability to recognise the risks, after-all the 'suspected hijacker' was not verified as the perpetrator until later, to do otherwise would have required technological and intelligence refinements not available at the time. But was nevertheless reported as human error, whilst ignoring the fact that intent is unpredictable and information sharing is hampered by poor resources.[4] Yet with the benefit of hindsight matching Atta's image in time to avert the attack would have been unlikely; and without other supporting data face recognition methods cannot guarantee security, they are merely adjunctive to existing intelligence.

---

[1]Lyon (2008), p. 8.

[2]Mohammed Atta.

[3]See Stikeman (2001). Cited by Gates (2011).

[4]See Eggen (2005).

Fig. 11.1 Identity silos

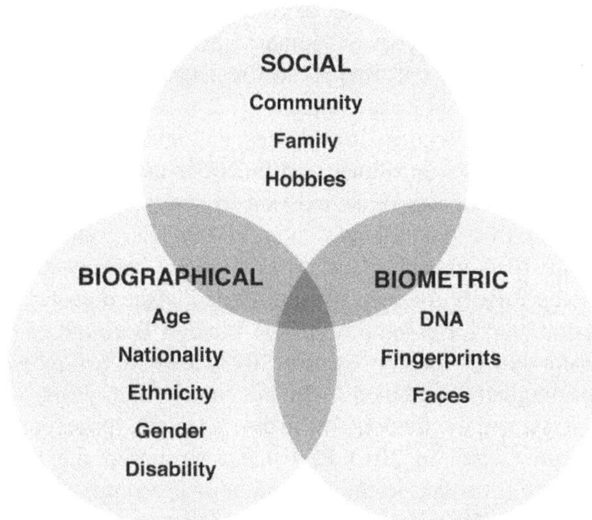

On the other hand, where face recognition technology is used to securitise identity it also homogenises disembodied identities by connecting the disparate and complex identities of individuals represented in these silos (Fig. 11.1):

These silos of identity overlap whereby the substantive aspects of identity: age, faces and the complexity of ethnicity are constant and are discernible across the boundaries. For instance, age is a physical attribute that is inseparable from the three identities, however some aspects of social identity are subject to choice and are thus flexible and relational; also individuals may have overlapping identities which may be expressed in different ways.[5] Given the diversity of attributes and how they are presented the dynamics of identity differ from each other and become increasingly complex when dissociated from physically social contexts, such as when interacting with organisations remotely either on-line or by telephone. Therefore, where verification of identity is required this necessitates a system of identity management that facilitates the interaction between individuals and the organisations[6] that securitises identity. This summarises the use of and the need for stable processes for securitising identity, but as the volume of data expands the demand for efficiency increases, and which maybe inversely proportional to the capacity to deliver the efficiencies required to sustain the process.

For instance, 20 CCTV cameras will produce 480 h of video footage in 24 h[7] and this exponentially increases the demand for monitoring the output which increases the cost of managing the surveillance. Therefore, to reduce the cost factors of capacity and labour the development of more intelligent systems has driven the

[5]See Foresight Future Identities (2013), p. 10.

[6]See Van Zoonen et al. (2012).

[7]Gates (2011), p. 64.

development of "anomaly detection" and "algorithmic" surveillance solutions[8] that can detect and recognise human faces from either video streams or still images.[9] Once captured, still images are matched or searched for against existing images stored in a facial image database.[10] This modality is representative of the demarcation between securitising identity and surveillance initiated face recognition. The former requires enrolment and functions in real-time at the point of access, whereas the latter searches other existing image databases to identify individuals thereby making this functionality akin to the DNA and police databases discussed in Chap. 10. Rather than merely embodying identity the surveillance applications are used primarily for security control and crime detection, which from 1998 had been operational for some time in the London Borough of Newham but has since been discontinued[11]; nevertheless in 2013 Newham had more cameras than Liverpool and Birmingham combined.[12] In the intervening years the Parliamentary Office for Science and Technology published a briefing paper in 2002 summarising the issues to date,[13] and in 2013 Parliament published the Surveillance Camera Code of Practice (pursuant to the Protection of Freedoms Act 2012).[14] This code is adjunctive to the 'Data Protection Code of Practice for Surveillance Cameras and Personal Information'.[15] Although the codes of practice benchmark best practice principles, and assume the capability and capacity of the technology, they are not proscriptive. However, they do set-out the requirements for compliance to the law that is supposed to engender public confidence in the uses of CCTV; whether public confidence equates to acceptance is another matter and is subject to the issue of choice. Moreover, if the purpose of CCTV is to protect the public, the risk of violating civil liberties for the sake of public safety should not be a zero-sum game, but rather CCTV should be a behaviour modifying influence that detects violations of public safety without any concomitant loss of civil liberty. Whether this is possible remains debatable and a significant feature of the wider ongoing discourse.

11.3 Identity Management

Whilst the foregoing has focussed on surveillance and the use of face recognition in crime detection; another major benefit of face recognition that is extolled by commercial enterprises is its use to replace passwords. Passwords are the principal

---

[8] *ibid.*

[9] See Visionics Corporation.

[10] See Brey (2004), pp. 97–109.

[11] London Borough of Newham (2015).

[12] BBC News (2013).

[13] Parliamentary Office for Science and Technology (2002).

[14] Home Office (2013).

[15] ICO (2014).

method of accessing personal online accounts which requires investment in identity management products and rely on the account holder's memory or password saving functions. Thus, if identity management processes only use passwords and login security measures for access, the proliferation of passwords and the need to remember them can defeat the security objectives when passwords are easily hacked.[16] For instance, to obviate the risk Cognitec's various 'FaceVacs' "face recognition applications can support secure login and authentication procedures" across platforms from computers to mobile devices thereby increasing efficiency when using mobile applications (apps) " to take biometric photos required for ePassports and other ID documents, to index photo galleries saved on mobile devices or in the cloud, or to communicate with an access control system".[17,18]

Ultimately, 'FaceVACS' and other products[19] are designed to achieve the maximum utilisation of their proprietary algorithms that perform similar functions, however further discussion about the differences between them is beyond the scope of this book. Nevertheless, they each purport to achieve real time functionality and provide behavioural indicators that exceed the basic requirements of password replacement, and therefore introduce new possibilities for proactive surveillance which will only be limited by the speed of response to the events captured, and which may only be ameliorated by pre-emptive crime prevention that was fictionally portrayed in 'Minority Report'.[20] But I digress to some degree because without robust safeguards in the dystopian world of Josef K (Chap. 4) the potential for such panoptical surveillance could become a reality and eliminate autonomy when the technical and operational obstacles are solved.

Conversely, in respect of passwords the domestic use of face recognition is prima facie second-order compliant because the software is reputed to improve users' experience, and is marketed as the solution to easier online access.[21] Using faces instead of passwords increases connectivity across platforms and functions, and further reduces the necessity for different passwords[22]; such an attractive solution for simplicity of access is problematic when associated with the concomitant effect on transparency and the loss of anonymity which consequently challenges autonomy and threatens privacy.

That is, passwords obscure identity and although potentially hackable, the user remains anonymous; conversely faces verify identity yet can reduce anonymity if successfully spoofed and thereby result in greater unintended transparency[23] when unauthorised disclosure or activity occurs. Therefore, reliance on face recognition *a*

[16]Hence the reason for substantial password strength that ensures data security.

[17]Cognitec (2013).

[18]Cognitec (n.d.) FaceVacs video scan.

[19]See Trepp (2019).

[20]Arthur (2010).

[21]For example: Key Lemon 'Oasis Face'.

[22]*ibid.*

[23]I am using 'transparency' to describe the loss of confidentiality and privacy.

posteriori is not second-order compliant when the risks are considered; but whether the risks of hacked passwords or spoofed faces exceed each other is unknown[24] and the trajectory of travel is that face recognition[25] is likely to replace passwords as more enterprises seek to streamline their identity management systems. Until face recognition enabled login becomes foolproof passwords (or passcodes) will remain a second level authentication process for accessing confidential areas, for instance Apple account holders are required to login by password even though their devices can be verified by a fingerprint or by face recognition.[26]

11.4 Face Recognition and the Human Interface

Face recognition software detects and captures two-dimensional (2D) images which are enough for identity verification in controlled environments where pose and lighting are stable, but where these elements are variable errors occur.[27] Recent research and commercial developments have concentrated on motion detection that utilises 2D images and enhances functionality. For instance, Microsoft have used motion detection in their consumer products,[28] and similarly motion detection is used in enhanced (smart) surveillance to distinguish non-threatening and threatening behaviour.[29,30] However, the video processing is not entirely reliable because of the variation in environments and low-resolution images challenge the efficacy of detection.[31]

In 2011, the ADDPRIV© project addressed the issues of (a) the use of intelligent image processing algorithms and (b) the social acceptance of surveillance systems, by evaluating existing smart surveillance systems. It concluded that whilst purpose of the project was to enhance privacy, none of the systems reviewed met the project's objectives.[32] Moreover, the demand for smart surveillance and the burgeoning expansion of securitised identity has dichotomised the face recognition discourse whereby on one hand: surveillance in the aftermath of September 11th 2001 has articulated the movement towards identification and classification of individuals

---

[24]This is conjectural as quantifiable risk data may be available but is not germane here. The general trend is towards face recognition, although passwords can be archived or saved to reduce the risks of hacking or forgetfulness.

[25]Other biometrics such as fingerprints or voice recognition have also been tried, mainly to log-on to protected devices (mobile phones and tablet computers) without using a password.

[26]Apple; see Dormehl (2014).

[27]Chapter 2.

[28]See Soper (2017).

[29]See Weiming et al. (2004).

[30]See Paul et al. (2013), pp. 12–13.

[31]*ibid.*

[32]ADDPRIV (2011), p. 8; 69.

suspected as terrorists; and on the other hand presents itself as a means of streamlining access to online services and potentially increase personal productivity and security.[33] There is also the possibility of convergence, because:

> [C]onsumer applications of biometrics may help people feel more comfortable not only using biometrics themselves, but also being subject to institutionalized forms of biometric registration and coming into contact with larger-scale biometric systems [such as smart surveillance] on a regular basis... [Therefore, it may] seem less like an invasion of privacy and more like obvious and necessary measures being instituted for their own protection.[34]

Hence, the prospect of submission towards a panoptic indexicality resembling the late nineteenth century's pursuit for representation, is analogous to Tagg's[35] view that photography and other technological advances empowered and increased State authority.[36] The camera was merely the device that provided the means to that end, and without its use to record evidence, photography may have remained a social activity unconnected with State power, but instead of being thus closeted "the power of the apparatuses of the local state which deploy it and guarantee the authority of the images it constructs to stand as evidence or register a truth"[37] becomes the driving force for advancing new technology.

From this perspective the partnerships between the State authorities and the technocrats who market and supply their face recognition modalities, are the current incarnations of their predecessors. Though unlike the late nineteenth century, the scope for a panoptic society has expanded, because the limitations of labour intensive photography have been replaced by automated systems that utilise the social aspects of photography that have created the human interface between State and individual power. Consequently, such convergence has generated post Snowden anxieties that have required calming whilst also justifying the need for increased vigilance.[38]

Before considering these anxieties, another technological development is likely to enhance face recognition and the concomitant smart surveillance. This development is evolving from Ekman and Friesen's 'Facial Action Coding System' (FACS).[39] Originally their system was devised to standardise facial expressions to eliminate inaccuracies and variables of "human-observer-based-methods"[40] used in psychology for behavioural research to investigate emotion. Given that potential and the political impetus to increase the effectiveness of face recognition and smart surveillance the ability to analyse emotion is marketed as a deception detection tool[41] which

---

[33]Gates (2011), pp. 100–101.

[34]*ibid* (2011), p. 136.

[35]Tagg (1988).

[36]*ibid* pp. 62–64.

[37]*ibid* p. 64.

[38]See President Obama (2014).

[39]Cited by Gates (2011), p. 168 *op cit.*

[40]*ibid* p. 169.

[41]Emotional Intelligence Academy.

awaits automation. In the meantime the US Transportation Security Administration (TSA) deploy 'Behaviour Detection Officers' who use FACS to "Screen[ing] Passengers by Observation Techniques"[42]; however this so-called SPOT programme initiated in 2007, was reviewed by the US Government Accountability Office (GAO) in 2013 and reported that the programme had been unsuccessful because the evidence did not support the use of behavioural indicators since a review of "over 400 studies over 60 years" found that using SPOT techniques was the same or only slightly better than chance.[43]

To overcome the failure of human observation automating FACS is regarded as potential solution.[44] In 2006 Ekman[45] predicted that such automation would be possible by 2008. This has yet to materialise. Although the University of California (San Diego) has invented an 'Automated Facial Action Coding System' for licensing and subsequent commercialisation[46]; the quest for a viable system is paradigmatic of motion detection and smart surveillance, but there will also be another variable when false error rates are compounded by the complexities of converging systems. Nevertheless, until the scepticism highlighted in the GAO report is substantively rebutted, the ability to identify behaviour remains elusive and the scepticism justified. Meanwhile the need to efficiently screen travellers continues to exercise the Department of Homeland Security's (DHS) strategists and to that end the 'Apex Air Entry and Exit Re-Engineering' (AEER) programme has been devised to screen travellers' entry and departure from the US using face recognition technology to verify identity.[47] These two programmes highlight the frontiers of the security discourse; the former purportedly offers a means of pre-emptive intervention without the need for identity verification, and the latter is expected to identify imposters if there is a mismatch between the entry and exit presentations; but unlike FACS, AEER is likely to succeed because the variables are controllable and measurable.

11.4.1 Data and the Human Interface

The anxieties that Snowden's revelations engendered concern issues of confidentiality and privacy and the subsequent likelihood of unexpected transparency when personal informational traffic flows are subjected to such scrutiny. To prevent this, resilient encryption protocols are recommended if the Internet is to remain open and free from interference. But given the need to surveille Internet traffic for potential

[42]Gates (2011), *op cit* p. 180.

[43]GAO (2013).

[44]Gates (2011), *op cit* p. 181.

[45]*ibid*; Ekman (2006).

[46]UC San Diego (2007).

[47]DHS Science and Technology Directorate (n.d.).

threats, such advice is rather ironic when it comes from government officials.[48] Therefore, whatever the level of encryption the methods are not entirely secure, because the resources available to government agencies will exceed personal cyber-security if the legislative framework permits the necessary counter-measures.[49] However, although communication service providers assure their customers of the inherent security of the service,[50] 25,229 respondents to the 2019 Centre for International Governance Innovation Global Survey on Internet Security and Trust, 53% were concerned about their online privacy, 66% and 61% were concerned about domestic and foreign Government agencies (respectively) secretly monitoring their online activities.[51] Whilst the survey quantifies the anxieties related to internet use there are only limited defences against intrusive government activities that can be reasonably taken; conversely governments need to take some measures for security purposes despite the concerns. However, balancing the concerns and government paternalism is problematic if people fear intrusion and if the only recourse is a life insulated from the public gaze by being confined to one's home and disconnecting telecommunication devices[52]; even when this is possible the ubiquity of CCTV and smart surveillance reconnects citizens to the watchers' gaze when venturing beyond the confines of one's home; and indeed for many the practicalities of disconnecting telecommunication devices would isolate them from their economic and social networks, comprising 4.4 billion users worldwide, of which 719.4 million are in Europe.[53] Consequently, in their 2015 report[54] the Intelligence & Security Committee of Parliament (ISCP) noted the volume and the enormity of the task to monitor communications and acknowledged that both the bulk collection of data, and where necessary the examination of targeted individuals is permissible,[55] subject to the Regulation and Investigatory Powers Act (RIPA).[56]

Nevertheless, although the legislative authority exists, privacy campaigners oppose bulk interception because of its infringement on privacy[57] even at the expense of security and the prevention of harm; their opposition therefore is at odds with Parliament's utilitarianism and questions about the greater good. The committee's new understanding of the constitutive value of bulk interception accords with my contention that images are both communication data and content-derived information analogously described in Chap. 7.[58] Subsequently, when face

[48]See Collier (2014).

[49]See Anonymous (2015), ISCP (2015).

[50]For example: Apple 'Privacy Policy'.

[51]CIGI-Ipsos (2019).

[52]Chesterman (2011), p. 244.

[53]Internet World Stats (2019).

[54]ISCP (2015).

[55]*ibid* paras 90–91, p. 33.

[56]*ibid* para 80, p. 32; and the later Investigatory Powers Act 2016 §136.

[57]*ibid* paras 92–94 p. 35.

[58]Section 7.6 Data Protection and Face Recognition.

recognition modalities (shortcomings withstanding) are factored into the practice of bulk interception the activity enhances the panoptical state collectively described in Chap. 4, which arguably stimulates the privacy campaigners' opposition,[59] irrespective of the potential threat when communication data includes identifiers such as user name and location.[60] However, since the government has a duty to protect its citizens, reducing security or preventing legitimate surveillance for the sake of maintaining privacy is potentially absurd, and indeed contentious. Yet, this should not devalue or be at the expense of privacy but is rather the exercise of protective liberty for the many, that balances paternalistic responsibilities against the personal autonomy of the few.[61]

11.5 Predicting Social Concerns and Reactions

Whilst the Parliamentary Committee's concern was commendable, their purpose was to examine the veracity of Snowden's revelations to review the current legal framework, and to further recommend a new legal framework that legitimises and regulates the intelligence community's activities.[62] This would be provided by an Intelligence Services Bill which would consolidate the intelligence and security related provisions contained in the existing, but separate legislation.[63]

In Chaps. 7 and 8, some aspects and provisions of these various Acts have been discussed. Whether the new Bill will materialise remains to be seen. Nevertheless, the social concern has also stimulated changes in attitude towards privacy and intrusion, and has and will alter behaviour in advance of any parliamentary response to Snowden. Concurrent with the ISCP Report, but unrelated to it, is the 2015 Market Research Society's (MRS) White Paper: "Private Lives? Putting the consumer at the heart of the privacy debate".[64] Their report focuses on the uses of personal (and therefore private) data that companies collect from their customers, for instance: free Apps that monetise an individual's data by selling the data to third (often unknown) parties. The MRS also note that peoples' lives are increasingly 'datafied' and that datafication is of greater benefit to the institutions. These benefits according to the MRS include: more sales, improved security risk assessments, and fraud prevention. Moreover, the disclosure of personal information supposedly improves customer experience such as specific marketing, which may or may not be progress. Because they caution that, although people may have become used to disclosing personal information in exchange for the benefits, there is a paucity of discussion about the

[59]ISCP *op cit*: para 94, p. 35.

[60]*ibid* at AAA, p. 105.

[61]See Sect. 9.3 Liberty and State Power.

[62]ISCP *op cit* paras ii & v, p. 1.

[63]*ibid* at XX, p. 103.

[64]MRS Reports (2015).

implications of surrendering so much information and the precise meaning of privacy.

The apparent notion that people may, or indeed, have become used to disclosing personal information is the likely effect of compulsory visibility[65] which Dixon[66] is vehemently opposed to and critical of; and the assumption that the benefits are second-order compliant is misguided, now that individuals are rescinding their data because the benefits of disclosure are unclear or untrustworthy. Without adequate trust frameworks that encapsulate second-order compliant terms and conditions that ameliorate the loss of trust, the potential for less engagement is compounded. Even as it is possible to limit personal 'datafication' by disclosing less information (where appropriate) face recognition accessible resources and devices erode anonymity when identities can be confirmed from other open sources that may not be possible to edit.

The antidote to passivity or indeed the laissez-faire attitude towards disclosure and/or bulk interception would be informed consent. Instead of assuming consent, either by plebiscite or agreeing to terms and conditions, a proactive social contract is necessary to frame the choices more openly and progress towards greater transparency whereby societal interests are better served.[67] For Chesterman a new social contract is predicated by transparency because it "help[s] educate the public so that better choices are made concerning the diminishing sphere of privacy. Education is essential if the consent of the population is to be informed".[68] Hence, he appears to accept that the diminishment of privacy is inevitable if people are not educated, which arguably accords with the increasing importance of privacy reported in the MRS White Paper. The stimulus for this increase is the loss of control felt by 70% of respondents to a YouGov survey.[69] Yet this suggests that the loss of privacy is unwittingly self-inflicted by naivety or insufficient diligence, but which can be remedied by self-awareness, because privacy relates to selfhood and the ability to be cognitively evaluating and independent.[70]

Therefore, the ability to be 'cognitively evaluating' is an essential feature of Dworkin's description of autonomy that is incompatible with the loss of control when limited choices of access dictate the level of disclosure, especially when a prerequisite of access is the surrender of information and the capitulation of autonomy. Although the data is likely to be secure and confidential and possibly disembodied, the converging silos of metadata, content and images are the basis of a maturing panoptical surveillance society that de-anonymises individuals.

Anonymity and privacy are synonymous in terms of knowledgeability when describing reclusiveness or strangers. However, when anonymity and privacy are

---

[65]See Chap. 6.

[66]Dixon (2010).

[67]Chesterman (2011), pp. 248–250.

[68]*ibid* p. 258.

[69]MRS (2015), p. 8.

[70]*ibid* p. 12.

separate components, by separating the person from their data, they remain anonymous; but when anonymity and privacy converge privacy remains (by reason of confidentiality) and anonymity is lost. The outcome is increased loss of control that is likely to become unremitting in scope and complexity given the political will to drive the agenda towards a mature surveillance society, even when subject to any new legal framework that may legitimise the use of face recognition surveillance modalities.

This has the semblance of Bentham's Panopticon, although the principal purpose of face recognition enhanced surveillance may not necessarily be behaviour modification, but rather the de-anonymisation of persons and the advancement of panopticism and compulsory visibility. Such visibility extends the reach and expansion of government and enterprise agencies, who unless restricted will autocratically presume citizens' consent unless albeit, the conditional 'right to be forgotten' is guaranteed.[71]

11.6 Constitutional Safeguards and Rights

The General Data Protection Regulation 'Right of access' Article 15 provides that:

> The data subject shall have the right to obtain from the controller confirmation as to whether or not personal data concerning him or her are being processed, and where that is the case, access to personal data and the following information [such as]: (. . .)
>
> (a) the purpose of the processing; (b) the categories of personal data concerned; (c) the recipients or categories of recipient to whom the personal data have been or will be disclosed, in particular recipients in third countries or international organisations; . . .(e) the existence of the right to request from the controller rectification or erasure of personal data or restriction of processing of personal data concerning the data subject or to object to such processing; . . .(g) where the personal data are not collected from the data subject, any available information as to their source.[72]

As noted in Chap. 7, a digitally captured image is personal data, but unlike alphanumeric data such as date of birth or an address which can be rectified, an image cannot be rectified as it is a different category of data because of its indexical relationship to the individual at the moment of capture; additionally, although the criteria for rectification includes incompleteness or inaccuracies, these criteria arguably do not apply. However, the image could be erased (deleted) from the database but only if the data controller is accessible, and the reason for doing so complies with the provisions stated in Article 17. Thus, the 'right to be forgotten' is principally associated with accessible personal information found via search engines and the deletion of the links[73] which would subsequently remove the information but only if:

---

[71]GDPR Article 17.

[72]*ibid* Article 15.

[73]*ibid* Article 17(2).

> (a) the personal data are no longer necessary in relation to the purposes for which they were collected or otherwise processed (b) the data subject withdraws consent on which the processing is based according to point (a) of Article 6(1), or point (a) of Article 9(2), and where there is no longer other legal ground for the processing; (c) the data subject objects to the processing of personal data pursuant to Article 21(1) and there are no overriding legitimate grounds for the processing, or the data subject objects to the processing pursuant to Article 21(2); (d) the personal data have been processed unlawfully; (. . .)[74]

Whilst this establishes clear principles, Article 17 is not a charter for reducing the visibility of celebrities in the public domain, as the exemption of 17(3)(a) permits freedom of expression and information; nor is it a charter for hiding criminality as 17 (3)(b) permits the exercise or defence of legal claims. Subject to the UK's interests Article 17 rights are incorporated in the UK Data Protection Act 2018.[75]

However, although celebrities are public figures, their personal information is confidential and the right to freedom of expression and information is contestable, if personal (that is private information) is published.

In Chap. 7 the Campbell and von Hannover scenarios were discussed, and arguably, on one hand, are justification for the increased protection of privacy and confidentiality; but, on the other hand any use of disseminated information that leads to criminals' convictions is not morally equivalent. Herein is the difficulty, ordinarily individuals are neither celebrities nor are they criminals, but the level of transparency and visibility imposed on them is not directly regulated because the expectation of privacy in public and its inversion poses significant challenges to the legislators, given that surveillance is not confined to public places and the tension between private and public space is fluid. This fluidity is potentially accelerated when face recognition systems ubiquitously identify individuals or provide the means of access across data domains, for instance: driver licensing and passports (Chap. 2). The UK Data Protection Act 2018 (DPA) regulates sharing data across domains by standardising compliance; and stipulates whether sharing data is justified and that organisations have the authority to share the data.[76] The earlier Data Protection Act 1998 applied only to the data not the person and therefore did not protect privacy per se,[77,78] conversely ECHR Article 8[79] protects privacy and was invoked by von Hannover (Chap. 7) to prevent publication of photographs and thereby maintain control "of scenes pertaining to family life".[80]

[74]*ibid* Article 17(1).

[75]Data Protection Act 2018 §§43-45.

[76]As per Data Protection Act 1998; see ICO Data Sharing Checklist.

[77]See University of California, Irvine (2011).

[78]Berle (2011), pp. 43–44.

[79]European Convention on Human Rights (and UK Human Rights Act 1998).

[80]Kindt (2013), pp. 192 §347.

11.7 Legal and Regulatory Safeguards

In addition to von Hannover, two other cases illustrate the dichotomy of privacy and confidentiality that relate to the face recognition discourse, because they have included a right to one's own image or at least the right to redress the interference incurred when photographs are taken or distributed without consent, such as Perry (Chap. 7) which rather spans both features of the cases below.

Hence the additional case law applying Article 8 to facial images provides both the backdrop from which protection can be derived and acknowledges autonomy by testing the boundaries of acceptability that are associated with second-order choice and or the nature of legality. For instance:

In *Sciacca v. Italy* 2005,[81] Mrs. Sciacca was prosecuted with others for criminal conspiracy, tax evasion and forgery. These facts were published in the press with a photograph of Mrs. Sciacca that were released by the tax inspectors from their file. The Court (ECtHR) judged that this interference was not "in accordance with the law" because "there was no law which regulated the matter but rather a practice governing the taking of photographs of people under suspicion or arrested". In 2009, after a child was officially photographed in a private clinic by a commercial photographer without parental consent[82] the Court ruled in *Reklos and Davourlis v. Greece*[83] "that there was a breach under Article 8 ECHR for the mere taking and registration of someone's facial image, even without any further use or publication" thus "an effective protection of the right to control one's image implies the need for consent" irrespective of its use.[84] Moreover,

> The Court reiterate[d] that, although the object of Article 8 is essentially that of protecting the individual against arbitrary interference by the public authorities, it does not merely compel the State to abstain from such interference: in addition to this primarily negative undertaking, there may be positive obligations inherent in an effective respect for private or family life. These obligations may involve the adoption of measures designed to secure respect for private life even in the sphere of the relations of individuals between themselves. That also applies to the protection of a person's picture against abuse by others (see Von Hannover v. Germany, no. 59320/00, §57, ECHR 2004-VI).[85]
>
> In addition, the Court finds that it is not insignificant that the photographer was able to keep the negatives of the offending photographs, in spite of the express request of the applicants, who exercised parental authority, that the negatives be delivered up to them. Admittedly, the photographs simply showed a face-on portrait of the baby and did not show the applicants' son in a state that could be regarded as degrading, or in general as capable of infringing his personality rights. However, the key issue in the present case is not the nature, harmless or otherwise, of the applicants' son's representation on the offending photographs, but the fact that the photographer kept them without the applicants' consent. The baby's image was thus

---

[81] Sciacca v. Italy (2006) 43 EHRR 400. Cited by Kindt (2013) *op cit.*

[82] See Hughes (2009), p. 163.

[83] Reklos and Davourlis v. Greece 27 BHRC 420.

[84] Kindt (2013) *op cit* p. 193 §347.

[85] Reklos and Davourlis v. Greece para 35 *op cit.*

> retained in the hands of the photographer in an identifiable form with the possibility of subsequent use against the wishes of the person concerned and/or his parents.[86]

This judgement sets no precedent that would dismiss the legitimate use of photography in criminal investigations, such as occurred in *Lupker and others v. The Netherlands*,[87] because:

> (1) the photographs "were not taken in a way which constitutes an intrusion upon the applicants' privacy", (2) the photographs were "kept in police or other official archives since they had been either provided voluntarily in connection with applications for a passport or a driving licence or taken by the police in connection with a previous arrest"; and (3) they were used "solely for the purpose of the identification of the offenders in the criminal proceedings against the applicants and there is no suggestion that they have been made available to the general public or used for any other purpose".[88]

The difference between Reklos et al. and Lupker et al. is discernible on the basis that the Court's judgement in Reklos emphasised that:

> [T]he applicants' son did not knowingly or accidentally lay himself open to the possibility of having his photograph taken in the context of an activity that was likely to be recorded or reported in a public manner. On the contrary, the photographs were taken in a place that was accessible only to the doctors and nurses of the clinic ... and the baby's image, recorded by a deliberate act of the photographer, was the sole subject of the offending photographs.[89]

Therefore, the court recognised that the clinic had engaged the services of a commercial photographer without parental permission or any clinical need for the photographs. Furthermore, noting that the plaintiff "did not knowingly or accidentally lay himself open to the possibility of having his photograph taken" and that as these mitigating facts prevailed the Court arguably acknowledged that ECHR article 8 provides protection because their right to privacy and family life (Art 8(1)) was entirely within the scope of the Convention, and therefore the interference permitted in article 8(2) did not apply. On the basis that Article 8 rights are conditional, the Courts' judgements illustrate how the GDPR Articles 15 and 17 balance the right to access against other considerations.

Additionally, balancing the right to privacy and the right to own one's image is problematic given that each can be framed in terms of property which implies ownership and protection, in this context of a person's identity being captured in a photograph.[90] In the former, privacy is breached by intrusion and in the latter by unconsented photography; although these may appear identical—that is without consent—any photography is an intrusion of privacy which depending on the emphasis of the law and its undergirding jurisprudence will frame the remedy accordingly. Generally, those remedies and safeguards are evident in Article 8 ECHR, and were effectively applied in Reklos and Davourlis:

---

[86] *ibid* para 42.

[87] Lupker and others v. The Netherlands. Cited by Vermeulen (2014).

[88] *ibid* § 5.

[89] Reklos and Davourlis v. Greece, para 37 *op cit.*

[90] See Chap. 7.

> A person's image constitutes one of the chief attributes of his or her personality, as it reveals the person's unique characteristics and distinguishes the person from his or her peers. The right to the protection of one's image is thus one of the essential components of personal development and presupposes the right to control the use of that image. Whilst in most cases the right to control such use involves the possibility for an individual to refuse publication of his or her image, it also covers the individual's right to object to the recording, conservation and reproduction of the image by another person. As a person's image is one of the characteristics attached to his or her personality, its effective protection presupposes, in principle and in circumstances such as those of the present case (see paragraph 37 above), obtaining the consent of the person concerned at the time the picture is taken and not simply if and when it is published. Otherwise an essential attribute of personality would be retained in the hands of a third party and the person concerned would have no control over any subsequent use of the image.[91]

This frames the Court's judgement to the right to one's own image from the onset in terms of personality, it is the permanence of personality that prohibits the taking of photographs without consent and also limits the use of consented photographs. The limits inferred here also apply to face recognition modalities and will be discussed below. Meanwhile, the judgement appears to imply that copyright of personality and indeed images is applicable which accords with Article 10 of the Belgian Copyright Act that states that "the author or the owner of a portrait or any other person who is in possession of a portrait or as such at his or her disposal is not entitled to reproduce it or communicate it to the public without the consent of the person portrayed".[92] Framing the decision from this perspective resonates with Samuelson's[93] moral rights approach where "as with the moral right of authors the granting of a moral right to individuals in their personal data might protect personality based interests that individuals have in their own data".[94]

A feature of copyright law is the delineation and distinction between authorship and ownership that are paradigmatically apparent in the foregoing judgement. In terms of copyright for instance: commissioning a painting or photograph does not assign copyright and therefore reproducing the image or exploiting the work is not permitted; with this purview the Court's judgement that "an essential attribute of personality would be retained in the hands of a third party" without protection "and the person concerned would have no control over any subsequent use of the image" is arguably applicable to the regulation of face recognition enhanced surveillance and also confers with Velu's expressed view:

> that the right to respect for private life covered a miscellany of rights that protected the individual against (1) attacks on his physical or mental integrity or his moral or intellectual freedom, (2) attacks on his honour and reputation and similar torts, (3) the use of his name, identity or likeness, (4) being spied upon, watched or harassed, (5) the disclosure of information protected by the duty of professional secrecy.[95]

---

[91]Reklos and Davourlis v. Greece, para 40 *op cit.*

[92]Kindt (2013), p. 194 §349 *op cit.*

[93]Samuelson (1999).

[94]*ibid* p. 10.

[95]Velu (1970) quoted by Loukaidēs L. Cited by Vermeulen (2014), p. 19 *op cit.*

Velu's analysis predates data protection and human rights law,[96] but which can be detected in the present legislation and ensuing jurisprudence in Reklos and Davourlis paragraph 40.

The foregoing has sketched the legal and regulatory safeguards that have emerged from national and European case law. Although the ECtHR jurisprudence has evolved, their judgments may not be adopted nationally because of the variations within the European states. English case law, for example has yet to establish a precedent for developing privacy law per se despite Campbell and Mosley,[97] and therefore is very different from French law that protects privacy holistically by cohering intrusion and confidentiality in civil and penal codes.[98,99,100]

A holistic approach to regulating the use of face recognition is possible when each of Velu's principles are operational by common law: such as the duty of confidence; or by statute that transforms moral rights into substantive positive freedoms (liberty), thus protecting personality and indeed self-hood. This accords with Solove's[101] contention that the "value of protecting the individual is a social one" and that "[w]hen the law protects the individual, it does so not just for the individual's sake but for the sake of society",[102] thereby recognising the need to balance individual and societal values that respect dignity and maintain self-hood. This could be achieved by acknowledging that data has become a commodity, and that the value of the data potentially exceeds the value of the data subject to the degree that commercial and governmental objectives have a dehumanising effect in their pursuit of securitising identity or categorising individuals for representational purposes.[103] Ironically, this potentially decreases effectiveness of the overall project in proportion to the cynicism that it engenders, such as was the impact of Snowden and the subsequent response from Parliament's Intelligence & Security Committee in 2015, which recognised that:

> While the UK public appear to – for the most part – be supportive of the Agencies, the National Security Agency (NSA) leaks have led to allegations, myths and misconceptions about the Agencies and these have damaged that trust. Many witnesses to this Inquiry felt that the Agencies need to move 'out of the shadows' in order to retain the confidence of the public over the longer term.[104]

---

[96]Which followed the Universal Declaration of Human Rights 1948 and the Convention for the Protection of Human Rights and Fundamental Freedoms 1950.

[97]Chapter 7.

[98]Laurent (2013).

[99]France: Penal Code - Article 226-1.

[100]See Logeais and Schroeder (1998).

[101]Solove (2011).

[102]*ibid* p. 50.

[103]Tagg (1988) *op cit.*

[104]ISCP *op cit* para 277.

To restore trust requires transparency and accountability which may be further enhanced with the regulation of data acquisition not in only in terms of protection but also by acknowledging individuals' moral rights.

11.8 Regulating the Commoditisation of Data

Acknowledging that data is a commodity challenges the status quo because whilst UK data protection law defines the parameters of legitimate data processing it does not equate at present to a rights-based duty such as is evident in the ECHR Article 8. This dichotomy is most apparent when considering the nature of face recognition enabled surveillance or identity security systems or commercial applications, which during their accrual of reified image data dehumanises or depersonalises the individual data subject; whereby, ultimately the subject becomes a template for future reference or a marketing target.[105] Reification of the image initiates the loss of anonymity whenever the image data is aggregated across data platforms; herein is the potential for misuse, if data protection does not clearly define the parameters of legitimate processing or protect the value of personality or acknowledge selfhood above the monetary value of the data held.

Generally, data is monetised when information is sold to third-parties without the data subjects' consent or knowledge. This is not the same as sharing information for screening or investigative purposes which are typically ethically justifiable, for instance safeguarding children or vulnerable adults, fraud prevention, or driver and motor vehicle matters. Accordingly, the United States 18 U.S.C. 2721—'Prohibition on Release and Use of Certain Personal Information from State Motor Vehicle Records',[106] permits the disclosure of the information, and the UK Driver and Vehicle Licensing Agency informs drivers that their information can be shared when there is reasonable cause for disclosure.[107] However, whatever the grounds for disclosure, when data is sold to those applying for it, this may in some contexts exceed consent and be unlawful.[108] Moreover, since the data is derived from drivers' personal details that are generally voluntarily provided, any unconsented secondary use of the data denies choice in the pursuit of furthering the agencies' ends, if reasonable cause is dubious. Therefore, since the licensing data dossiers include an identity photograph in response to this asymmetry another approach to regulating and safeguarding data is required and will be considered in the final chapter.

---

[105] *Vis-à-vis* 11.4 above.

[106] United States Crimes and Criminal Procedure 18 USC §2721 Chapter 123.

[107] DVLA.

[108] Adams (2011). From a UK and EU perspective, how similar activity plays-out in the new data regulation landscape remains to be seen.

References

Adams B (2011) Legal Theft: Florida DMV Makes Millions Legally Selling Personal Information. https://www.theblaze.com/news/2011/07/29/legal-theft-florida-dmv-makes-millions-legally-selling-personal-information. Accessed 30 Aug 2019

ADDPRIV (2011) Automatic Data Relevancy Discrimination for a Privacy-sensitive video surveillance. 'Review of existing smart video surveillance systems capable of being integrated with ADDPRIV project'. Deliverable 2.1 Gdansk. pp. 8, 69 http://www.addpriv.eu/uploads/public%20_deliverables/149%2D%2DADDPRIV_20113107_WP2_GDANSK_Scoreboard_R11.pdf. Cached on Google 30 August 2019. The project closed in 2014, see CORDIS EU research results https://cordis.europa.eu/project/rcn/98125/factsheet/en. Accessed 30 Aug 2019

Anonymous (2015) GCHQ will circumvent encryption no matter what. Here's how. http://www.wired.co.uk/article/how-spies-will-circumvent-encryption-anyway. Accessed 30 Aug 2019

Apple. https://www.apple.com/uk/privacy/approach-to-privacy/. Accessed 28 Aug 2019

Apple: privacy policy: https://www.apple.com/legal/privacy/en-ww/. Accessed 30 Aug 2019

Arthur C (2010) Why Minority Report was spot on. The Guardian, 16th June 2010. http://www.theguardian.com/technology/2010/jun/16/minority-report-technology-comes-true. Accessed 28 Aug 2019

BBC News (2013) Newham Council wants to add to its 959 CCTV cameras. http://www.bbc.co.uk/news/uk-england-london-21822080. Accessed 28 Aug 2019

Berle I (2011) Privacy and confidentiality: what's the difference? J Visual Commun 34(1):43–44 (March 2011) https://www.tandfonline.com/doi/abs/10.3109/17453054.2011.550845?journalCode=ijau20. Accessed 30 Aug 2019

Brey P (2004) Ethical aspects of facial recognition systems in public places. J Inf Commun Ethics Soc 2(2):97–109. https://doi.org/10.1108/14779960480000246. Accessed 28 Aug 2019

Chesterman S (2011) One nation under surveillance: a new social contract to defend freedom without sacrificing liberty. Oxford University Press, Oxford, p 244

CIGI-Ipsos (2019) CIGI-Ipsos Global Survey on Internet Security and Trust. www.cigionline.org/internet-survey-2019. Accessed 30 Aug 2019. For comparison see also CIGI (The Centre for International Governance Innovation) and IPSOS '83% of Global Internet users believe affordable access to the Internet should be a basic Human Right'. November 24, 2014. https://www.cigionline.org/internet-survey-2014. Accessed 30 Aug 2019

Cognitec (2013) Face Recognition SDK Now Available for Android. http://www.cognitec.com/news-reader/product-release-7-2013.html. Accessed 28 Aug 2019

Collier K (2014) America's top spy department: You need better encryption. Daily Dot, March 2014. https://www.salon.com/2014/03/06/u_s_intelligence_officials_nevermind_us_maybe_you_need_encryption_partner/. Accessed 30 Aug 2019

Data Protection Act 2018, §§43–45. https://services.parliament.uk/bills/2017-19/dataprotection.html. Accessed 30 Aug 2019

DHS Science and Technology Directorate. 'Apex Air Entry and Exit Re-Engineering' http://www.dhs.gov/sites/default/files/publications/Apex%20Air%20Entry%20and%20Exit%20Re-Engineering-AEER-508_0.pdf. Accessed 30 Aug 2019

Dixon P (2010) The One-Way-Mirror-Society Privacy Implications of the new Digital Signage Networks. http://www.worldprivacyforum.org/wp-content/uploads/2013/01/onewaymirrorsocietyfs.pdf. Accessed 30 2019

Dormehl L (2014) Facial recognition: is the technology taking away your identity? http://www.theguardian.com/technology/2014/may/04/facial-recognition-technology-identity-tesco-ethical-issues. Accessed 28 Aug 2019

Drivers and Vehicles Licensing Agency Release of information from DVLA's registers, p 12. https://www.gov.uk/government/uploads/system/uploads/attachment_data/file/390088/Website-Release_of_information_from_DVLA__2_.pdf. Accessed 30 August 2019

Eggen D (2005) Pre-9/11 Missteps by FBI Detailed. Washington Post. 10 June 2005. http://www.washingtonpost.com/wp-dyn/content/article/2005/06/09/AR2005060902000.html. Accessed 28 Aug 2019

Ekman P (2006) How to Spot a Terrorist. October 29, 2006. http://www.washingtonpost.com/wp-dyn/content/article/2006/10/27/AR2006102701478_2.html. Accessed 30 Aug 2019

Ekman P, Friesen WV (n.d.) Facial Action Coding System. https://www.paulekman.com/product-category/facs/. Accessed 30 Aug 2019

Emotional Intelligence Academy. https://www.eiagroup.com/. Accessed 30 Aug 2019

European Convention on Human Rights. https://echr.coe.int/Pages/home.aspx?p=basictexts&c=. Accessed 23 Sept 2019

Foresight Future Identities (2013) Future identities –changing identities in the UK: the next 10 years. Final Project Report, Government Office for Science, London, p 10 https://www.gov.uk/government/uploads/system/uploads/attachment_data/file/273966/13-523-future-identities-changing-identities-report.pdf. Accessed 28 Aug 2019

France: Penal Code - Article 226-1. Available in English from: http://translate.googleusercontent.com/translate_c?act=url&hl=en&ie=UTF8&prev=_t&rurl=translate.google.com&sl=auto&tl=en&twu=1&u=http://www.legifrance.gouv.fr/affichCodeArticle.do%3FidArticle%3DLEGIARTI000006417929%26cidTexte%3DLEGITEXT000006070719%26dateTexte%3D20090415%26fastPos%3D6%26fastReqId%3D381967113%26oldAction%3DrechCodeArticle&usg=ALkJrhjvqSiy3zh99zR29fjKFSaeFR0oAQ. Accessed 30 Aug 2019

GAO (2013) Aviation Security: TSA Should Limit Future Funding for Behavior Detection Activities. https://www.gao.gov/products/GAO-14-159. Accessed 30 Aug 2019

Gates KA (2011) Our biometric future: facial recognition and the culture of surveillance. New York University Press, New York, p 1

GDPR. (General Data Protection Regulation) Article 17. https://eur-lex.europa.eu/legal-content/EN/TXT/?qid=1528874672298&uri=CELEX%3A32016R0679. Accessed 30 Aug 2019

Home Office (2013) Surveillance Camera Code of Practice, June 2013. https://www.gov.uk/government/uploads/system/uploads/attachment_data/file/282774/SurveillanceCameraCodePractice.pdf. Accessed 28 Aug 2019

Hughes K (2009) Photographs in public places and privacy. J Media Law 2:159–171, 163. http://stu.westga.edu/~cbailey4/databin/photos_public_privacy.pdf. Accessed 30 Aug

ICO (2014) Information Commissioner's Office. In the picture: A data protection code of practice for surveillance cameras and personal information Version 1, 15/10/2014. https://ico.org.uk/media/1542/cctv-code-of-practice.pdf. Accessed 28 Aug 2019

ICO (n.d.) Data Sharing Checklist. https://ico.org.uk/media/for-organisations/documents/1067/data_sharing_checklists.pdf. Accessed 30 Aug 2019

Intelligence and Security Committee of Parliament (ISCP 2015) Privacy & Security: A modern & transparent legal framework. http://isc.independent.gov.uk/news-archive/12march2015. Accessed 30 Aug 2019

Internet World Stats (2019). http://www.internetworldstats.com/stats.htm. Accessed 30 Aug 2019

Key Lemon 'Oasis Face'. http://www.discoversdk.com/products/keylemon#/overview. Accessed 28 Aug 2019

Kindt EJ (2013) Privacy and data protection issues of biometric applications. Springer, Heidelberg, p 192 §347

Laurent O (2013) Protecting the right to photograph, or not to be photographed. The New York Times, April 23, 2013. http://lens.blogs.nytimes.com/2013/04/23/paris-city-of-rights/?_r=0. Accessed 30 Aug 2019

Logeais E, Schroeder J-B (1998) The French right of image: an Amiguous concept protecting the human persona. http://digitalcommons.lmu.edu/cgi/viewcontent.cgi?article=1366&context=elr. Accessed 30 Aug 2019

London Borough of Newham (2015) Responding to a Freedom of Information request (FOI/E22073) "The London Borough of Newham does not use face recognition technology. It is understood there was a short trial of face recognition cameras in the borough many years ago, but we no longer hold any recorded historical information on this". Received 16th March 2015

Loukaidēs L (1995) Essays on the developing law of human rights (international studies in human rights). Martinus Nijhoff Publishers

Lupker and others v. The Netherlands, 18395/91, 07/12/1992. http://hudoc.echr.coe.int/eng?i=001-1433. Accessed 30 Aug 2019

Lyon D (2008) (1st published 2003) Surveillance after September 11. Polity Press, Cambridge, p 8

Mohammed Atta, image available online from Getty Images: https://www.gettyimages.co.uk/license/51093486. Accessed 28 Aug 2019

MRS Reports (2015) Private lives? Putting the consumer at the heart of the privacy debate. https://www.mrs.org.uk/pdf/private%20lives.pdf. Accessed 30 Aug 2019

Obama B (2014) Remarks by the president on review of signals intelligence. http://www.whitehouse.gov/the-press-office/2014/01/17/remarks-president-review-signals-intelligence. Accessed 30 Aug 2019

Parliamentary Office for Science and Technology (2002) 'CCTV 2002 Number 175' http://www.parliament.uk/briefing-papers/POST-PN-175.pdf. Accessed 28 Aug 2019

Paul M, Haque SME, Chakraborty S (2013) Human detection in surveillance videos and its applications - a review. EURASIP J Adv Signal Proc 176:12–13. https://doi.org/10.1186/1687-6180-2013-176. Accessed 28 Aug 2019

Reklos and Davourlis v. Greece 1234/05, [2009] ECHR 200, 27 BHRC 420, [2009] EMLR 16. Council of Europe/European Court of Human Rights – Conseil de l'Europe/Cour européenne des droits de l'homme. http://hudoc.echr.coe.int/sites/eng/pages/search.aspx?i=001-90617. Accessed 30 Aug 2019

Samuelson P (1999) Property as intellectual property. Stanf Law Rev pp 1126–1173 52 Stan. L. Rev. 1125, p 1146–1151. https://works.bepress.com/pamela_samuelson/. Accessed 30 Aug 2019

Sciacca v. Italy (2006) 43 EHRR 400 s29-30. Case summary available from: http://www.5rb.com/case/sciacca-v-italy/. Accessed 30 Aug 2019

Solove DJ (2011) Nothing to hide: the false trade off between privacy and security. Yale University Press, New Haven

Soper T (2017) Goodbye, Kinect: Microsoft stops manufacturing motion-sensing Xbox camera. https://www.geekwire.com/2017/goodbye-kinect-microsoft-stops-manufacturing-motion-sensing-xbox-camera/. Accessed 28 Aug 2019

Stikeman A (2001) Recognising the enemy. Technology Review, December 2001. https://www.technologyreview.com/s/401300/recognizing-the-enemy/. Accessed 28 Aug 2019

Tagg J (1988) The burden of representation: essays on photographies and histories. Palgrave Macmillan, Basingstoke

Trepp P (2019) Face recognition: the future of personal identity management. https://www.facefirst.com/blog/face-recognition-the-future-of-personal-identity-management/. Accessed 28 Aug 2019

UK Human Rights Act 1998. http://www.legislation.gov.uk/ukpga/1998/42/contents. Accessed 23 Sept 2019

United States Title 18—Crimes and Criminal Procedure 18 USC §2721 Chapter 123 —Prohibition on release and use of certain personal information from state motor vehicle records. http://www.gpo.gov/fdsys/pkg/USCODE-2011-title18/pdf/USCODE-2011-title18-partI-chap123-sec2721.pdf; and https://www.law.cornell.edu/uscode/text/18/2721. Accessed 30 Aug 2019

University of California, Irvine (2011) Privacy vs. Confidentiality: What is the Difference? UCI Researchers (Summer) 2011. Listed as 'privacy-confidentiality-hrp.pdf'. https://www.research.uci.edu/cascade/compliance/human-research-protections/docs/. Accessed 30 Aug 2019

University of California, San Diego (2007) Office of Innovation and Commercialisation. Automated Facial Action Coding System. http://techtransfer.universityofcalifornia.edu/NCD/22278.html. Accessed 30 Aug 2019

Van Zoonen L et al (2012) Scenarios of Identity Management in the Future Report. IMPRINTS (Public responses to Identity Management Practices & Technologies). Department of Social Sciences, University of Loughborough, Leicester UK. http://www.imprintsfutures.org/assets/images/pdfs/Scenarios_of_identity_management_in_the_future_Report.pdf. Accessed 28 Aug 2019

Vermeulen M (2014) European University Institute: SURVEILLE. Surveillance: Ethical Issues, Legal Limitations, and Efficiency. https://surveille.eui.eu/wp-content/uploads/sites/19/2015/04/D4.7-The-scope-of-the- right-to-privacy-in-public-places.pdf. Accessed 30 Aug 2019

Visionics Corporation, 'FaceIt® will Enhance & Compliment your CCTV Surveillance System' http://valy.1ka.eu/ruzne/tash/tash.gn.apc.org/Visionics_Tech2.pdf. Accessed 28 Aug 2019

Weiming H, Tieniu T, Liang W, Maybank S (2004) A survey on visual surveillance of object motion and behaviors. IEEE Trans Syst Man Cybern Part C Appl Rev 34(3). https://ieeexplore.ieee.org/document/1310448. Accessed 28 Aug 2019

Chapter 12
Conclusion

Abstract This chapter summarises some of the key issues raised. Especially as error free face recognition technology and other biometric technologies have become a major pursuit for technology companies as they seek to perfect their products to satisfy commercial and government expectations. Such expectations will require justifying, since the data ecosystems are evolving, and new ways of thinking become necessary. For instance, data ownership and rights, and how the democratising of technology has started to challenge the status quo. Additionally, the right to image ownership is an issue, that like Cinderella is in need of recognition, if data protection law is to fully acknowledge the status of personal identifiable images.

12.1 Face Recognition Technology and the Right to Personal Image Ownership

Error free face recognition technology and other biometric technologies have become a major pursuit for technology companies as they seek to perfect their products to satisfy commercial and government expectations. This drive for flawlessness coupled with the anxieties to successfully create products that can help detect and prevent crime and protect citizens from various harms has stimulated a concern for individual privacy and the counterbalancing need for accountability and transparency. However, the burgeoning use of FRT in some of its applications requires a new approach to freedom of choice if that freedom is to be valued and sustained. To that end, establishing the right of personal image and data ownership in the UK and elsewhere will enhance that freedom by recognising the value of consent and consolidate the disparities discussed above.

I. Berle, *Face Recognition Technology*, Law, Governance and Technology Series 41,
https://doi.org/10.1007/978-3-030-36887-6_12

12.2 Data Ownership: A New Legal and Moral Rights Framework

The disparate and conflicting arguments associated with face recognition technology and its various applications discussed either directly or paradigmatically have a common denominator. Common or central to my concern is the failure of the discourse to recognise the centrality of autonomy and acknowledge selfhood that Article 8 ECHR invokes. From the UK perspective to apply the principles of Article 8 rights requires support from other existing legislation and case law that currently recognises certain moral rights to autonomy and selfhood. For instance, the meaning of private information has been determined in *Campbell v MGN*,[1] *von Hannover v Germany*,[2] and in *Mosley v News Group Newspapers Ltd*.[3] These are relevant in respect of face recognition for two reasons. Firstly, they broaden the discourse of privacy to include the misuse of photographs and the intrusive use of covert cameras or similar imaging devices.

Secondly, because Campbell's photograph was ostensibly evidence of rehabilitative treatment which, although to some extent is within the ambit of healthcare, her claim presents a suitable precedent for engaging Article 8(1) for there to be a cohesive and consistent approach for redressing the misuse of photographs such as might occur on social networks. Although these cases are landmarks in the public interest versus confidentiality discourse and exceed the scope here,[4] they are nevertheless significant because of their association with the loss of personal control. The disclosure of information breaches privacy in these cases; however non-disclosure of information is still a breach of privacy because the information was obtained without consent such as was analogously evident in *Reklos and Davourlis*.[5] Furthermore, the separation of personal identifiable images from the person denies choice and diminishes autonomy whenever facial images are captured involuntarily.

This loss of control, I contend can be rectified if the 'right to one's own image' is recognised in UK law. Arguably the current absence of this right is archaic. It is likely that the dissociation of identity images from alpha-numeric data is historically based on the disconnection of text-based information from film and print generated photographic representation.[6] The two are associated only in terms of data protection when digital images are included in data dossiers as personal data. If the data is

[1]Campbell v MGN Limited.

[2]Von Hannover v. Germany.

[3]Mosley v News Group Newspapers Ltd.

[4]See Stanley (2008).

[5]Reklos and Davourlis v. Greece.

[6]Before digital photography became routine, photography used film and print processes. The resultant prints would be filed with the respective documentation. But, the Data Protection Act 1998 did not include photographs, nor did it adequately define consent. However, the GDPR and the UK Data Protection Act 2018 requires consent where it 'signifies agreement to the processing of personal data relating to him or her'. Therefore, if photographs are included in the data or are to be

anonymised, it is beyond the scope of the GDPR and the Data Protection Act 2018 (DPA), and consequently this further dissociates ownership by not attributing any rights to the image even when the data is allegedly anonymised. Given that the data subject can be identified using face recognition software, an anonymised[7] image becomes oxymoronic and is therefore no longer anonymous, and arguably is protected by the data regulations.

The circularity of this argument may at first glance seem rather facile, but my contention is intensified when the misuse of the image does not constitute a breach of confidence or privacy because it is isolated from the alpha-numeric components that comprise personal information, whether anonymised or not. However, if misuse is only defined as unauthorised disclosure, data protection does not apply because nothing is disclosed in an unidentified image, but where the image is used to verify information, protection is applicable. Therefore, a further circularity of this argument rests on the dichotomy between data protection and privacy that are, or have been potentially, separated in UK law. The 'right to one's own image' resolves this separation by attributing moral and legal rights that are similar to copyright, thus by adopting this strategy second-order choices are recognised and acknowledged, and additionally confers the right to protect anonymised information. And since both General Data Protection Regulation (GDPR)[8] and the DPA[9] require data controllers and processors to be cognisant of data provenance, by default images are protected; yet, the potential for re-identification is possible when separate databases are combined, and the provenance of the images is unverified.[10]

Whilst the notion of copyrighting personal data is unusual, since the UK Copyright, Designs and Patent Act 1988 (CDPA) affirms both authorship[11] and ownership[12] of original works, its provisions are paradigmatically applicable on the basis that the data subject is the author and owner of the information provided. Moreover, the information is generally provided voluntarily, and the subsequent use consented to. In these terms, the data controllers would be licensed to disclose information subject to the provisions and permissible contractual arrangements, this would alleviate the complexities of anonymisation because the modified CDPA would protect the data subject not just the data per se. Furthermore, this is justified by the precedent set by Professors Brian Cox and (the late) Stephen Hawking who have trademarked their names, (presumably because they could not patent their

---

added to existing data, consent is necessary. Generally, otherwise, any photographs that are not included in personal data files remain beyond the scope of data protection law.

[7]That is: an image dissociated from the data subject.

[8]Information Commissioner's Office.

[9]Data Protection Act 2018.

[10]Big Brother Watch (2015), p. 43. Citing Narayanan and Shmatikov (n.d.).

[11]Copyright, Designs and Patents Act 1988, Ch.1 §9(1) (the) '"author", in relation to a work, means the person who creates it'.

[12]*ibid.*

likenesses) to protect their interests from commercial exploitation.[13] Other celebrities have lucrative image rights earned from endorsing products which Viera[14] has reviewed in his analysis of the economics and legalities of such profitable images.[15]

Aside from success, the de facto use of informed consent is another facet that assists this proposal and highlights the earlier 1998 Data Protection Act's[16] deficiencies. For instance, the Information Commissioner's guidance[17] to educational institutions regarding the taking of photographs at events is typical of de facto consent, especially when the guidance is incorporated into local policies and practice and are (latterly) essential for GDPR compliance. For instance, in 2010 one UK university[18] advised that it was necessary to:

> Obtain the subject's consent in writing before photographing [people]; this is the easiest and safest way of proving you have obtained the image fairly and in accordance with the individuals' rights, both key elements of DPA compliance. If consent is inappropriate or not possible then informing people that their photograph is to be taken and explaining how it is to be used should be enough to ensure 'fairness'. To get consent, use the standard image release form.[19] This form ensures that when you collect the image(s) you are not only acquiring their consent, but also telling people what is being collected, why, the limits on processing (use, disclosure and disposal).

Interestingly, in addition to data protection guidelines the university's guidance is indicative of the 'fair practice' principle that is associated with copyright conventions and law which permits limited use of copyrighted material for study or review etcetera.[20] Both copyright and informed consent when combined provide the means and method for my assertion that all identifiable images should be 'owned' by the data subject who will 'license'[21,22] their image for specified uses.[23] However, contrary to privacy rights campaigners, rights to ownership and usage would not exceed other legislative instruments that have precedence over privacy if by due process interference is morally, lawfully and judicially justified such as those

---

[13]See Burrows (2015).

[14]See Viera (1988), pp. 135–162.

[15]Gross (1988), p. vii.

[16]Data Protection Act 1998.

[17]ICO (n.d.).

[18]University of Reading (2010) Guidelines on the collection, use and storage of photographic images. This dates from 2010 (so should not be assumed to reflect a current policy position), (ii) was intended for an HEI audience and (iii) does not constitute legal advice.

[19]*ibid* Consent form for film/video, audio & photography with notice of copyright.

[20]Copyright, Designs and Patents Act 1988, c.48 Part 1, Ch.3.

[21]*ibid* Ch.4 §90.

[22]Licensing implies a contract which is agreed after obtaining consent.

[23]Furthermore, this is analogous to safeguarding policies that schools have adopted to control the photography of children on school premises by parents, relatives or friends. Such policies require that each child's parent or guardian consent to photography prior to an event.

described in the key findings of the Parliamentary Intelligence and Security Committee's Report[24] and comply with HRA 1998 Article 8(2).[25]

The purpose of combining copyright and consent is principally to acknowledge the moral right to self-determination *vis-a-vis* images that had been overlooked in the previous data regulations, and which is missing in the Privacy by Design principles described in Chap. 7. Moreover, the right to copyright creates a quid pro quo between the parties that has hitherto been absent until now; inasmuch that the GDPR requires consent or at least an unambiguous approach to consent where both parties agree to comply.

Additionally, perhaps instead of copyright, of major consideration is the issue of apportioning property rights to 'facial ownership' as the basis for owning one's image. That is, do individuals by right own their faces? If so, we might ask if such a right should not be understood as identical with or similar in important respects to intellectual property rights? We might then consider whether the use of someone's face without consent is plagiarism. Although this might seem an absurd suggestion, the idea that a person's face can be plagiarised is not so far-fetched where such action is considered equivalent to spoofing.[26] Therefore, based on the premise that FRT diminishes personal autonomy, apportioning property rights could redress the balance in favour of supporting it if the concept is framed within the boundaries of a coherent approach to privacy and confidentiality, which is within the scope of the GDPR. This would ameliorate the burgeoning UK privacy case law and create consistency that applies to everyone, and which is not dependent upon celebrities to defend and would obviate the need to trademark their faces. Therefore, since images are commoditised and valuable, the complexities of confidentiality and data ownership in UK law,[27] requires a reappraisal of how personal identifiable images have affected the notion of proprietorship in that they need considering as intellectual property on one hand and confidential information on the other.

12.3 Democratisation of Technology Development

A potential driver for this could be the nascent democratisation of technology that is changing society by conjoining knowledge with power.[28] Generally, this is an asymmetrical relationship because the limitations imposed on individuals' autonomy

---

[24]Intelligence and Security Committee of Parliament (ISCP).

[25]*ibid* p 1, iv iv "...Some rights are not absolute: the right to privacy, for example, is a qualified right – as all the witnesses to our Inquiry accepted – which means that there may be circumstances in which it is appropriate to interfere with that right. In the UK, the legal test is that action can be taken which intrudes into privacy only where it is for a lawful purpose and it can be justified that it is necessary and proportionate to do so".

[26]Chapter 2.

[27]See Stanley (2008).

[28]See Feenberg (2009).

as a form of social control disenfranchises citizens who may wish to have more control of their data and is illustrated in Fig. 4.1 above, in terms of tension between the T1 and T2 boundaries.

Nevertheless, I believe that some point in the near future society will have to confront the issue of the democratisation of technological development. As technology development accelerates with the innovation demands of 'economic growth' the public are increasingly left out of the evaluation; the weighing up of risks and benefits, and the prioritisation of emerging technologies and their application as Hunt and Mehta have emphasised in the case of nanotechnology.[29] Anne Chapman says in her book, 'Democratising Technology'[30] that some citizen groups are now focussing on changing how choices about innovation are made; and that, if social and political institutions are to endure they need to intellectually justify their existence. Hence their rebuttals, for instance, when they are challenged by citizen groups such as the privacy campaigners.

Therefore, to facilitate changing the status of personal identifiable images: firstly, social and political institutions need to acknowledge that images are data, and respect the data subjects' privacy; secondly, if privacy is to be respected informed consent is necessary; thirdly, whether, or not images are copyrighted the moral right to them is justified; fourthly, the case for legitimate over-riding of privacy of images needs to be clearly and publicly argued for. Given that the GDPR harmonises European data law and modernises the law in the UK, these may be one of its benefits, as each in are within its scope.

12.4 Personal Identifiable Images and Street Photography

Street Photography is an unmediated and spontaneous photographic art form otherwise known as 'candid photography' that records decisive moments in peoples' lives, sometimes for purely documentary purposes or to fulfil an artistic or illustrative purpose. Whatever the purpose, candid photography generally does not require consent because privacy in public spaces is not protected, although it is good practice to obtain consent to use the images commercially as publishers may be reluctant to publish images without a model release form or license. However, street photographs, many taken as snapshots are often posted on social media sites and the ability to identify individuals increases the risk of breaching privacy. What then the future of street photography? How can the risks of identification be ameliorated?

Street photography will remain a social phenomenon due to the ubiquity of cameras and users' curiosity or artistic license. Therefore, the risk of identification must be managed by social networks proactively limiting access to peoples' profiles

[29]See Hunt and Mehta (2006).

[30]See Chapman (2007).

and the prudent verification and provenance of the image, and its source by data processors.

12.5 Recommendations

The previous chapters have discussed the ethical, legal and political aspects of face recognition technology and its modalities from which broadly three major themes vie for attention. These are: identity securitising and verification, civil liberties and surveillance. Arguably the justification for securitising identity is well established yet the perceived dichotomy between privacy and security is yet to be fully resolved, especially when privacy campaigners challenge the veracity of the intelligence community's demands[31] many of which can be resolved by incorporating Privacy by Design[32] (PbD) principles in the ISCP's proposed legal framework discussed above, and which are equally applicable elsewhere. Although PbD was formulated to embed data protection practices an essential feature of PbD is the user-centricity of processes that recognise the value of privacy, and which caveats (above) withstanding would not be at odds with the overall aims of effective security and the maintenance of privacy and autonomy. But this would necessitate a new legal framework that recognises the moral agency of persons, and which also obviates the divisiveness of opinion between the civil libertarians and Parliament. To those ends, in addition to those described in Chap. 10, the following recommendations are proposed:

- Develop practices and functions that incorporate Privacy by Design with the attribution of inclusive moral rights to one's own image
- Establish property rights to personal data that strengthens data protection provision and increases awareness of personal responsibility
- Improve communication and accountability between Parliament and the agencies, to control excessive or unauthorised use of devolved powers.[33]

The three facets of the discourse demand different responses which do not pit one against the other. There is clearly a need for a mature conversation between the opposing sides, and eventual reconciliation of some by now entrenched positions which I have described. But until the legislators recognise that face recognition

---

[31] *ibid.*

[32] Cavoukian (n.d.) Privacy by Design The 7 Foundational Principles. These include anticipating privacy invasion, and therefore making privacy the default setting and embedding this in the design and architecture of IT systems and business practices.

[33] See Chap. 8; Brad Smith (2018), the President of Microsoft has highlighted the need for public regulation and corporate responsibility. He writes about the need for government regulation of face recognition technology, such as the need to ensure the 'right to know' what identifiable images have been collected and stored. By alluding to PbD principles Brad Smith emphasises the need for transparency that is fostered by corporate responsibility.

modalities will not solve the surveillance questions, which the technologists hyperbolically espouse, and accept that this problem is potentially insurmountable the longer the entrenched positions will remain. Furthermore, privacy campaigners defend privacy rights as expected, but until the moral right to personal data is legally established the dissonance between first and second-order choice remains, and the trade-off between privacy and security is unresolved.

Ultimately, without adequate public accountability and transparency the FRT project will continue to diminish citizen autonomy, because public debate and approval is denied, and therefore the majority in democratic western societies are likely to lose their understanding of, and their ability to control the use of their personal identifiable images in the form of digital data despite the GDPR.

In conclusion, the ethics of Face Recognition Technology is complex and multifaceted, and wherever the dividing line between privacy and security is drawn, personal autonomy expressed as personal liberty and choice is reduced. Yet, although the GDPR requires explicit consent for biometric data,[34] that is arguably predicated by second-order preferences[35] and which potentially rectifies some of the concerns I have raised. Yet, if in the UK explicit consent only applies to biometric applications that are chosen for convenient access to services or border controls; then a substantive ethical and legal framework that does not include recognising the status of personal identifiable images is incomplete, and the opportunity to enhance peoples' choices not fully realised.

The recommendations that are offered here seek to redress some of these tensions and omissions though some of the fundamental issues and philosophical questions will likely remain at the centre of such controversies as the new data landscape matures. Such maturity needs to encompass and include greater transparency, an understanding of the importance of privacy protection that acknowledges the ownership of personal identifiable images,[36] and an understanding of the importance and the value of liberal democratic principles that are foundational to human flourishing, not only in societies that have observed them, but also in societies that may differ but where their citizens in the twenty-first century are part of the global community.

References

Big Brother Watch (2015) Protecting Civil Liberties Big Brother Watch 2015 Manifesto. http://www.bigbrotherwatch.org.uk/wp-content/uploads/2015/02/manifesto.pdf. Accessed 30 Aug 2019

Burrows T (2015) Big brand theory for professors Brian Cox and Stephen Hawking who trademark their own names to turn themselves into brands. Mail Online 29th March 2015. http://www.

[34] General Data Protection Regulation, Article 9.

[35] See Sect. 9.5 Citizen and State and Sect. 11.5 Predicting social concerns and reactions.

[36] Where ownership or rights to personal images do not exist at present.

dailymail.co.uk/news/article-3016648/Brian-Cox-Stephen-Hawking-turn-brands.html. Accessed 30 Aug 2019

Campbell v. MGN Limited [2002] EWHC 499. http://www.bailii.org/ew/cases/EWHC/QB/2002/499.html. Accessed 30 Aug 2019

Cavoukian A (n.d.) Privacy by Design The 7 Foundational Principles. https://www.ipc.on.ca/wp-content/uploads/Resources/7foundationalprinciples.pdf. Accessed 30 Aug 2019

Chapman S (2007) Democratising technology: risk, responsibility and the regulation of chemicals. Earthscan, London

Copyright, Designs and Patents Act 1988 c.48. http://www.legislation.gov.uk/ukpga/1988/48/contents. Accessed 30 Aug 2019

Data Protection Act 1998 c.29. http://www.legislation.gov.uk/ukpga/1998/29/contents. Accessed 30 Aug 2019

Data Protection Act 2018. https://services.parliament.uk/bills/2017-19/dataprotection.html. Accessed 30 Aug 2019

Feenberg A (2009) Marxism and the critique of social rationality: from surplus value to the politics of technology. Camb J Econ pp 37–49. http://www.jstor.org/stable/24232019. Accessed 30 Aug 2019

General Data Protection Regulation, Article 9. http://data.consilium.europa.eu/doc/document/ST-5419-2016-INIT/en/pdf. Accessed 30 Aug 2019

Gross L (1988) Preface. In: Gross L, Katz JS, Ruby J (eds) Image ethics: the moral rights of subjects in photographs, film, and television. Oxford University Press, Oxford, p vii

Hunt G, Mehta M (2006) Nanotechnology: risk, ethics & law. Earthscan, London

ICO (n.d.) Taking photographs in schools. https://ico.org.uk/media/for-organisations/documents/1136/taking_photos.pdf. Accessed 30 Aug 2019. See also: https://ico.org.uk/for-organisations/education/. Accessed 30 Aug 2019

Information Commissioner's Office (ICO) Guide to the General Data Protection Regulation (GDPR). https://ico.org.uk/for-organisations/guide-to-the-general-data-protection-regulation-gdpr/. Accessed 30 Aug 2019

Intelligence and Security Committee of Parliament (ISCP 2015) Privacy & Security: A modern & transparent legal framework. http://isc.independent.gov.uk/news-archive/12march2015. Accessed 30 Aug 2019

Mosley v. News Group Newspapers Ltd [2008] EWHC 1777 (QB), [2008] EMLR 20. http://www.bailii.org/ew/cases/EWHC/QB/2008/1777.html. Accessed 30 Aug 2019

Narayanan A, Shmatikov V (n.d.) Robust De-anonymisation of Large Sparse Datasets. https://www.cs.utexas.edu/~shmat/shmat_oak08netflix.pdf. Accessed 30 Aug 2019

Reklos and Davourlis v. Greece 27 BHRC 420, [2009] EMLR 16, [2009] ECHR 200. http://hudoc.echr.coe.int/sites/eng/pages/search.aspx?i=001-90617. Accessed 30 Aug 2019

Smith B (2018) Facial recognition technology: The need for public regulation and corporate responsibility. https://blogs.microsoft.com/on-the-issues/2018/07/13/facial-recognition-technology-the-need-for-public-regulation-and-corporate-responsibility/. Accessed 30 Aug 2019

Stanley P (2008) The law of confidentiality: a restatement. Hart, Oxford

University of Reading (2010) Guidelines on the collection, use and storage of photographic images. https://www.reading.ac.uk/web/FILES/imps/collectionuseandstorageofimages22-11-10CURRENT.pdf. Accessed 23 Sept 2019

University of Reading (n.d.) Consent form for film/video, audio & photography with notice of copyright. https://www.reading.ac.uk/internal/imps/Copyright/imps-Publishing_AV_material_to_the_Web_1.aspx. Accessed 30 Aug 2019

Viera JD (1988) Images as property. In: Gross L, Katz JS, Ruby J (eds) Image ethics: the moral rights of subjects in photographs, film, and television. Oxford University Press, Oxford, pp 135–162

Von Hannover v. Germany (2005) 40 EHRR 1, [2005] 40 EHRR 1, 40 EHRR 1, [2004] EMLR 21, 16 BHRC 545, [2004] ECHR 294. http://www.bailii.org/eu/cases/ECHR/2004/294.html. Accessed 30 Aug 2019

Bibliography and Further Reading

Agamben G (2005) State of exception (trans: Attell K). The University of Chicago Press, Chicago

Amos M (2006) Human rights law. Hart, Oxford

Amos M (2014) The impact of human rights law on measures of mass surveillance in the United Kingdom. In: Davis F, McGarrity N, Williams G (eds) Surveillance, counter-terrorism and comparative constitutionalism. Routledge, London

Beauchamp TL, Childress JF (2001) Principles of biomedical ethics, 5th edn. Oxford University Press, New York

Brennan P, Berle I (2011) The ethical and medical aspects of photo-documenting genital injury. In: Gall J, Payne-James J (eds) Current practice in forensic medicine. Wiley-Blackwell, Chichester

Brin D (1998) The transparent society. Addison-Wesley, Reading

Brogan C (2016) Data protection in Europe: why UK companies must prepare now for the GDPR. In Risk UK September 2016, Pro-Active Publications

Chapman S (2007) Democratising technology: risk, responsibility and the regulation of chemicals. Earthscan, London

Chesterman S (2011) One nation under surveillance: a new social contract to defend freedom without sacrificing liberty. Oxford University Press, Oxford

Cole D (2014) Preserving privacy in a digital age: lessons of comparative constitutionalism. In: Davis F, McGarrity N, Williams G (eds) Surveillance, counter-terrorism and comparative constitutionalism. Routledge, London

Collingridge D (1981) The social control of technology. Open University Press, London

den Boer M, Goudappel F (2014) How secure is our privacy in seceurope? European security through surveillance. In: Davis F, McGarrity N, Williams G (eds) Surveillance, counter-terrorism and comparative constitutionalism. Routledge, London

Dershowitz A (2004) Rights from wrongs: a secular theory of the origins of rights. Basic Books, New York

Dostoevsky F (1864) (Wordsworth Classics Edition 2015) Notes from underground and other stories (trans: Garnett C). Wordsworth Classics, Ware

Doyal L, Gough I (1991) A theory of human need. Macmillan, Basingstoke

Driessen B, Dürmuth M (2013) Achieving anonymity against major face recognition algorithms. In: De Decker B, Dittmann J, Kraetzer C, Vielhauer C (eds) Communications and multimedia security. CMS 2013. Lecture Notes in Computer Science, vol 8099. Springer, Heidelberg

Dworkin G (1988, reprinted 1997) The theory and practice of autonomy. Cambridge University Press, Cambridge

Edgar TH (2017) Beyond Snowden: privacy, mass surveillance, and the struggle to reform the NSA. Brookings Institution Press, Washington DC

I. Berle, *Face Recognition Technology*, Law, Governance and Technology Series 41,
https://doi.org/10.1007/978-3-030-36887-6

Fabre C (2006) Whose body is it anyway? Justice and the integrity of the person. Oxford University Press, Oxford

Fine B (1984) Marx's capital. Macmillan, London

Foucault M (1975) Discipline and punish, birth of the prison (trans: Sheridan A). Allen Lane, London. Republished by Penguin 1991. First published as Surveiller et punir: Naissance de la prison (1975)

Garfinkel S (2000) Database nation: the death of privacy in the 21st century. O'Reilly & Associates Inc, Sebastopol

Gates KA (2011) Our biometric future: facial recognition technology and the culture of surveillance. New York University Press, New York

Gerstein R (1978) Intimacy and privacy. Ethics 89:76–81. University of Chicago Press

Gregory P, Simon MA (2008) Biometrics for dummies. Wiley, Indianapolis

Gross L (1988) Preface. In: Gross L, Katz JS, Ruby J (eds) Image ethics: the moral rights of subjects in photographs, film, and television. Oxford University Press, Oxford

Haggerty KD, Ericson RV (eds) (2006) The new politics of surveillance and visibility. University of Toronto Press, Toronto

Hague R (2011) Autonomy and identity, the politics of who we are. Routledge, Abingdon

Han J, Kamber M (2002) Data mining concepts and techniques. Morgan Kaufmann, California

Hobhouse LT (1964) Liberalism. Oxford University Press, London

Hunt G (2013) Civil servants and whistle-blowing: loyal neutrality and/or democratic ideal? In: Neuhold C, Vanhoonacker S, Verhey L (eds) Civil servants and politics. A delicate balance. Palgrave Macmillan, London

Hunt G, Mehta M (2006) Nanotechnology: risk, ethics & law. Earthscan, London

Inness J (1992) Privacy, intimacy and isolation. Oxford University Press, Oxford

Kafka F (1925) Der prozess. The trial first published in Germany 1925 (UK trans: Parry I 1994). Reprinted by Penguin Classics 2000, London (USA trans: Mitchell B 1998). Schocken Books Inc, New York

Kindt EJ (2013) Privacy and data protection issues of biometric applications. Springer, Heidelberg

Kluge Eike-Henner W (2001) The ethics of electronic patient records. Peter Lang, New York

Kremer J (2014) On the end of freedom in public spaces: legal challenges of wide-area and multiple-sensor surveillance systems. In: Davis F, McGarrity N, Williams G (eds) Surveillance, counter-terrorism and comparative constitutionalism. Routledge, London

Kroeger CC (1989) The classical concept of *Head* as "Source". In: Hull GG (ed) Equal to serve: women and men in the church and home. Scripture Union, London

Laurent M, Levallois-Barth S (2015) Privacy management and protection of personal data. In: Laurent M, Bouzefrane S (eds) Digital identity management. ISTE Press/Elsevier, London/ Oxford

Lyon D (2003) (reprinted 2004 & 2008) Surveillance after September 11. Polity Press, Cambridge

Lyon D (2007) (reprinted 2011) Surveillance studies: an overview. Polity Press, Cambridge

MacKinnon C (1989) Toward a feminist theory of the state. Harvard University Press, Cambridge

Manson NC, O'Neill O (2007) Rethinking informed consent in bioethics. Cambridge University Press, Cambridge

Marshall J (2009) Personal freedom through human rights law? Autonomy, identity and integrity under the European Convention on Human Rights. Martinus Nijhoff, Leiden

Marx GT (1996) Ethics for the new surveillance. In: Bennett CJ, Grant R (eds) Visions of privacy 1996, Toronto, University of Toronto Press

Mill JS (1859) On liberty. In: Gray J, Smith GW (eds) JS Mill on liberty in focus. Routledge, London, p 1991

Nelson LS (2011) America identified: biometric technology and society. Massachusetts Institute of Technology, Massachusetts

Nissenbaum H (2010) Privacy in context: technology, policy and the integrity of social life. Stanford University Press, Stanford

Patil AM, Kolhe SR, Patil PM (2010) 2D face recognition techniques: a survey. Int J Mach Intell 2 (1):74–78
Pomeroy SB (1994) Goddesses, whores, wives, & slaves: women in classical antiquity. Pimlico
Rawls J (1971) A theory of justice. Revised edition 1999. The Belknap Press of Harvard University Press, Cambridge
Regan P (1995) Legislating privacy: technology, social values and public policy. University of North Carolina Press, Chapel Hill
Rule JB (2007) Privacy in peril. Oxford University Press, Oxford
Schoeman FD (1992, reprinted 2008) Privacy and social freedom. Cambridge University Press, Cambridge
Schwartz PM, Solove DJ (2014) Reconciling personal information in the United States and European Union. Calif Law Rev 102:877
Sclove RE (1995) Democracy & technology. Guildford Press, New York
Smart JJC, Williams B (1973) Utilitarianism: for and against. Cambridge University Press, Cambridge
Solove DJ (2008) Understanding privacy. Harvard University Press, Cambridge
Solove DJ (2011) Nothing to hide: the false trade off between privacy and security. Yale University Press, New Haven
Stanley P (2008) The law of confidentiality: a restatement. Hart, Oxford
Syndercombe-Court D (2011) DNA analysis: current practice and problems. In: Gall J, Payne-James J (eds) Current practice in forensic medicine. Wiley-Blackwell, Chichester
Tagg J (1988) The burden of representation: essays on photographies and histories. Palgrave-Macmillan, Basingstoke
Van de Veer D (1986) Paternalistic intervention: the moral bounds of benevolence. Princeton University Press, Princeton
Veak TJ (ed) (2006) Democratizing technology. State University of New York Press, Albany
Viera JD (1988) Images as property. In: Gross L, Katz JS, Ruby J (eds) Image ethics: the moral rights of subjects in photographs, film, and television. Oxford University Press, Oxford
Von Hippel E (2005) Democratizing innovation. MIT Press, Cambridge
Von Schomberg R (2011) Introduction. In: Towards responsible research and innovation in the information and communication technologies and security technologies fields. European Commission Publications Office, Brussels
Wacks R (1989, revised 1993) Personal information: privacy and the law. Clarendon Press, Oxford
Westin AF (1967) Privacy and freedom. Bodley Head, London
Whitehead JW (2013) A government of wolves: the emerging American Police State. Select Books Inc, New York
Wicks E (2007) Human rights and healthcare. Hart, Oxford

Index

I. Berle, *Face Recognition Technology*, Law, Governance and Technology Series 41,
https://doi.org/10.1007/978-3-030-36887-6

GPSR Compliance
The European Union's (EU) General Product Safety Regulation (GPSR) is a set of rules that requires consumer products to be safe and our obligations to ensure this.

If you have any concerns about our products, you can contact us on

ProductSafety@springernature.com

In case Publisher is established outside the EU, the EU authorized representative is:

Springer Nature Customer Service Center GmbH
Europaplatz 3
69115 Heidelberg, Germany

www.ingramcontent.com/pod-product-compliance
Ingram Content Group UK Ltd.
Pitfield, Milton Keynes, MK11 3LW, UK
UKHW021030041026
15470UKWH00013B/1107
* 9 7 8 3 0 3 0 3 6 8 8 6 9 *